# The Priority of Justice

AF184023

# The Priority of Justice

## Elements for a Sociology of Moral Choices

Michel Forsé & Maxime Parodi

Translated by Constance Bantman

PETER LANG
Oxford · Bern · Berlin · Bruxelles · Frankfurt am Main · New York · Wien

**Bibliographic information published by Die Deutsche Bibliothek**
Die Deutsche Bibliothek lists this publication in the Deutsche National-bibliografie; detailed bibliographic data is available on the Internet at ‹http://dnb.ddb.de›.

British Library and Library of Congress Cataloguing-in-Publication Data:
A catalogue record for this book is available from The British Library, Great Britain, and from The Library of Congress, USA

Cover design: Thomas Jaberg, Peter Lang AG

ISBN 3-03910-658-9
US-ISBN 0-8204-7172-0

Original Edition *La priorité du juste. Eléments pour une sociologie des choix moraux*
© Presses Universitaires de France, Paris 2004

© Peter Lang AG, European Academic Publishers, Bern 2005
Hochfeldstrasse 32, Postfach 746, CH-3000 Bern 9, Switzerland
info@peterlang.com, www.peterlang.com, www.peterlang.net

All rights reserved.
All parts of this publication are protected by copyright.
Any utilisation outside the strict limits of the copyright law, without the permission of the publisher, is forbidden and liable to prosecution.
This applies in particular to reproductions, translations, microfilming, and storage and processing in electronic retrieval systems.

# Table of Contents

# Introduction

The advent of modern societies is the product of a moral revolution which has consisted in giving priority to the right over the good. It is their most basic characteristic, beyond their most often quoted other traits, such as democracy, individualism, secularisation, and many others, according to a great deal of authors. All these traits make for an (often) apt description of social changes since the dawning of modernity, but the priority of the just is the principle of legitimacy without which democratic institutions would have no real substance. The Moderns assemble into a society, solve their conflicts and overcome their divergences in a way which is radically different from that of the Ancients. Or, more accurately, the *legitimate* way out of a conflict rests on a new foundation, where one's personal efforts to get along and live with others comes before everyone's private axiological convictions.

If we focus only on the broad types of societies, this constitutes a break away from a form of collective life whose main elements Plato had already highlighted. Reading *The Republic*, one understands how and why, according to the Ancients, the existence of a well-ordered society depends on the knowledge of man's true nature. What each person must do is inferred from such a knowledge. The contemplation of what is gives access to what ought to be. By leaving the cave, the philosopher and all those who follow him can contemplate the True and the Good. They know what they have to do to achieve perfection. The principle of order is therefore simple: there is such a thing as the Good in itself. But this principle can only have any social reality if the (traditional) community within which it prevails unites individuals who share an essentially similar substantial conception of the good, and therefore a similar vision of the world. For the Ancients, this seems 'natural'. In other words, the situation appears as an obvious fact, whose force stems from the fact that it is very often linked to a revelation. Myths, sacred texts, or, even better, a Church are here as reminders of their true nature. Those who are different can only be barbarians, beings partaking in a different humanity. There cannot be any life in common with them, unless they become converted to the 'true' good.

In a modern society, it is out of the question to establish collective life on a conception of the good which would be shared by everyone at once. Faced with the ever-threatening conflict between visions of the world and of the life that is worth living, the Moderns have decided on making those convictions relative by granting everyone the freedom to think. Consequently, moral certitude as to the good in itself, as to man's true nature or even as to true religion can no longer be the single axiological criterion to judge one's or somebody else's actions. Each person must also be able to justify their point of view on others. And this is impossible without an attempt at *impartiality* towards other conceptions of the good, even if one values them only because someone else believes in them. Such an effort simply amounts to trying to give justice the priority over the good.

If this perspective is indispensable to understand modern societies, which, as a matter of fact, are meeting points between various conceptions of the good, it is necessary to recognise that the most spontaneous models to explain morality and solidarity are still a matter for a sociology (mainly of Durkheimian inspiration) which does not take these notions into account. On the one hand, society is supposed to maintain itself thanks to norms which have been inculcated to people; this is what enables it to reproduce itself unaltered and to keep up a minimum level of social cohesion. On the other hand, since this change also has to be explained, the most frequent – and the simplest – explanation consists in seeing it as the result of the rise of individualism. Of course, other hypotheses can be devised. In this context, they are *ad hoc* anyway. But with such an approach, it is actually impossible to figure how unity could endure for long. Here, unity is nothing but some old remnant from the past, while the diversification of aspirations and perspectives confirms itself unrelentingly and shapes the society to come. This is what leads some to speak of the decline of morality and traditional values within contemporary societies, in order to defend, on a nostalgic mode, an idealised traditional moral order, while according to others in the same league, this disappearance of morality through the advent of 'post-modern' societies is something one should rejoice over.

However, far from reflecting recent social evolutions, such judgments simply come from the shortcomings of this spontaneous theory. One of these shortcomings stems from a lack of understanding of what the moral dimension encompasses. Morality is reduced to a judgment of good and evil, when it also bears upon what is fair and what is unfair. By not being unduly simplistic, we understand easily that what disappears within modern societies is not morality, but the identity of views on good and evil, on what is worth living, on the world's religious values and images, because it is now the acceptance of the pluralism of values and the search for rules respecting other people's right to evaluate differently which have a privileged place in them. It is not enough to speak of the rise of generalized benevolence or of moral relativism to account for this. All things are not equal, something which most people are actually perfectly aware of, as evidenced by the fact that they can tolerate other people having beliefs that are different from theirs, and therefore being entitled to decide for themselves, while they remain opposed to the various religious fundamentalisms or to other ideologies negating freedom of thought. In doing so, they give the priority to the right and display an informed moral judgment. It is therefore surprising to note that this moral competence is ignored by the most widespread and dominant theories in social sciences.

The problem is first of all located at the microsocial level, where an attempt is made to explain what determines the actor to act. For some theorists, actors are supposed to act only according to their interests or to their conception of the good life, without caring about the fact that others may have legitimate claims to put forward as to the resulting social order, which obviously involves everyone. Trapped in their vision of the world, these actors are unable to conceive of life in common; they lack the ability to take into account other people's perspectives in order to achieve a 'well-ordered society' (Rawls, 1971), that is a fair social order. The notions of social order and social justice mean nothing to them. For other theorists, as if by symmetry, individuals are expected to stick to a social order which they inherited, without even being really conscious of it. They have become some sort of reflex-guided beings, now overwhelmed by ideologies, now manipulated by the unconscious's obscure forces, when they are not likely to be actuated by reasons which 'should not' be theirs. This time, the social order is no longer absent, it is oppressive. It annihilates everyone's reflection and deprives them of their critical mind – except in the paradoxical case of the scientist.

Each of these perspectives has its specialists. Economics has made much of the hypothesis of an individual rationally finding her way into the world, perfectly enlightened as to where her well-being lies, though remaining strangely blind to the demands of life in common. On the contrary, sociology has in one way or another often considered the individual to be determined by norms that 'reflect' the social order, and whose source sometimes springs from religion, the family, class relationships, socialisation (sometimes restricted to infancy), culture, values, etc. In practice, however, it is often an *ad hoc* juxtaposition of these two types of action that one notices. In his book, *The Cement of Society*, Jon Elster (1989) opposes the rationally-oriented agent to the culturally-oriented agent. But it is not enough to simply reduce the choice of a sociological model to a confrontation between one form of methodological individualism, which can only explain the social order through isolated cases, and a form of methodological holism which starts by admitting the social order with no further explanation. This amounts to leaving the crucial problem of the continuous construction of the social order in the dark. This is a theoretical void. Between a rational choice where the individual seeks to make the most of the situation and a cultural determination where she remains faithful to what cements society, we also have to consider an orientation where she regards the social cement as fresh again. In other words, it is still necessary to shed light on the dimension whereby the individual is the producer of the law or, more precisely, the co-producer of this law.

In this respect, we have to bear in mind that an institution (in the broad sense of the term) is not only something that is passively received. It can be taken up in a critical way. Individuals display their *autonomy* and they do not necessarily back up the tradition, or they adopt it for reasons which they deem appropriate, or still they adapt it through repeated adjustments. They do not necessarily give their agreement, and always retain the ability to challenge the legitimacy of such or such institution on this or that specific point by invoking *reasons*. Therefore, the state of the law or of norms can indeed be seen as a state, but it must also be considered as the result of a process aiming at *agreement*. And, even if such an aim may entail disappointments and failures, this reflexive process remains at work in the 'social fabric'. The social order is of course empirically given at the beginning but, if we want to account for change, we also have to consider that this order is, in actors' minds, a social order *in the making*.

Why have most social sciences refrained from endowing individuals with a full ability to reflect on the social order which they create? The reason lies in a consequence of positivism. With a view to establishing firmly the objectivity of those who took the society of men as their object, it seemed to be the easiest way to just copy their exteriority from that of those whose object was nature, by pretending that this reduction had no implications. However, it is not possible to forget that an individual, as opposed to an atom, can question the maxims of her actions, and give herself new ones. To put this in a nutshell, social sciences deal with freedom, and natural sciences do not. And if we admit this point, its effects should not be underestimated. All the more as, thanks to this 'omission', it has quickly been assumed that in order to study human beings objectively, the scientist is seen as being endowed with a critical faculty, whereas, in principle, being a man, he should not possess that faculty. This is obviously a problem for, as Fichte wrote, 'the scientist is a scientist only insofar as he is considered in society' (1794, third conference). The point is of course not to deny the knowledge of the scientist, but to found it altogether differently, in order to avoid falling into this unsustainable conception of his exteriority. To this end, it seems that social sciences have no other choice, but to make their Copernican revolution: it is necessary to start from the basic situation of a finite reason which presupposes the existence of another one, of a freedom presupposing another one – in other words, to focus on an autonomous subject. Otherwise, the scientist cannot avoid setting himself up as an infinite reason, soon pretending to infer freedom and what is reasonable in other people from this. He has reified the social.

Of course, not reducing freedom and reason *a priori*, leaving room for anyone's criticism, do not mean we live in a pure society of free and critical spirits. It is only a regulating principle for life in common, which can have more or less weight – and even no weight at all in certain circumstances. But this cannot be decided on *a priori*. No definite opinion can be formed without observing the social world with the help of the relevant tools. For the detractors, it is no use taking so many precautions since by definition actors do not make any effort to decentre themselves and escape the numerous sociological determinisms which occupy scientists' minds. At such a cost, social sciences could do without the idea of the priority of the right.

In the following developments, we will adopt precisely the opposite research perspective, but of course, in order to argue in its favour, it will be necessary to specify this notion of the priority of justice. To do so, the many questions this raises will be organised around two main interrogations, each corresponding to one part of this book. First, what are the reasons of an actor who gives priority to the right? If one admits as a starting point the Copernican revolution which has just been described, it will certainly be difficult to find convincing elements of explanation in the theories which confute it – whether methodologically holistic or individualistic. They will always fail to fully bring to light individuals' moral faculties. It will therefore be necessary to set up another model to analyse actions or opinions, using a non-restrictive theory of rationality as a framework. The problem is not only theoretical however, and it will be important to measure the validity and relevance of this model in order to analyse empirical data. And indeed, we will see that it can account for these data whereas other approaches only deliver interpretations either incorrect or insufficient.

It will then be possible to tackle the second interrogation. What principle of justice does an actor want to put into practice when giving priority to justice? To sum it up briefly, this principle can be reduced to that of justice, perceived as a unanimous agreement on some rules in order to overcome a conflict. In spite of its clarity, it gives way to frequent confusions, especially because the logic which necessarily underpins it is rather easily forgotten. After explaining this logic, it will be possible to show that it is always because they try to avoid its consequences that the opposing theories of justice are faced with strong and often damning objections. But above all, it will be necessary to establish the reasons why, contrary to what appearances may suggest, this principle of unanimous agreement cannot accommodate moral relativism. It could indeed look as if, by willing that justice rests on the idea that men are free to build the agreement they want, we ineluctably ended up lapsing into subjectivism or relativism, even with a unanimity constraint. But it is purely and simply the reverse which is true: unanimous agreement is a source of objectivity in the practical domain. By arguing in favour of this view, we will establish a sociology of moral choices which, in order to maintain its axiological neutrality, will have neither to be restricted to the mere description of moral pluralism, nor to justify it by implicitly or explicitly indulging into relativism.

# Part I

# The Reasons of the Fair Spectator

# Chapter 1

# The Fair Spectator Model

The principle of the priority of justice over the good is indispensable to grant everyone the ability to think over their interactions with others under *all* their modalities, and to establish this, we have to focus on analysing actors' reasons. By following this orientation, we will be able to understand not only how these actors can solve their conflicts fairly, but also the failure of traditional approaches in social sciences which, while accepting the hypothesis of a rational actor, always embrace conceptions of this rationality which are far too narrow. Hence the fact that they cannot grasp how and why justice as fairness is a solution to conflicts. In this perspective, the weak points of utilitarianism will be closely examined, since this doctrine is still widely used in economics, while it proves definitely unable to fill the gaps of the *homo œconomicus* model. In its claim to generality, the rational choice theory which goes with it leads to difficulties that cannot be overcome, simply because it does not take into account the moral reasoning of an actor who gives priority to justice. In order to go beyond such impossibilities, and since falling back on a holistic determinism is obviously not the solution, we will be led to develop the alternative model of a fair spectator. Nevertheless, we will be able to use such a model only by founding it on an extended theory of rationality which, without rejecting the rational choice, will not forget the reasonable that constitutes its frame.

There ensue many consequences, two of which should be emphasised now. First, by virtue of this very principle of extended rationality, the position of a fair spectator cannot simply be one position among others in a conflict. Though it is indeed a position, the fair spectator is more fundamentally a *horizon* which we get closer to as partiality biases preventing its expression are removed. Secondly, and still in conformity with this principle of extended rationality, the fair spectator model is also a *method* for social sciences. This is what will allow us, in the next chapter, to apply it to the analysis of empirical data to check that what will have been expounded here in theory does have a practical value, and especially that the reasons of a fair spectator constitute a horizon because it is through them that unanimity can be obtained when conceptions of the good life and everyone's private interests no longer ambition to impose themselves as such to others.

## 1. The Priority of Justice over the Good

### 1.1 *The rational and the reasonable*

In everyday life, when people argue about morality, they wonder what they should do and look for the reasons which justify what they think or do. Sometimes, in the discussion, one of them will say: 'this may be rational, but it is not very reasonable'. What difference is she trying to emphasise? Which principle does she implicitly support? When we say that someone is reasonable, we want to underline that she can be reasoned out of or into something, that she is willing to listen and to take into account the reasons put forward by others. On the contrary, saying that someone is rational is to admit that she acts methodically and can reach successfully the goal she pursues. Sometimes, it is also to imply that she calculates only according to her interest or without great considerateness for others. The common image of a rational, but not reasonable, being is that of a cold calculator acting like a machine: reasoning her is out of the question. One has to be stronger to make her stir away from this line of conduct, and at the smallest weakness, her advantage will prevail. We could also think that this individual should always fear potential twists of fate, and that it is because she has failed to take in the impending risks that she can be described as unreasonable. However, if this individual fails because of a lack of caution, it was simply a wrong calculation: she acted irrationally. This is therefore not how one should define the term reasonable. In the context of a moral discussion, being reasonable consists in taking into account other people's reasons in order to try and adopt a position which is justified from everybody's perspective, while being only rational is equal to not asking oneself whether one's actions or opinions are as acceptable to others as they are to oneself. It thus appears that the person saying 'this may be rational, but it is not very reasonable', beyond the distinction she establishes, implies that, in a moral argument, the reasonable should prevail over the rational. In a sense that is beginning to appear, we may as well say that she endorses the principle that the right should be given priority over the good.

However, this somewhat common way of looking at things does not correspond to the one advocated by many social sciences theorists, for whom reason can be reduced only to its rational dimension. The reasonable is only an appendix of the rational. It is mistaken for a cautious behaviour, a reluctance to any form of risk. Certain contemporary forms of irrationalism can therefore be understood. Since a fundamental dimension of practical reason is ignored, there are no other ways out than finding a palliative for the reasonable. However, this conclusion is hasty, and even erroneous according to a Kantian conception of reason, or to its various contemporary reinterpretations. On the contrary, what we find here is a distinction between the rational and the reasonable which owes a lot to the one which we have just expounded. We will have to come back to this many times, but let us insist on several points now.

A rational actor endeavours to solve problems of orientation in nature. She seeks to devise methods enabling her to forecast what nature's reactions to her actions will be. She aims to reach a given goal with efficiency. She has an idea of what will make her happy, of what is good for her, and she tries to get as close to it as she can. Borrowing from an economical vocabulary, we can also say that she maximises her utility. If she has to deal with other people, we can add that she is a strategist, in particular if she has long-term foresight. But, in doing so, she only regards others as a nature. In any case, the end justifies the means. *Alter* is here for *ego* only a means, a nature hazard which she has to master, to manipulate, or even to tame as suits her. Nothing else counts, but the rational pursuit of a given or possible aim through the use of adequate means.

When an actor is reasonable, and not only rational in this restrictive sense, his reason's activity is not defined towards a nature, but towards another being, who is regarded as free and capable of reasoning. Practical reason thus moves to another level. Before, *ego* did not have to restrict himself while pursuing a goal. It would have been irrational for him not to do anything necessary to reach the target he had set himself. He was limited only by a nature which could resist him and which he was not skilful enough to bend to his will or cautious enough to control in all its dimensions. Now, *ego* discovers a new possibility: that of teaming up with a free and rational being by means of an agreement deemed acceptable by both of them. Far from considering the other as a natural hazard, he recognizes him or her as an *alter ego*. He is therefore going to restrict himself.[1] The question is no longer to submit *alter* by cleverly taking of the ratio of forces into account. The question is to act according to shared reasons. An economist would say that *ego* accepts not to maximise his utility. This does not mean that a reasonable actor becomes irrational. In the long term, he will always have to find the adequate means to the aims he pursues. Each actor still pursues his idea of happiness, but, here, he accepts to do so under the auspices of what is fair for everyone.

## 1.2 *Deontology* v. *teleology*

When this is the case, the reasonable frames the rational (Rawls, 1980). And to endorse this idea in a general way means to adopt the deontological perspective which admits the priority of the right over the good, or of pure practical reason over empirical practical reason (Kant, 1785). As we have seen, if individuals seek to satisfy their conceptions of the good life, they also endeavour to justify themselves to others – at least in the circumstances of morality. If we want to be able to account for this, we have to admit that rationality in the narrow sense of the term is only one part of an extended rationality, which includes the reasonable. Moreover, if a reasonable actor does not restrict herself to optimising the means to attain a goal that she considers to be pleasant or congruent with her conception of the good life, but also aims at bringing together several ends, so that everyone's life plans can coexist, we also have to admit that she thereby gives priority to the just over the good (or to the reasonable over the rational).

The deontological position would only be normative if it came down to advocating the (reasonable) point of view that actors should adopt. But it leaves this domain, as soon as we recognize that in order to solve a conflict between various conceptions of the good, in the end, there is only one basic alternative: force (or an equivalent, such as cunning or manipulation)

1 It is noteworthy that this idea of self-restriction is applied by Simmel (1917) to analyse sociability and is essential (Forsé, 2002) to understand his point of view. It is, according to him, thanks to this self-restriction that uniting relations of sociability can be undertaken, beyond objective and subjective separating differences.

on the one hand, justice on the other.[2] To withdraw is a behaviour which is outside the perspective we are dealing with: living together, making up a society. If one wishes to maintain this standpoint, without resorting to force to obtain the other person's agreement, *there is no other stable solution* than everyone's agreement to give justice precedence over the various rational conceptions of the good held by each of the parties involved. The priority of justice is therefore not only one possible viewpoint among others. It emerges as the only viewpoint which can bring together everybody's will. According to us, it is even the only one which, when explaining the social order, avoids the black boxes of a so-called hidden or already-given harmony or of a nature which, no matter how the process occurs, imposes itself to men. But this also has to do with the debate between liberalism and perfectionism, which will be dealt with in the next section.

For the time being, let us just observe that the opposite of deontology consists in a teleological perspective (or, which amounts to the same, a consequentialist one simply judging the morality of an act by its empirical consequences) which takes the good for granted and only gives a second-rate role to the right. The good, which tells us what is worth living, is therefore supposed to solve problems of associations between individuals. The right will consist only in maximising the social good and will therefore be only a by-product of the good. The appeal of such a perspective is linked, among other things, to the fact that it turns collective problems into individual ones – which makes it much easier to solve them. As we will see, this presupposition makes it possible to extend the principles of the rational choice theory[3] to moral issues. But this extension will stumble against a major stake, that is the plurality of life plans. The coexistence of ends is actually only a false problem here. An individual's rationality can be reduced to the maximisation, on a measuring scale, of the gratification of the end he set himself, and this can therefore appear as reason in all its modalities. As a

2 This was already clearly established by Karl Popper (1945, p. 236). According to him, if a dispute arises: 'There are only two solutions; one is the use of emotion, and ultimately of violence, and the other is the use of reason, of impartiality, of reasonable compromise.'

3 The phrases 'Rational Choice Model' or 'Expected Utility Model (or Theory)' are also used sometimes to describe the same perspective of a rationality which is restricted or which excludes the reasonable. As we shall see, it is simply a form of explanatory utilitarianism.

matter of fact, for the main part, this is what explains the hyperbolic use which is often made of the rational choice theory by its champions.

The non-consequentialist point of view is nevertheless frequently misunderstood or misinterpreted. For instance, it seems the deontological approach leads to the claim that an actor thinks or acts without contemplating the consequences that could ensue. Far from exploring an aspect of reason, this approach is said to see the actor only as an individual who just respects laws and rules. This claim entails, among other things, the old notion that Kantism is rigorist since the actor supposedly limits himself in the pursuit of his idea of happiness through his blind respect of established rules; this perspective is therefore considered to pave the way for legal positivism. And yet, this is a misunderstanding. For Kant, as for Rawls or any other author in the deontological current, an action has meaning only if it is oriented by a finality. As John Rawls writes (1971, p. 26): 'All ethical doctrines worth our attention take consequences into account in judging rightness. One which did not would simply be irrational, crazy.' The deontological position holds it that a reasoned action is necessarily aimed at an interest, but only if the simply rational, empirical practical interest is not mistaken for what Kant called pure practical interest, which is also reasonable (Rawls, 2000). In the first case, the actor uses reason to satisfy his preferences; in the other, he also uses his reason, but this time in order to solve, with a respect for others, a problem of coexistence between various life plans. There is nothing mysterious about this. It is simply necessary that, before optimising anything at all and going in search of the most efficient means, the actor checks that he has reasons for doing so which are acceptable by others.[4] In other words, he has to take into account certain consequences of his actions, which cannot be simply measured by a scale of individual or collective preferences.

If we take a closer look, it is rather the consequentialist position which corresponds to a form of blindness as to the unreasonable consequences of actions. Here, only the consequences which optimise a good must be taken into account. But it is one thing to say that acting out of moral duty consists in making a decision according to *a priori* principles (which are not derived from experience), and another to pretend that this amounts to refusing to consider the consequences of one's actions. It is actually even the

4 One can also say, like Thomas Scanlon (1998), that these are reasons which 'no one could reasonably reject'.

opposite, since it is in order to reach a fair end that an actor determines his position according to deontological principles, while on the contrary a radical consequentialism holds that it is reasonable to just optimise a given end, which must not be renegotiated by regard for its consequences on someone else. For instance, a supporter of consequentialism, observing that an actor behaves fairly, will only conclude in favour of a lucky coincidence, as a result of which the useful action, in its 'optimal' form, is also the fair or just action.

Within the social sciences, consequentialism is defended chiefly by economists.[5] Even if some of them – a small minority – point out, down to the very titles of their works (Hirschman, 1984; Sen, 1999), that economics is a moral science, the majority does not (yet?) go as far as to leave for good the realm of teleology. In a conference given in 2001 to celebrate the twentieth anniversary of the *Observatoire Français des Conjonctures Economiques*, Amartya Sen advocated a radical promotion of freedom of speech in developing countries. He stated all the good reasons – including economic ones, but of course not these only – to support such a point of view. But how could the defence of this freedom of speech make sense outside any deontological context? If we have to wait for it to maximise some utility or to be regarded as the good which one will eventually aim for, where it would obviously be a miracle, chances are we will be disappointed. Defending freedom of speech only in the name of its benefits (whether economic or other) is an error of category: it means believing that we *already agree* on the society we want, whereas freedom is a *condition for this agreement*. It also means believing that it is not, in such a hypothesis, a mere waste of time that one would barter for. On the contrary, for the deontological position, the moral law is, as Kant might have said, 'a law of freedom': it is because it is *reasonable for all* that it imposes respect for the dignity of any human person, as a free and equal moral person, and therefore, among other things, that it imposes equal respect for freedom of speech.

5 One of the reasons for the reluctance towards deontology comes from the fact that it leads to relativizing the role of optimisation drastically. But optimisation is a key-instrument in economics, at least as it is currently taught.

## 1.3 *Liberalism as the opposite of perfectionism*

Through this reasoning, the deontological standpoint appears to be closely related to liberalism which, as a moral theory, is opposed to perfectionism. The differences between these two approaches are so great that they can be summarized quite easily. The term 'perfectionism' can be used to refer to a moral doctrine which supposes that there already is an agreement on what the good is. For the perfectionist, in the end, there is only one conception of the good – usually the one he stands for. On the contrary, liberalism recognizes the *plurality* of conceptions of the good and, to a large extent, sets out to reckon with them. From an empirical perspective, if all individuals shared the same interests or the same moral conception of the good, there would hardly be any difficulty. Perfectionism would be neutral. Inversely, this ceases to be the case as soon as there are – as is the case in any mass society or in relationships between various communities – divergent interests or ethical orientations which are, at least potentially, conflicting.

Let us imagine a society in which everybody considers that nothing is more important than music, and is willing to sacrifice everything to it. The priority will be to build concert halls and music instruments, to the detriment of football (soccer) stadiums for instance. The rule of justice is simple: 'You like music like the rest of us, so you cannot complain.' In a mass society, it is hard to believe in such a community of taste, and the football fan can legitimately complain that he is not allowed to do what he wants. Two positions can be held in this conflict. First, in a perfectionist perspective, it can be argued that music is better than football and, treating the individual as a minor, people can explain to him that it is in his interest to learn music rather than football, that it is for his own good. Then, if he does not give in to 'reason' by changing his tastes, he can be pressured 'in the name of music', for instance through incentives. In other words, because only one conception of the good is admitted, the individual is bullied into being virtuous in the name of one's own conception of the good. On the contrary, the liberal perspective admits by principle the plurality of substantial conceptions of the good and seeks compromises. The agreement will be established over reasons which are neutral because they are acceptable to all parties. In the grotesque event of everybody recognizing that people must either play music in order to set up a complete orchestra, or play football to have 22 players, but that it is impossible to do both, a rule of justice which could unite everybody would consist in drawing lots. If there is a unanimous agreement on this procedure, the result, whatever it is, will be regarded as fair by all.[6] Other solutions are of course imaginable, for instance adapting football rules and playing chamber music only, so that everyone can perform the activity they like.

This example shows that, to the perfectionist, only a coercive solution is perfectly rational. If there is only *one* good, those who do not recognize it are mistaken. Either, by better adjusting their judgment to their moral intuition, they will eventually discover it (pure intuitionism), or they can be helped to do so, and then there are two ways of doing so. The soft way offers a method to discover the good in itself. This is of course a certain form of Platonism, in which this good actually exists independently from us. The hard way is none other than coercion, which makes it possible for the strongest of the lot to impose his conception on the weakest one.

It is not necessary to discuss this coercive solution at length. As long as the weakest is merely compelled to yield to the strongest, there is no unanimous agreement and therefore no justice. As Rousseau already very sharply observed (1762), the so-called 'right' of the strongest is simply not a right. It is simply a *de facto* situation. Now, if we stick to facts, a perfectionist conception that would not be in one way or another coercive is hard to contemplate.

It is unlikely that in the event of a conflict, and without resorting to force, one of the parties could accept the other person's point of view as such. It will be necessary to come to an agreement, that is, to negotiate a compromise after which each party will have backed down on their initial demands. Now, if this is completely possible in a deontological and liberal context, where there is no reason there for a reasonable conception of the good to coincide with a merely rational conception, this is impossible for the perfectionist, who, in order to remain consistent, finds himself obliged to cling to his convictions. In fact, perfectionists are already in the process of discussing the rational means of attaining the 'true' good life when liberals are still wondering how to bring together different life plans in a reasonable way, that is by being careful to restrain a freedom only if it infringes upon another. In doing so, only the latter are discussing justice. The former discuss the means to reach a good which, they hope, will be wanted by everyone. But it is impossible to reach it without banishing life plans that do not enhance this good, and a theory which ends up negating reasonable

6 This is called a pure procedural justice (cf. chapter 3).

life plans in such a way negates the moral personality of the individuals who have formed these plans.

Perfectionism cannot overcome this negation without losing its consistency. But it is not the only doctrine for which this is the case; it is also true of the utilitarian doctrine, because, among other things, of the consequentialism which it underpins and which leads it, by definition, to admit no principle making it possible to avoid sacrificing an individual plan when this is instrumental to the optimisation of the good. This is the reason why Rawls (1971, I, 1) starts his reflection on justice with a total rejection of this dogma:

> Each person possesses an inviolability founded on justice that even the welfare of society as a whole cannot override. For this reason justice [...] does not allow that the sacrifices imposed on a few are outweighed by the larger sum of advantages enjoyed by many. [...] the rights secured by justice are not subject to political bargaining or to the calculus of social interests.

In this passage, Rawls summarises what can be called the 'deontological objection', but, in order to grasp all its implications, we have to examine more closely the utilitarian theses.

## 2. The Pitfalls of the *Homo Œconomicus*

### 2.1 *Normative utilitarianism, explanatory utilitarianism*

When he published *A Theory of Justice* in 1971, Rawls put an end to the domination of utilitarian thinking in the Anglo-Saxon world. This was no small achievement. The simplicity of the initial principles of utilitarianism and their congruence with the standard approach in economics exerted a powerful attraction. In sociology, the influence of utilitarianism had always been less important, though not non-existent (Coleman, 1990). The flexibility of a notion like that of 'utility' and the endless refinements it opened onto had led people to believe that it would be possible to overcome certain contradictions, in particular those between the morality of 'everybody's utility' and the liberal principle to which some adhered (Mill, 1859). Since then, nobody would have dreamt of supporting a utilitarianism in the tradition of a Moore (1912) or a Sidgwick (1874). As for those who refused to cross the line for good and give up on the teleological contents of this doctrine, they found themselves compelled to give such toned-down formulations that one can wonder what is really left of it.[7]

It is not superfluous, however, to discuss utilitarianism. The idea that it could be enough to look for 'the greatest happiness for the greatest number' – to quote Hutcheson's words (1725), which were later sanctioned by Bentham and his followers – is enticing at first sight. A critical reflection on this principle is a simple way of getting to the crux of the matter. Besides, such a critic necessarily leads to a discussion of the shortcomings of explanatory utilitarianism, that is, of the rational choice theory.

Historically, the utilitarian theory provided substantial support to secular and humanist parties. By claiming to judge everything afresh from the standpoint of mundane happiness, it opposed traditional morals, which rested on religion and 'revealed' principles. It presented itself as a 'science of morality' which could determine what a rational individual in search of happiness on earth ought to do. Calculating the happy and unhappy consequences for everyone and maximizing total happiness was enough to do so.

Beyond the variations of the doctrine from one author to the next – which are sometimes significant since the doctrine is so flexible – two difficulties can be made out. First, having to add up 'goods' (or, in its more neutral version, 'utilities') makes it necessary to apply a similar scale of values. Even if utilitarianism initially seems to accept a form of deontology, which consists in leaving to everyone the freedom to define their idea of happiness and in making sure that every person counts for one, the practice of maximisation inexorably leads this doctrine back within the field of perfectionism. Moreover, as a science of morality, utilitarianism claims to determine rationally what ought-to-be, without taking into account what is reasonable. This makes it necessary to admit the notion that there is such a thing as human nature, hence a mechanistic and slightly simplistic explanatory project. As soon as we assume that all morality rests on the maximisation of the total of individual utilities, a perfect information on the consequences of a given action is indispensable. It is necessary to be able to predict the variations caused by this action on everyone's utilities. On the scale of a society, it is necessary to build a true mechanics of man because it

7 Some have therefore spoken (Slote, 1985, 1989) of '*a minima* consquentialism' or of 'satisficing rationality' – that is, allowing non-optimal choices.

is necessary, for each action, to be able to deduce precisely enough the sequence of all the individuals' reactions. The question is no longer to find out how to live together by using *general* rules. It is to solve a problem of logistics where individuals are mere cogwheels of a plan devised to increase utility ('everybody's utility', that is).

These difficulties have an epistemological side, which deals with the knowledge of morality, and a motivational side, which endeavours to account for reasons to act. These are of course different things. What is of public utility, or everybody's utility, or even which is a utility *for us* does not necessarily match up with what is personally useful *for me.* In this perspective, normative utilitarianism (defined as the optimisation of the sum[8] of utilities) is distinct from explanatory utilitarianism (understood as the optimisation of individual utility). For Bentham (1789), they still had to be brought together by a skilful balance of offences and sentences. This relation had to be built judicially. As for political economy, it contented itself with supposing the existence of the relation. But the compatibility between private happiness and public interest must still be ensured. In order to do so, it is necessary to draw all the consequences of what Mandeville (1714) had already suggested in his *Fable of the Bees* ('private vices, public benefits') by introducing an 'invisible hand' guaranteeing that every person's pursuit of their private happiness should maximise the collective well-being. The main result of this quest for an 'invisible hand', a quest that remained fruitless, is nothing else than the frequent confusion between a normative utilitarianism and an explanatory utilitarianism.

The rational choice theory has inherited those difficulties. It is not enough to claim to ignore normative utilitarianism to hope to come out unscathed. By not making conflicts the starting-point of his analysis, the rational choice theorist, who must say something about utility or collective preferences, almost always sticks to the myth of pre-established harmony or of 'everything is for the best in this best of all possible worlds' (Leibniz, 1710). *A world without conflicts is a world which does not need justice.* This is quite clear. But as soon as it sets down that there is a conflict between individual utilities, the rational choice theory stumbles upon the contradiction between the rational pursuit of individual well-being and the rational pursuit of everyone's welfare.

8 Some prefer to speak of the 'maximization of the average of utilities' (Harsanyi, 1977), but this variation does not prevent the difficulties reviewed here from arising.

Historically, this deadlock is located in the extensions of two perspectives which find their origins in Hobbes's writings, among others: the state of nature or a social pact deriving exclusively from this state of nature. In the first case, agents are endowed with a *natural* psychology (selfishness, will to power, etc.). They have no critical distance as to the conflicts they provoke and they live in the present by following their inclinations. If we leave this naturalistic version, it is enough to say that we are in the case where individuals pursue their well-being rationally. In such hypotheses, conflicts are solved by force (or some equivalent for it). In the second case, men are free. Nevertheless, such a 'tearing-away' from immediate nature only aims at preserving the 'vital process'. The agent does not follow his inclinations for the mere reason that he doubts his strength vis-à-vis others and has anxieties over the future. Agents are pushed towards a prudential logic (an aversion to risk) which leads them to *deny their nature in the name of their nature*: they accept to sign a pact which deprives them of some of their immediate desires in order to preserve their lives. They have a greater interest in doing so.

The rational choice theory has obviously detached itself from strictly naturalistic presuppositions, but it could not go as far as to give up the idea that social dynamics essentially came from springs. The choice of a mechanistic modelling led it to take little notice of other motives. Such a restriction has heavy consequences because it also banishes a mode of conflict resolution founded on the *idea* of the social contract and eventually of justice. It is therefore hardly surprising that one of the greatest stumbling blocks of the rational choice theory is moral reasoning and, more specifically, the reasoning on what is fair. This is because the social contract, far from accompanying nature, dramatically breaks away from it. As Rousseau wrote (1762, I, 9):

> […] the fundamental pact, rather than destroying natural equality, on the contrary substitutes a moral and legitimate equality for whatever physical inequality nature may have placed between men, and […] while they may be unequal in force or in genius, they all become equal by convention and by right.

This is something which a calculation of pleasures and pains, or an aversion to risks, or a generalised benevolence or malevolence, or an optimisation of utility, or any other totally empirical apprehension of human nature cannot account for. In the best case, the result is a rational 'natural' pact which merely optimises everyone's interest. But there will always lack a public space to find agreements, and as a result, this 'natural' pact will always be a fake agreement, to be read in terms of cunning and strategic behaviours. Instead of this, and to put things as Kant did, if the social contract is an Idea of reason, it must find a foundation in (the practical) reason. It cannot be rational only in an empirical way. It must imperatively be reasonable too, and it must therefore respect the *a priori* principles of reason, in particular the one which compels it to rest on a *unanimous agreement*.[9] But the social contract can aim for such unanimity only if every party accepts to consider the others' perspectives. In other words, the question here is not to know which principle of organisation or which institution maximises everyone's interest, but which principle or organisation respects each person' equal freedom; and this will never be derived from an optimisation of the good, even at the cost of elaborate mathematical endeavours.

There have been many efforts to solve, within the context of such an optimisation, the question of how rational, but not reasonable, individuals manage to serve a common interest. We will examine in detail in chapter 4 the model proposed by Robert Axelrod (1984) to explain social cooperation. But since it is neither possible nor actually necessary to dwell on any of these attempts, as the same logic is always at work, we will only take one example here. It is linked to the way in which Mancur Olson (1965) intends to account for the production of a collective good or, more broadly, for collective action.

According to him, it is possible to achieve this by sticking to the axiom whereby individuals only know how to serve their personal interests. In such a hypothesis, how could they produce a collective good, or engage in collective action, if the resulting benefits, in the event of a success, are a profit to all, even those who took no part in it (as in the case of a strike leading to an increase of wages for all, the strikers as well as the non-strikers)? At first sight, and with a certain number of general conditions, it is of course impossible. Every rational individual will act as a free rider. If we want to avoid resorting to coercion (which is not a general answer, and which would actually not be explained by this model), and since individuals clearly produce collective goods or engage in collective actions, it is necessary to try to understand how it remains possible not to act as a free rider (without the individuals ceasing to maximise their utility, of course). The

9 Unanimous agreement represents in substance what the categorical imperative demands, but we will come back to this later.

answer is simple: an individual will produce a collective good or take part in a collective action only if she finds a personal benefit in it, which those who did not engage will not find. Those benefits are chiefly material or financial. But, as Olson acknowledges, they cannot be reduced to that. There are countless cases where individuals engage in a collective action without being paid in any way. These goods can therefore be symbolical. Morality appears there, but only as the strict functional equivalent of a financial incentive. If an individual's ethics dictates her to serve a common interest, she will do so, provided she considers that this will maximise her well-being, in a better way than free riding. For instance, Olson tells us, she can gain self-esteem or some prestige from it, she may not be able to cope with the idea of being 'ostracised' from society, she may be in need of social recognition, etc. – as many individual and non-collective goods.

Even if we admit this, one would have to explain why 'social recognition' (or any other good of the same kind mentioned by Olson) would come to those who are not free riders. Nothing in this model helps us to understand it. One has to suppose that actors, those who provide the recognition as well as those who receive it, already agree on this point. How could actors who are selfish by hypothesis reach this agreement, tacitly or not? We are not told anything about this, and such a deadlock is hard to admit. In a mafioso group, being a free rider or carrying out a swindle without being caught, or performing a theft with talent are on the contrary worthy of recognition. Why are we not in this situation? The problem is obviously regarded as already solved, while it was precisely what needed to be explained.

Moreover, while we had started with only one type-behaviour, it has now evolved into two opposite directions: maximising one's utility by free riding because the utility of following a moral imperative (in the full sense of the word, that is supposedly non 'mafioso', but for an unknown reason) is inferior, and maximising one's utility by not free riding because the utility of following the same moral imperative is superior. The mystery of the individual's participation or non-participation to a collective action is then 'solved'. Individuals serve only their private interests, and therefore act as free riders by not participating to the production of a good benefiting everyone, but among those free riders, some are not free riding, were it only because of the mere personal satisfaction of having followed a moral imperative, a satisfaction which the former cannot experience (Olson puts it very clearly, morality is introduced here only as a 'selective incentive'). True free riders are free riding, but there are fake free riders, who do not grant enough value to free riding and therefore take part completely naturally in collective actions. In other words, those who cease to be free riders cooperate, and those who remain free riders do not cooperate. This is a highly expectable tautology.[10] However, there is no explanation about what called for one: the miracle whereby some free riders enter the 'magic circle' of cooperation – to quote Olson's phrase. It is obvious that the willingness to cooperate is in fact already there among those free riders who are not true ones. Reasonableness has been excluded, but the social order which should have been accounted for was only presupposed.

## 2.2 *Utilitarian impartiality, deontological impartiality*

Because of the difficulties raised by an anthropological model which reduces actors to absolutely ego-centred individuals, social sciences and a certain tradition in utilitarianism have tried from the very beginning to find an alternative model. There has always been a need to understand not only what opposes individuals, but also what brings them together. Hume (1739–1740) and Smith (1759) have thus tried to go beyond selfishness, and to extend human psychology by relying on the notion of sympathy. The maxim with which Smith launches his *Theory of Moral Sentiments* is very clear in that respect: 'How selfish soever man may be supposed, there are evidently some principles in his nature, which interest him in the fortune of others, and render their happiness necessary to him, though he derives nothing from it except the pleasure of seeing it.' The point is to introduce as much as possible the idea that we put ourselves in other people's position *mentally*, and to infer the existence of moral principles from there.

10 It will be noted that since morality or any other 'good' of the same kind is introduced as an equivalent to a financial or material incentive to cooperate, we cannot overcome the problem by falling back on purely material or financial goods to account for participation in a collective action. We understand that a free rider can be paid to stop free riding, but we cannot understand why this works for some and not for others, so that in the end, the tautology has not been overcome. Besides, supposing it is possible to bring any incentive down to the equivalent of a financial incentive means supposing, without saying so, that the problem of the interpersonal comparison of utilities has been solved. But this problem is far from having been solved, insofar as it can be solved at all, as many utilitarians actually acknowledge.

Hume's or Smith's sensualist and empirical presuppositions nevertheless orientate them towards a simple analysis of the feelings transferred from one individual to another. To sympathise, for these actors, is to experience from other people's behaviours the same feelings as them. Typically, pity or compassion are the product of an individual's sympathy when facing another human being's suffering. The underlying psychological principle is clear but it raises several problems, especially because the sympathetic transfer cannot be purely mechanical. It cannot be seen only as a mere contagion of emotions. First, an individual's suffering is not the *same* feeling as the pity experienced by a spectator. Sympathy not only transfers the feeling; it transforms it. Moreover, depending on the closeness between the individual at stake and the spectator, sympathy does not lead to the same result. Hence two other problems, which are probably more crucial when it comes to founding a morality. First, sympathy negates any attempt at overcoming our differences: I feel pity because I am similar to the person I am looking at, and because I see him in a situation which makes me infer that he is suffering as I would suffer in his position. However, he may not be suffering, and our tastes may be radically different. We come upon the ambivalence of the idea of putting oneself in other people's position. This may mean that I put myself in their position with my tastes, my fads, and my idea of happiness; this may also mean that I put myself there with their tastes, fads and idea of happiness. Besides, sympathy mainly expresses partial feelings. As a result of sympathy, we experience feelings which are similar to those who are close to us or like us, who share the same culture, the same language, the same customs, etc. These are undeniably important aspects for the study of feelings; and yet, morality cannot rest exclusively on this type of feelings. How impartiality can be deduced from partiality still has to be explained.

To that effect, Hume invokes a 'Judicious Spectator', while Smith uses an 'Impartial Spectator'. In both cases, they try to compensate sympathy's shortcomings and to add a form of regulation of feelings to an approach only based on the circulation of feelings. But it is necessary to assume the existence of an authority to judge and arbitrate between all feelings. From there, it is possible to draw parallels between Hume's position and the classical utilitarian theory. In the context of these parallels, the judicious spectator forms her moral evaluations from a calculus of utility, which is simply postponed or indirect, which distinguishes it from the selfish individual's calculus.

At first sight, Smith does not bring the impartial spectator's judgment to considerations of utility. Starting from the idea that I not only put myself in the other person's position, but that I also put myself in the position of the person putting himself in my position – that is, from the idea that the individual involved sympathises with her spectator, Smith makes this situation the Archimedes' point explaining the well thought-out judgment of his impartial spectator. The explanation comes down to admitting the idea that individuals seek the spectators' approval, even if this approval has no utility. This aspect is indeed important, but still does not explain moral judgment: seeking everyone's approval does not say anything about what could trigger such approval. Besides, at a formal level, the operator of sympathy can again, and in spite of everything, be retranslated into the context of classical utilitarianism. It just requires introducing other people's preferences into the utility function. A certain form of benevolence can thus be explained. The impartial spectator corresponds to an ideal individual, perfectly rational and informed, who brings into the utility function other people's utilities with equal weighting. This is the perfect sympathiser who takes sides for no one in particular, so that eventually, in accordance with normative utilitarianism, what will be regarded as fair will be what maximises the sum of uniformly weighted utilities.

As a result, we come upon a difficulty which echoes the one posed by classical utilitarianism. In no way does sympathy as it is generalised here make it possible to settle conflicts. It accounts very well for partiality, but it is not enough to consider a sort of 'generalised partiality' to account for impartiality.[11] While the deontological perspective defines unanimously

11 This criticism also runs counter to some contemporary feminist theories of justice. According to them, liberal theories, which are mainly due to male thinkers, rest on an overly 'abstract' or 'public' fairness, impartiality, or subject because the public sphere is the one where men rule. The feminine point of view is more 'concrete' and is related to the domestic sphere where the maintenance of personal bonds is left to or imposed on women (Friedman, 1987). From the perspective of this feminine sphere, justice therefore appears to be an ethics of solicitude, towards close people according to some (Tronto, 1987), but more 'generalised' according to others (Gilligan, 1982). However, there is a misunderstanding here. Contrary to its 'rigorist' reputation, it is easy to show that justice as impartiality or fairness does not make solicitude impossible in principle. But inversely, it cannot be founded on or deduced from such an ethics, which is only a form of altruism. We will examine this more closely later; for now, it is enough to underline that partiality, which consists in favouring another person (whether close or otherwise), cannot found impartiality.

accepted rights and duties to settle conflicts, sympathy operates a depersonalisation by merging all preferences, and therefore denies conflicts. Either we always are sympathisers because no actions can harm us; and we live in an ethereal universe. Or we all are pure altruists and we always decide to do what others desire, which, at this level of generalisation, is paradoxical,[12] and shows well how the issue of justice is avoided. If no one desires to become selfish, there is nothing to be arbitrated on because there are no primary preferences to make operational the sympathy which is a second-rate preference, a preference of preference.

In order to come out of this deadlock, some have tried to find a standard which is *common to all*, from which an accounting operation on pleasures and pains could be undertaken. This perfectionist solution returns more directly to classical utilitarianism. Here, a conflict can be settled by comparing an individual's pains to the pleasures resulting for others. If pains prevail, the latter will become sympathisers and curb their desires. On the contrary, if pleasures prevail, they will sacrifice the former to their desires. And yet, the measuring of pleasures and pains can be called fair only if the standard good is acknowledged as such by all. The conflict must be a conflict between equals. Such a presupposition is nothing but a new way of enforcing harmony. It evacuates conflicts between life plans which do not enhance the same goods.

Utilitarianism thus proves unable to account for the solutions found by actors to overcome their differences and solve their disagreements. If we return to the example of a community which must choose to invest into either music or football, we see that utilitarianism misses the point. Its 'solution' consists in asserting that a compromise is already found in the weighting of pleasures and pains derived from music and football. But individuals rarely agree on weightings, rather on rights and duties. More fundamentally, interpersonal comparisons of utility, which are a prerequisite, are highly problematic. Even if utilitarianism succeeded in providing an empirical procedure (for example, a system of auctions) to compare objectively subjective utilities, it could not account for sentiments of justice.

12 A real altruism, that is one which does not hide some selfishness more or less artfully, cannot be generalised in logic. Indeed, this would make it a sort of infinite mirroring that could stop only if it came across selfishness – by principle excluded from such a process of generalisation. This paradox of 'living for others' as a duty for mankind, according to Comte's wish (1852), has often been underlined (see Spencer, 1879; Dupuy, 1992).

Imagine a judge showing clemency towards a sadist who tortured a mentally deficient individual by arguing that he feels less pain than another person would – in this case, the weighting of pleasures and pains would back up his point. This is usually regarded as unfair because the judge is expected to *objectify* the offence and treat the moaning victim and the impassive victim in the same way. Considerations on justice are not necessarily related to pleasures and pains or even, more generally, to utility.

## 2.3 *Justice below unanimity?*

If, originally, utilitarianism was presented as a hedonistic doctrine, it is nonetheless possible to get rid of this aspect while retaining its model of reasoning. The rational choice theory did not fail to do so. It is indeed possible to formally avoid attributing to individuals a supreme good which they all should desire, or a type of natural psychology. By not considering that the agents' choices are based upon reasons which give meaning to their actions, the rational choice theory avoids taking sides for these motives. It does not matter whether the individuals' motivations are selfish or altruistic, whether they aim at fairness or not, and neither do the ends which individuals set themselves matter. It just registers that the latter have this or that order of preference, rather than another one. It is therefore not forbidden – according to the theory of revealed preferences – to grant more utility to the action 'voting' than to 'not voting', to the action 'throwing money down the drain' than to 'saving'. In this case, optimising a utility function is only a formal translation of the maxim 'act as you prefer' and the issue at stake in the model rests entirely on the aggregation of behaviours.

It appears as obvious, however, that this reduction of rational choice to a mere formal claim does not satisfy anyone. It is enough to see how little interest an empirical approach to the construction of the order of preferences arouses. In practice, this order is always devised *a priori* and exempted from any justification. This implicit area is of course problematic, since the relevance of this or that utility function rarely seems to be at stake. In particular, it makes it possible never to question the 'intrinsic value' of an action. It is taken for granted, for instance, that work never is a calling, but only a labour whose attraction only rests on the matching remuneration. Similarly, it seems that social integration through work depends only on financial incentives rather than on setting up life plans to which agents give meaning. In other words, the value is extrinsic and rests on the law of supply and demand. This amounts to mistaking the value for the price. Such a definition of value is far from being self-evident and entails at least one difficulty. It requires that an order of preferences should at least be established. The principle of least spending (or least effort) is indeed a motivation, but a second-rate one, since this motivation requires a definition of the ends first.

Still, let us start from the idea that the order of preference is the result of a revelation. In this case, the utility encompasses realities which differ according to each individual, following the non-normative ambition of the rational choice theory. As long as there are no conflicts, nothing prevents individuals from doing whatever they wish. This idea is at the origin of Pareto-optimality, which is defined as the social state in which it is impossible to increase an individual's well-being without harming another one. The strength of this principle comes above all from the fact that it generates *unanimity*. By construction (there is no harmful interaction between *ego* and *alter*), nobody can complain that others are improving their lot. It can also be said that in this situation, fairness is suggested by the fact that no one is envious. It is admitted that the improvement of each person's welfare is a private matter, which does not have anything to do with others. But such a hypothesis purely and simply comes down to regarding conflicts as null and void, not to say as illegitimate.

Since conflicts are denied, in order to account for the individuals' feelings of fairness, one has to go beyond Pareto-optimality. If we stay in the utilitarian context, the problem is therefore as follows: knowing that everyone is free to rank their preferences as they wish, how can we aggregate individual preferences to deduce the fair way of solving a conflict? Or still, how can we set up a function of social choice which respects the moral standpoint? In Rousseau's terms, this amounts to wanting to build the general will through the mere addition of particular wills, and therefore, to confuse straightaway the general will with the will of all (Philonenko, 1968, chap. 19). From the outset, the type of solution sought by the rational choice theorist is opposed to the idea of the social contract. Instead of building the general will through a *reasonable compromise* between all the particular wills, the utilitarian goes in search of a *rational operation* to determine the general will. Instead of regarding the general will as the result of an intersubjective, creative, constructive and well thought-out effort to integrate differences between individuals into a collective life, the rational choice theorist wants to obtain it through calculus, and this inevitably leads him to assume that the problem is solved at the level of axioms. Such a quest is analogous to the search for a machine which will solve any moral problem. This of course has no solution and will never have one.

This is actually the conclusion which utilitarianism itself must accept, in the wake of Kenneth Arrow's works (1951). His famous theorem establishes that there is no accounting procedure which is neither dictatorial nor imposed from outside, which does not use interpersonal comparisons of utility and which still makes it possible to build, from individual preferences, an order of collective preferences respecting certain usual criteria of rationality. A unanimously acceptable compromise cannot be achieved only from an automatic procedure (which can be represented by a mode of ballot). Hoping to reach unanimity by relaxing the obligation of unanimity has proven vain. As a matter of fact, this was already Flaubert's conclusion in *Bouvard and Pécuchet*: truth is not what is voted by a majority; it demands an argumentation aiming at everyone's agreement. It was also Rousseau's starting point (1762, I, 5), who did not intend to obtain fairness from a ballot: 'Why would a hundred who want a master have the right to vote on behalf of ten who do not want one?'

## 2.4 *Action or rule, the deontological objection remains*

Some have thought it possible to get out of all these dead-ends by leaving direct or act utilitarianism for indirect or rule utilitarianism. But the deontological objection, whose formulation we re-stated above as it was given by Rawls (1971), persists. Without a loss of consistency, no utilitarianism finds in its model the means to warrant that any human person's rights will not be sacrificed on the altar of utility. According to direct act utilitarianism, agents choose *in effect* actions which maximise utility. But it could be argued that, if they do not calculate at every moment what makes it possible to maximise the utility, they follow principles which happen to have the 'lucky' effect of leading (sooner or later) to this maximisation. This is the world of 'everything happens as if'. Therefore, for Mill (1859), the principle of liberty allows each individual to do what they please in their private lives. And, according to him, if everyone follows this principle, it turns out that the collective well-being will eventually be maximised. So far, it has not been demonstrated that it happens this way as a matter of fact; it is thus necessary to stick to the belief in a pre-established harmony. Conversely, it is easy to show that ignoring this principle could be optimal from the viewpoint of act utilitarianism. With no deontology, it will therefore be necessary to infringe upon it. In fact, the principle of liberty has no other guarantee here than the principle of utility. The observance of rights therefore remains purely contingent and we have made no progress at all in trying to reply to the deontological objection.

Contemporary rule utilitarianism (Harrod, 1936; Harsanyi, 1977) is a little more precise. Agents do not always act directly towards utility maximisation of, but they behave 'fairly' by choosing a (moral) rule which, as long as it is observed by everyone, maximises utility. The persons' rights are indeed present, but since they are nothing else than what results from rules which ensure an optimisation, this leaves the bulk of the deontological critic unanswered. For instance, what guarantees that a given rule entailing a strong negative discrimination will not pass, in certain circumstances, the maximisation test? In this case, without deontology, we have no reason not to adopt it, and the individual's most basic rights may therefore be sacrificed again. Either we finally give up and forsake these rights, or there is no other solution but to develop an *ad hoc* argument for each rule, which is hardly satisfactory. Richard Hare (1981) would answer however that there is always an alternative, that is another rule which, in order to go on with the same example, would ensure with no negative discrimination the same utility maximisation. Admitting that this can always be the case – which is far from having been proven – this only amounts to putting off the day of reckoning anyway, since why, still without deontology, should we choose this new rule rather than the one implying negative discrimination?

The critic can be stopped here, since it is clear that utilitarianism always misses the real point, which is not to wonder why we should choose such or such rule rather than another one as a means to maximise utility, but why a moral rule should be the *mere* means to anything at all? As long as fairness is only a means, even if it serves the good, it is in fact impossible to warrant that the rights of any human person will always be respected. To really take these rights or fairness seriously (Dworkin, 1977), there is no other solution but to always make them ends as well, and to give them priority over the good or utility.

All the arguments mentioned until now are enough to show that the rational choice theory cannot be expected not to be undermined by the criticisms which a liberal and deontological theory is led to formulate against it. The hope that, with respect to the shortcomings of normative utilitarianism, it could be possible to fall back on a 'purely' explanatory utilitarianism without relying on any deontology, this hope, which is actually slightly strange, is pointless. In metaphorical terms, abandoning Bentham in the hope that it is enough to embrace Pareto and that the latter does not need Kant to account for moral choices, is illusory. Even unanimous, Pareto-optimality is not justice, for the latter does not consist, unless accidentally, in optimising the good.

All things considered, the rational choice theory cannot overcome the following dilemma. Either it sets out objective springs (such as the vital process or the supreme good), which leads to call some specific ends 'rational', along with the processes which are efficient to reach an end. It then becomes normative. Or it starts from subjective springs, but does not manage anymore to give itself a social choice which is stable because it is fair or objective. In both cases, it evacuates some of the reasons which individuals use to live together. Since these cannot be forgotten without leading to inextricable difficulties, on the contrary, it is to these reasons that we will appeal to formulate the hypothesis of a fair spectator.

## 2.5 *Falling back on a holistic strategy is not the solution however*

Utilitarianism has failed to account for the path which leads from explanatory utilitarianism to normative utilitarianism or, which amounts to the same, for the 'leap' from selfish motivations to moral motivations,[13] and yet, despite this failure, we owe it, at least partly, to the lack of any idea of a precedence of the right over the good in social sciences. This of course had many consequences on their methodology.

Seeing only the rational pursuit of one's individual good often leads to dubious moral contortions. Instead of a balanced judgement taking both interest and morality into consideration (or the rational and the reasonable), the theorist may now go in search of an increasingly unlikely and empirically evanescent hidden interest. It is then impossible to say that the rational dimension of an action or an opinion has been truly highlighted. All

13 Including moral preferences into utility functions makes them more complex, but is of course not a solution since they are added arbitrarily (see Wolfelsperger, 2001).

that is obtained is an incomplete – not to say false – interpretation. In practice, most rational choice theorists do not draw all the consequences of their approach, and express some reservations as to their conclusions.[14] As data generally resist their hard-line technique, this naturally leads them to set a 'bound' to the actor's rationality (Simon, 1957). Establishing such a bound (because information is incomplete, imperfect, etc.) leads to a greater realism towards the *homo œconomicus'* absolute rationality, but it does not solve any of the difficulties that have arisen so far. As a result, for some sociologists, the conclusion seems obvious: the actor's rationality, methodological individualism and the idea of a comprehensive approach should be abandoned, as if those principles really were at stake (Boudon, 2003), in order to lapse into holism. For them, there is no other solution, but to leave the *homo œconomicus* (bounded or not) and to put on the glasses of the *homo ideologicus*. However, this strategy only barely covers the lack of understanding.

In a certain way, the dead end in which utilitarianism finds itself is only cropping up again under a different form here. One of the problems of utilitarianism stemmed from the impossibility of linking epistemological and motivational aspects of morality. Unless one presupposed social harmony, it was impossible to understand what makes an actor serve social or collective interests. The holistic strategy only consists in putting the latter away as some form of unconscious, without caring about whether the actor has access to it, and even less about the mechanisms of this access. How do superstructures (of which morality is a part), often themselves determined by techno-economic infrastructures, hovering above individuals, find their way into their minds, to the point of turning them into mere puppets? Of course, there are always exceptions to what this strong determinism orders individuals to think (according to their social class, their race, etc.), but the reply is 'unanswerable': it is that these individuals only have a false consciousness (their real behaviour is devalued by comparison with what they should think or do if they were willing to conform to the theorist's theory). In a metaphorical way, such reasoning shows well that the holist is after all only a rational choice theorist who just sweeps the 'dust' under the carpet. And of course this is only tantamount to pretending to solve the problem.

14 Damien Broussolle (2001) remarks in this respect that, even if they do not go as far as to confront it fully, economists are not unaware of the difficulties of the rational choice theory.

We will come back to this in greater detail when discussing the communitarian theories (see chapter 4). Let's say, for the time being, that one should be careful not to conclude too hastily that other people are irrational (stupid, mad, hypocritical, etc.). This generally indicates an excessively narrow conception of rationality. Many theorists thus circumscribe thoughts and actions which have reasons – not forgetting to include theirs – and put the others away into the irrational or the unconscious, with no further discussion. This amounts to taking it upon oneself to say in an elitist way what reason is, and such a strategy entails a major difficulty. Either we consider that actors find their way in the world thanks to their lights, however weak these are. And in this case, it is the sociologist's or the economist's duty to endeavour to share his lights, while using other people's to do so, which implies that we accept a broad rationality (thus including the reasonable). Or we admit that some have access to lights to which some cannot by principle aspire. Consequently, theorists form an elite which has to be taken at its own word. Such a claim can indeed be met, it is as old as Plato's myth of the cavern, but it is incompatible with the processes of modern sciences, which precisely suppose a well-argued debate between actors relying on their own lights.

## 3. The Fair Spectator Hypothesis

### 3.1 *Reasons relative to the agent and neutral reasons*

Let us leave there the holistic strategy and return to the idea that individuals can solve their conflicts through the search for a reasonable compromise between everyone's demands. In that context, we admit that while actors have reasons to pursue their idea of happiness, they also have reasons to restrict themselves in this pursuit in the name of life in common.

To account for this, we have to start from the principle that individuals perform an action or endorse an opinion for good reasons. On one side, reasons that are only *relative to the agent*, and related either to his particular interest or to his conception of the good life (these are the only reasons that rational choice theorists are willing to take heed of). On the other side, *neutral* reasons (Nagel, 1991), which are likely to convince others, even if they have neither the same interests, nor the same conception of the good life. It can also be said that the first reasons are simply subjective, while the second reasons are objective (in a sense that will be specified in chapter 5). So, just as neutral reasons aim at the truth when fact judgments are concerned, they aim at fairness when it comes to value judgments. And of course, truth and the just are not unrelated (Boudon, 1995*a*).

The phrase 'neutral reasons' does not refer to a neutralisation of reasons which would no longer be connected with individuals. On the contrary, it leads to emphasise that certain reasons are shared and conducive to unanimity. In this sense, a neutralisation of reasons involves a well thought-out integration of the various individual perspectives into a common point of view. In other terms, speaking of neutral reason leads to pure practical reason, as Kant (1788) defined it. It means that individuals are not *determined* by their desires and natural inclinations, but simply *affected* by them, and that they have other reasons to act which fulfil *other ends*, whose coexistence needs to be thought over. It then appears that determining oneself according to neutral reasons amounts to abiding by the claims of the categorical imperative (Kant, 1785): 'Act in such a way that you always treat humanity, whether in your own person or in the person of any other, at the same time, never simply as a means, but always at the same time as an end.' These other ends are other people; and neutral reasons are those which are the object of a unanimous agreement, which precisely supposes that every person should indeed be treated as an end. The equivalence between unanimous agreement and the categorical imperative may appear in an even better way in Kant's first formulation[15] of this imperative: 'Act only on that maxim through which you can at the same time will that it should become a universal law.' By following this rule, an actor defends an opinion, on the basis of neutral reasons, because its terms are regarded as acceptable by all and because it covers no preference for the interest or the ethical conception of a specific individual. The actor thus gives priority to the right over the good and his opinion or his way of acting lends itself to a unanimous agreement whereby, as Kant (1797, §46) also remarked: 'Each [person] decides the same thing about all and all decide the same thing about each.'

15 In this respect, it should be remarked that there is only one categorical imperative. The three phrasings which Kant gives (1785) in the *Groundwork of the Metaphysics of Morals* are only, as Rawls perfectly shows, reformulations from different angles.

In the context of this non-restrictive approach to rationality, the epistemological aspect (knowledge of the moral law) and the motivational aspect of morality happen to be linked, since what is conceived to be fair (categorical imperative) is not an oppressive duty that one could not want to do. On the contrary, since justice is a unanimous agreement which takes into account my own ends as well as other people's, since justice also expresses my own will, I have the will to be fair. This is the reason why Kant considers that, in the intelligible world, I will do in all liberty what is fair (autonomy of the will) but that, being also placed in the sensible world, and submitted to the heteronomy of nature, that is to various springs, my will to be reasonable may turn out to be secondary or immaterial in my action (heteronomy of the will). Hence two consequences, linked to the very nature of this principle of an extended rationality. In the first place, since the procedure through which the right can be found also makes the motive of an action explicit, it can be used as a method *for social sciences*, and not exclusively for moral philosophy. In the second place, on this basis, it becomes possible to provide a non-reductive typology of the solutions to conflicts.

## 3.2 *A typology of the solutions to conflicts*

In the theories expounded above, conflicts have always been negated in one way or another. The utilitarian ended up presupposing harmony. The holist could not see conflict as a practical problem. Eventually, there was nothing to choose between, and it resulted in a very incomplete theory of action – when it was not non-existing. We can get out of these narrow conceptions of practical reason by starting again, from the practical question *par excellence*: 'What ought I to do?' It has to be regarded under three different aspects, which in the wake of Jürgen Habermas (1991) we will describe as pragmatic, ethical and moral. A judgement bearing on the means to an end can be called pragmatic. A judgment on what is worth living according to an individual is called ethical. A judgment about a maxim of action which must gain everyone's agreement is called moral. A typology of the solutions to conflicts can be brought down to these.

(i) *The egoist solution.* Every individual can of course choose to give his or her own rational good the priority over what would be reasonable for all. His behaviour or opinion is selfish in the sense that his reasons are only convincing for him or those who share the same interests. The underlying reasoning is above all pragmatic. Such selfishness can also occasion sophisticated strategies when it implies a calculus involving someone else's well-being or behaviour. While giving himself a preference, an actor can indeed attempt to associate some of the others by offering them a mutual interest contract. However, as long as the reasons put forward do not aim to convince everyone, the contract at stake remains a coalition against at least one individual whom people are willing to sacrifice. This behaviour can be found under various guises, especially according to whether other people are regarded rather as a means or rather as an end. The compassionate individual proves sensitive to the reasons of those who do not – or hardly – benefit from the contract. He is affected, at least emotionally, by their situation, and it would therefore not go against his well-measured interest if this situation was improved. However, with respect to his other interests, which he would then have to relinquish, he is not willing to commit personally. The cynic is on the contrary willing to contribute, but in order to maintain, and even to add weight to, the terms of the contract in his favour. Under the cover of altruism, compassion and cynicism eventually turn out to be second-degree selfishness. This is why they are sometimes described as 'rational altruism' (Ballet, 1998). The emphasis on this type of approach is due among other things to the fact that it is the only one which keeps up the hope of explaining moral choices in the context of a rational choice theory.

(ii) *The altruistic solution.* Altruism, this time real or pure, the reverse of selfishness, cannot be excluded from the domain of rationality. As a matter of fact, the altruist does not seek to convince anyone to follow her. She decides, in the name of ethical conviction, to favour another person in a given conflict. Her reasoning includes an ethical dimension, since it implies reconsidering her priorities. The individual adopts a sacrificial, angelical, or supererogatory behaviour, without expecting others to do the same. She performs a pure gift which *does not demand reciprocity.* Contrary to what the utilitarian could think, this behaviour is no more 'irrational' than pure selfishness, since neither rely on reasons which appear convincing to everyone else.

(iii) *The fair solution.* So far, *ego*'s or (exclusive) *alter*'s conception of the good life was decisive. It is actually this reference to a unique conception of the good which makes it possible to stay in the realm of utilitarianism (with its maximisation of the good). The only solution left is therefore the one which consists in giving precedence to the right over the good, since it appears that individuals can still resort to a solution which they regard as unanimously fair. This does not mean that everyone's aspirations to happiness (such as everyone estimates it) are denied: they are simply made relative for the sake of life in common. The conception of the good is no longer the decisive element, because we are in the situation where actors devise a fair compromise and choose among the preferences which ones can be allowed to go on and those which have to be repressed or expressed differently to make society life bearable to all. The reasoning no longer bears on *my* preferences or *your* preferences, it bears on *bringing together our* preferences. In this respect, it corresponds to the moral reasoning. As Raymond Boudon (2000) points out, in this situation, every actor seeks to establish his reasons on solid justifications, that is, such that they are likely to be endorsed by any other person, in other words by all of us, as a result of which we truly find ourselves in the realm of fairness.

Such a typology is a necessary instrument to find out whether such or such moral opinion is the product of an optimisation of the good, or if it seeks to submit itself to a deontological principle of fairness – but how can this second orientation be recognised in practice?

## 3.3 *A justice as fairness or impartiality*

As we already know, to find an agreement is to negotiate a compromise after which everyone will in a way have backed down on their initial maximal expectations. Now, if this is perfectly possible in a deontological context, it is impossible in a perfectionist one, where it is necessary, to remain consistent, to stick to one single conception of the good. Nothing allows us *a priori* to claim that there exists a consensual conception of the good. This is why the perfectionist can always be suspected of being partial. A perfectionist judge wishing to give the lie to the suspicion of partiality which may then arise in those tried by him, will have no other solution than to convince them that he is the only to be one entirely right. Empirically, and as soon as several rational conceptions of the good prevail, this endeavour proves so hard that it is very likely to fail. His position will be considered as partial by all those who do not share his views. If the point is to solve a conflict, it is simply not settled as far as its contents are concerned. Conversely, a justice defined as a unanimous agreement on the right leads to principles (norms, rules or laws, it does not matter here) which, since they are by definition shared by all, allow any judge who wishes to be fair to do so without any difficulty.

Fairness therefore plays an important part in recognising justice, and it will be our first criterion. However, it can be understood in two different ways. In general, and since Aristotle, the maxim 'to each person their due' makes it possible to sustain an equal treatment of everyone. When equity is the principle of a distributive justice, it must be understood as a proportionality between contributions and retributions[16] (Homans, 1974). It is however necessary to know what the fair proportion is and what the contributions regarded as relevant are, before compensations are dealt with. In other words, for equity to be put into practice, it is necessary to have already agreed on a perfection criterion acceptable to all. For instance, about wages: to each according to his deserts, to each according to his seniority, or a mixture of both? And if we choose deserts, what are their components? According to the selected criterion, we end up with different empirical pictures of equity, as has been very well shown by Jean Kellerhals, Josette Coenen-Huther and Marianne Modak (1988) in their study on the construction of norms of social justice among groups.[17] Now, if we want to be able to use a neutral or *a priori* fairness, it is obviously impossible to presuppose any perfection criterion. Claiming it is known in advance would amount to imposing it. It can only appear *a posteriori*, after the agreement. When this agreement is known, it is possible to speak of perfect equity, in the sense of a perfect justice (see chapter 3). It is only imperfect if it is not certain that the way it is put into practice will lead to respect the desired proportionality. But when the agreement is not concluded yet, only general and universal rules can be proposed; and as far as fairness is concerned, this translates into the principle: 'similar cases must be treated in a similar way'. This time, fairness rests entirely on agreeing on what is general (what are similar cases?) and on what must be made universal (why should these cases be treated in the same way?).

16 In the case of a retributive justice, this proportionality applies to offences and compensations, but the issue of equal treatment remains the same. This equality is attained only if the same proportionality rules apply to all.

17 It is also possible to derive a phenomenology of justifications from this, as Luc Boltanski and Laurent Thévenot (1991) have done, and it then appears to be focused on the notion of agreement, or a comparative social semantics of the word 'justice', as does Patrick Pharo (2001) who actually observes that beyond the various meanings of the term there appears an 'objective logical meaning which constrains its many expressions'.

Formally, then, impartiality is the same as this fairness. A judgment resulting from an *a priori* bias cannot respect this rule, just as, conversely, a non-fair judgment, in this procedural sense, is formally identical to what it would be if it had been produced by a pure bias. If the principle of justice only defines one equivalence class, that of all those who are submitted to it in an identical way, it becomes obvious. This remains true, even if it is less simple, when the principle of justice defines several equivalence classes, which is always possible as soon as there is a unanimous agreement on this division.

An equivalence class is made up of all the individuals who have the same rights and duties. The reciprocity rule ('what is valid for one is valid for the other') is here applied by construction. Let us suppose, to simplify things, that unanimity leads to creating only two equivalence classes of individuals who have the same rights and duties. For instance, in the Highway Code, those who, at a crossroads, are coming from the right and those who are coming from the left. Surely, in the event of an accident, fairness does not consist in thinking that the rights of the person coming from the right were equal to those of the one coming from the left. On the contrary, impartiality or fairness consists in respecting differences of rights and duties between equivalence classes. Only then are similar cases treated in the same way. Not being impartial or fair amounts to negating the principle of justice at stake and therefore the unanimous agreement on this principle too. All in all, impartiality or fairness is only justice in action, and it can be said that an individual founding his opinion or action on a search for fairness uses a principle of justice.

The conflict between the partial judge – whom we supposed to be perfectionist in the example above – and those who disagree with him is not solved however. This conflict can spring from the fact that, relatively to the problem at stake, the judge and the others do not make up the same number of equivalence classes. For instance, for the judge, in the name of his conception of the good life, there are two classes, the virtuous ones and the non-virtuous ones, while for others there is only one. They deny that his distinction criterion should be applied *in this context*. But, in their own point of view, everyone has the impression of being impartial. And as a matter of fact, they are, if they grant themselves neither more nor less than what their principles of justice allow them to grant to others. To disentangle this confrontation of impartialities, it is therefore necessary to allow a second criterion in order to recognise an opinion founded on justice.

## 3.4 *The position of a spectator*

Finding such a criterion amounts to asking ourselves how to evidence the will to reach an agreement behind partial preferences. This idea is quite simple and has been expounded in different forms in moral and political philosophy. For instance, the social contract principle starts from the idea that fairness in rules for life in common must be judged from a specific position – the original position – where every person only has neutral reasons to further. The aim is to decentre the actor and to put him in the position of a spectator where, ideally adopting each of the other persons' perspectives, he tries to find an acceptable compromise. Such decentration[18] deserves more attention than it has received so far in sociology, all the more as it can be turned into a method without any difficulty.

One way of accounting for the reasonable then consists in giving close attention to the opinion of individuals who are not, or less, concerned by comparison to others who lie at the heart of a conflict. It is enough to list up the arguments of these spectators, that is of the individuals whose opinion is not the mere (rational) product of their material interest or conception of the good life. In this way, we give ourselves the means of knowing the most convincing justification of an act or an opinion, that is the one which is most likely to be accepted by everyone (oneself as well as someone else).

Such a research method stands opposed to the one which results from the rational choice theory by resting on its limits. Instead of trying to explain in what respect such or such action maximises an expected utility, a methodical use of the spectator enables to set a limit to these explanations by considering that there are still other reasons to take into account. The rational choice theory is 'neutralised' in a way and, by doing so, its anthropological hypotheses are avoided. In particular, it is now out of the question to claim that an involved individual remains unable to take distance from himself to judge from a moral point of view. The reasons of the non-

18 Psychological studies on moral development during childhood almost all insist on decentration, which makes it possible, after going through different stages during infancy, to form a moral judgment detached from egocentrism. The 'reversible (or reciprocal) adoption of a role' theorised by Lawrence Kohlberg (1981) is close to this idea of decentration, without being exactly the same as what Jean Piaget (1973) calls from the same viewpoint 'reflexive abstraction', nor actually as the Golden Rule ('do not do to other people what you would not want them to do to you').

involved actor are *at first sight* less biased, but the involved actor can perfectly take some distance and even pronounce himself against his own interest. In other words, the ability to appeal to neutral reasons does not belong to some sort of ideal observer living an ethereal life outside of our world. There is no reason to doubt systematically, as the rational choice theory demands, the morality of an individual with interests. But since in practice it is difficult to distinguish morality from interest, a good method requires this use of a *spectator* to establish the power of conviction of reasons which happen to be agreed on by everyone, by aiming at a *fair* treatment of each person – hence actually the name 'fair spectator' which we have given to this model of analysis.

Eventually, it is precisely this total reversal of perspective which will allow us to understand why the involved actor does not always maximise her utility, and we will be able to do so without using an *ad hoc* hypothesis, such as aversion to risk, which is generally paradoxical ('negating one's nature in the name of one's nature'). Neutral reasons underline what is objective in backing down on one's maximalistic claims.

### 3.5 *The fair spectator as a method of analysis*

To be more specific, the 'fair spectator' must still be distinguished from Smith's 'impartial spectator' or Hume's 'judicious spectator'.[19] As opposed to the latter, we do not need to make an anthropological hypothesis as to individuals' sympathy. We thus avoid the subsequent problems of utilitarianism which imply some weighting between selfishness and sympathy. Fundamentally, neutrality is here guaranteed because no particular conception of the good life is advantaged *a priori*. It is only *a posteriori* that one may observe some unanimous agreement on a specific good or life plan. The methodical effort to evidence the self-distancing from one's own conception of the good life represents precisely what inscribes the 'fair spectator', or according to Kant's phrase (1785) the 'both reasonable and impartial spectator', in the deontological current. It ensures the priority of justice

19 This is actually the reason why we use the phrase 'fair spectator' and not 'impartial spectator' or 'judicious spectator', even if, as we have shown, from the purely procedural point of view, it does not seem to us that there is a major difference to make between fairness and impartiality.

over the good and thereby radically distinguishes this approach from that Smith's 'impartial spectator' (or Hume's 'judicious spectator').

Neither do we have to presuppose some aversion to risk. This hypothesis, which underpins the introduction of the *maximin* principle adopted by any actor behind the 'veil of ignorance' in Rawls's theory, is problematic too. When, for instance, I cut a cake into equal pieces, this is not necessarily because I am afraid of being given the smallest piece. A principle of indifference can be just as relevant: I cannot find any reason to favour someone in particular, so I apply a rule which remains unvarying under any permutation between the aspiring candidates. Nothing either prevents the group from recognising that one of the aspirers has greater needs, and from entitling him to a special treatment. Rawls is forced to admit that the goods at stake behind the veil of ignorance are so crucial that we must do as if it was our worst enemy who gave us our share or our place in society. According to us, it is preferable not to make any substantial hypotheses on the mode of reasoning of individuals in the original position and, therefore, to be contented with a guarantee of their neutrality. But this also demands to pay attention to what these individuals really think.[20]

In order to grasp everything that separates this point of view from that of utilitarianism, we can also base ourselves on the distinction suggested by Rousseau between the will of all and the general will. As he writes in *The Social Contract* (1762, II, 3): 'There is often a considerable difference between the will of all and the general will; the latter looks only to the common interest, the former looks to private interest, and is nothing but a sum of particular wills.' If the individual can only reason in terms of her own interest, there can be no general will, only a simple[21] count of particular wills, leaving us no other choice than a utilitarian perspective. The path taken by Rousseau does not expect anything from such a count. *The Social Contract* does not propose to build the general will through sums, but to recognise it from a specific position (original position), from which it is

20 This is an important matter in the International Social Justice Project (Kluegel, Mason and Wegener, 1995) and David Miller (1999, pp. 51-59) shows that if we admit, with Rawls, that reflective equilibrium and public justifiability are key elements in a theory of justice, it follows: 'that such a theory is to be tested, in part, by its correspondence with our evidence concerning everyday beliefs about justice.'

21 'Simple' being only a manner of speaking as a result of the paradoxes evidenced by Condorcet and developed lately, as we mentioned earlier, by Arrow, on the inexistence of an univocal accounting procedure to determine the wishes of a group of individuals.

easier to see the right – that is, in the last analysis, from what we call the position of a fair spectator.

The distinction proposed by Rousseau offers a way of interpreting public opinion. It is clear that, today, the breakdown of opinion polls often just highlights the 'will of all' and only indicates to which group of interest or which ideological group it belongs. Although we are not doomed to such an interpretation, the question still remains, of how we can hear the 'general will', or justice as unanimous agreement, or the voice of the fair spectator in the field of opinion polls. As Rousseau (1762, I, 7) also observes: 'Each individual may, as a man, have a particular will contrary to or different from the general will he has as a Citizen. His particular interest may speak to him quite differently from the common interest.' How can we therefore be certain that it is the 'citizen' who expresses himself? We know the dangers of the tyrant claiming to be the only citizen among men.

Two solutions are possible. The first one, contemplated by Rousseau (1762, II, 4), consists in only wondering about general rules '[...] because there is no one who does not appropriate the word *each* to himself [...]'; the second one, which can perfectly be practiced by someone studying an opinion poll, consists in listening more carefully to the opinion of those who have no interest at stake – the spectators – or those speaking against their interest – the committed ones. In the field of opinion polls, forming the fair spectator hypothesis is therefore to provide oneself with a method of analysis whereby, if particular interests normally orientate partial actors' opinions, non-perfectionist impartiality is nonetheless present and constitutes an efficient motive of opinion.

However, there are two ways of understanding it, and both must be taken into account. Some individuals, because they feel little or not involved by a given question raising a problem of social justice, adopt the point of view of a purely procedural fairness. They are therefore fair spectators. Others, now involved, may have interests which are convergent with the latter's. But others, finally, who are yet implied *de facto*, attain the same position because they try neither to impose their interests nor their conception of the good life. Therefore, the fair spectator is not only a position, but also a horizon. In other words, if the standpoint of the fair spectator is reached when interests and conceptions of the good life vanish in front of the priority of justice, the fair spectator is a horizon which gets closer as this fading progresses.

With this last point, the whole of the hypotheses which had to be formulated about the fair spectator can be regarded as established. The question is then to know what their empirical validity and efficiency are. This is the focus of the next chapter, in which the model which has just been built will be applied to the analysis of a statistical opinion poll serving as an example.

# Chapter 2

# An Application to the Analysis of a Poll on Economic Opinions

Opinion polls are such an important source of data for sociologists that it can be surprising to find oneself compelled to notice the weakness of the theoretical models which underpin their interpretation more often than not – in so far as such models *are* actually used. With no exaggeration, commentators from any background sometimes lose their usual methodological wariness when it comes to reading a poll, and yield to an individualistic reading, in terms of *homo œconomicus* or to a holistic reading, in terms of *homo ideologicus*. Since neither the rational choice theory, which is restricted to an interest-based reading, nor holism, which is restricted to the idea that totalities impose themselves on individuals, fail to take seriously the reasons why individuals find such or such act fair or unfair, it is no wonder that these reasons should be relegated to one form or another of fake consciousness, or even of unconscious or lack of understanding, or that one should eventually be contented with only denouncing the pharisaic nature of feelings of justice by looking at all costs for some selfish calculation. Morality, considered exclusively in its perfectionist sense, can only translate a 'war of gods' between different conceptions of the good life which it is impossible to apprehend objectively, and, at best, it is impossible to go beyond the acknowledgment of a plurality of moralities. However, this amounts to forgetting that while it is probably not possible to debate on the good life ('everyone has their idea of happiness'), it remains possible to agree on conditions which make various ideas as to the good life compatible, and therefore agree on justice. In short, in the field of polls, it is possible to make the hypothesis that if self-interest explains opinions, morality is just as necessary and that it intervenes not only as a conception of the good but also of justice.

In order to test the relevance of this hypothesis, we will base ourselves on the example of a statistical poll on economic opinions, and show that the fair spectator model, as it was presented in the previous chapter, accounts perfectly for these data, whereas a strict application of the rational choice theory is insufficient and the holistic theory leads to a failure. To do so, our method will be threefold. First, we will select from the poll a large class of opinions, so as to bring out its overall logic and begin to see that if economic self-interest partly accounts for this logic, it seems to fail to do so completely, so that it is also necessary to resort to the moral dimension as well as to some demand for justice. The second step will consist in showing that, for a given opinion (in this specific case, about the level of RMI/income support),[1] not only is a moral model at work, all things being otherwise equal, but is indispensable in order to explain it. Finally, after seeing in which respects this model is linked to what fairness requires, we will only have to verify that beyond all the reasons of the partial actors, this fairness, when it is that of a spectator, constitutes the horizon – in other words, that opinion tends to justice as fairness when economic interests and conceptions of the good life recede.

## 1. The Emergence of a Moral Position in the Face of Economic Self-Interest

The study we will be using to back up this theory is an opinion poll carried out, in France in February 2000, by IFOP[2] at the request of DREES[3], on a representative sample by quota of 4,000 individuals aged 18 and more. The questionnaire seeks to appreciate public assent towards the Welfare State

1 Translator's note: The RMI (*Revenu Minimum d'Insertion*, i.e. 'Minimum Income for Social Integration') which will be called from now on *Income Support*, after the English term, was created in France in the late 1980s. It can be allocated to any person living in France, above the age of 25 (or in charge of at least one child), and whose income is below about 400 euros (for a single person). Its amount is equivalent to this upper limit. To receive RMI, claimants must sign a 'contract for social integration' with social services, whereby they formally commit to take part in the activities which these services will offer them in order to find some employment. In the early 2000s, there were about 1 million beneficiaries of RMI.

2 Translator's note: IFOP is one of the main French opinion poll institutes.

3 Translator's note: DREES is a research department in the Ministry for Employment and Solidarity.

and its achievements. Its scope is broad, therefore, and the problems discussed in concrete terms with the interviewees are plenty.

| *List of the main topics selected for the factor analysis* | |
|---|---|
| – General opinions on society, the State, or Europe | – Compensations for benefits |
| – Feelings as to the future and preoccupations | – Retirement pensions |
| – Moral opinions | – Social welfare |
| – Perceptions of inequalities, poverty, and their causes | – Health |

By selecting about thirty questions (that is more than a hundred response items), related to each of the major issues tackled by the study (see the above list), and by then submitting them to a multiple correspondence analysis (abbreviated from now on as *factor analysis*), in order to reach afterwards a hierarchical clustering of respondents, we will have a representation of the overall structure of opinions. We will not undertake here a thorough commentary of the detailed results, as this is not our purpose. We will limit ourselves to a presentation enabling us to understand how, even at this level of generality, the question of the respective places of morality and self-interest and finally that of a fair spectator come up and account for the logic of opinions and will thus have to be dealt with through more targeted statistical explanatory approaches, in a second stage.

It is worth noting that this study is repeated in a generally similar form every year. As we are writing these lines, we have been able to analyse the results of 2001 and 2002 and to observe that, to the exception of very subtle variations, they are roughly similar to those of 2000. To avoid overloading this presentation, in all that follows, we will only stick to the results of the year 2000, but this will not entail a loss of generality since studying 2001 or 2002 would not have made a difference.

### 1.1 *Judgments as to what is and what ought to be*

First, factor analysis reveals that while the opinion is structured, it is not excessively so. The first principal axis only accounts for 5.6% of the inertia. It is necessary to go as far as the 18th axis for 50%, and to the 40th for

90% of the inertia to be explained.[4] This indicates, not that the opinions of the French are incoherent, but rather that respondents have not unfolded a single pattern of response which they consciously wanted to emphasise throughout the interview. It seems that they have thought afresh for each sub-group of questions.

The first factorial axis (horizontal in figure 1) evidences quite clearly an opposition between those who think that French society is quite fair, and the others. The former are rather confident in the future both for themselves and for society in general; they interpret France's social situation as overall positive, more usually judging that inequalities and social exclusion are steadily decreasing. They are also more inclined to trust the State rather than individuals. Such satisfaction usually translates into a certain conservatism, politically speaking: it is here that one will find the minority (8.6%) claiming that 'French society should remain as it is'; or still the 22% claiming that 'we have exactly as much as we need in terms of social or economic State intervention'. The sociodemographic variables show that these tend to be mainly the respondents with the highest educational levels, professionals or senior executives, with high incomes and living in Paris.

At the other end of this first axis, the opposite response items can be observed. Here we find above all those with a pessimistic view of their future and of the fate of future generations; those wishing for radical reforms; or still, those who think that the health condition of the French has deteriorated over recent years. This last opinion, which is generally upheld by the oldest group of the French, proves a lot more determining than the item which represents those of 65 and more. Let us add too – but these answers are less characteristic, since they are almost commonplace in France – that a majority in this part of figure 1 thinks that there is not enough State, that the level of funding of social welfare is insufficient, that society is unfair or that the problems regarding the great sanitary crises (such as the mad cow, dioxin chicken or asbestos crises) are not being exaggerated. They also claim more often that social exclusion is explained by a shortage in jobs, an opinion often set next to the claim that there are too many immigrants in France. The categories of the population which stand out here are the most socially vulnerable (single parents with an income below the minimum wage, unemployed people, unemployed people living

4 Empirically, it can be said that these figures correspond to a 'standard' link between variables in a multiple correspondence analysis, that is, neither too strong nor too weak.

on benefits, etc.) as well as the least academically qualified, the least well-off and the oldest.

The second axis (vertical in figure 1) accounts for 4.2% of the inertia and describes a double contrast. First of all, it accounts for an opposition, which can also be found in many other studies (Forsé, 1999), between an interventionist vision and a more free-market oriented one. The free-market one is quite unambiguous. Respondents supporting it (at the bottom of figure 1) very clearly think – and this is very determining – that the funding of the Welfare State is excessive and that in terms of social and economic interventions there is too much State. For them, the monopoly of the *Sécurité Sociale*[5] is a bad thing and the existing pension system should be replaced with insurance or a system of individual saving. One also finds here the idea that those living in deprivation are reluctant to work. Greater selectiveness is therefore needed when it comes to the attribution of benefits. Solidarity is not rejected, but it must be accompanied by compensations asked from the beneficiaries. The opposite interventionist pole is more difficult to interpret because one does not observe, along the vertical axis, the expected order between the three items 'too much State', 'sufficient State', and 'not enough State'. These last two opinions can be found roughly at the same level on this axis. People living in deprivation are not seen as ill-willed or work-shy. The most determining responses, and therefore the most relevant ones to qualify the interventionist dimension, mostly insist on the idea of unconditional solidarity: with a refusal to ask for a public-good contribution from the unemployed or to demand compensations for income support, for instance.

The second axis evidences, in the second place, the usual opposition between economic liberalism and 'cultural liberalism' (Grunberg and Schweisguth, 1990). We would actually rather talk about moral liberalism in this case, since its position can be found mainly through opinions involving a morality and, on the other hand, because deep down it is moralities rather than cultures, in the anthropological sense, which are at stake. By principle, morally liberal individuals (located at the top of the factorial graph) reject all norm of differentiation taking into account ethnic criteria or sexual practices – such as homosexuality. Moral liberalism corresponds to a refusal to pass judgments on people's private lives, to the idea that every individual has a right to pursue the life plans they aspire to, as long as they are respect-

5 Translator's note: The State department in charge of medical insurance.

ful of other people's own schemes. This position can go as far as refusing that the economic sphere should hinder these life plans. The opposition on the vertical axis could therefore be the consequence of a judgment on the link between economic resources and life plans: on one side are the individuals who perceive economic resources almost as a 'right to live', a right to carry out one's projects; and on the other side, those who consider that these resources are above all the financial retribution for some achievement (or some risk) – personal well-being as opposed to deserts, in a way.

Table 1 – *Moral opinion and conditional solidarity (row %)*

| | | *Asking the unemployed to take part in some general-interest task* | | |
|---|---|---|---|---|
| | | *Yes* | *No* | *Total* |
| Homosexuals are like other people | Yes | 75.7 | 24.3 | 100.0 |
| | No | 83.8 | 16.2 | 100.0 |
| | Total | 77.9 | 22.1 | 100.0 |

Chi-sq = 28, degree of freedom (df) = 1, probability of a greater Chi-sq (p) < 0.0001

Overall, the superposition of the two contrasts upheld by the second factorial axis translates the strong congruence between economic opinions and moral ones. Moral particularism is paired with economic liberalism[6] because it leads to trusting one's own norms rather than those of some superior instance when one deems that it does not guarantee enough selectiveness. Inversely, refusing a selective (or overly selective) norm by basing oneself on moral principles rejecting the discrimination of mores, leads to seeking a solidarity for all, without any selection, including in the economic sphere. According to the chi-square test,[7] table 1 provides a highly revealing example among many others. However, if, as we have already noticed, economic liberalism and moral particularism form a rather unimodal pole, interventionism combined with universalism splits into two, since one can think

6 Translator's note: In French, the word 'liberalism' has a double meaning which has no English equivalent. There is no distinction in the French usage between doctrines of minimal State (libertarianism) or of free market (neo-classical economics) and a position which is strictly liberal in a political, moral or philosophical sense.

7 The Chi-square is a statistical index which makes it possible to measure the significance of a link between nominal variables. For instance, it is said to be significant at the 1% level if the link observed between the variables has less than one chance in a hundred to be a mere random result.

either that the situation is satisfactory, and therefore that there is enough State with respect to social and economic interventions, or that it is unsatisfactory, especially because there is not enough State.

This leads to a first overall interpretation, with the help of the opposition between insiders and outsiders, that is to say between those who are well-insured by the Welfare State, and those who tend to be left out of its benefits. The first axis testifies primarily to the feeling of *being an insider or not*. It is a degree of satisfaction with the distribution of social benefits, a judgment on a gap between needs and the help actually received. The second axis evidences the same opposition, but as reformulated on the mode of a judgment on *what ought to be*. The economically-liberal pole vindicates the idea of being more selective in the attribution of benefits: there should be fewer *insiders* and they should be 'better' selected, while the interventionist or morally-liberal pole rejects the very idea of selection. The redevelopment of State benefits must be calculated for the profit of all. It is interesting that this opposition between restricted and wider selectiveness also appears clearly in a factor analysis based on a poll carried out in Belgium in 1993, which includes several questions quite similar to those selected here (Jacquemain, 1995).

### 1.2 *Three opinion clusters*

We will not study the third axis, whose interpretation is more intricate. It may account for an opposition between radicals and moderates, but this is not certain. To go further, we will carry out a hierarchical cluster analysis (according to Ward's method) based on the first five factorial axes. This method consists in grouping individuals according to their proximity in terms of opinions (as judged from their factorial scores). It must be noticed that by restricting ourselves to the first five axes, which represent 20% of the total variance, we lay the emphasis on the most determining opinions. The others are as it were filtered because of their lack of relevance; they are regarded as 'noises' and therefore as inadequate when it comes to highlighting affinities.

We will stick to a clustering in three groups because this number has proven both necessary and sufficient to describe correctly the structure of opinions. These three groups are placed easily enough around each of the three points of the triangle formed by the items 'too much State', 'sufficient

State' and 'not enough State' (see figure 1). A cross-tabulation (chi-sq = 599, df = 4, $p < 0.0001$) confirms that the first group think more than the average that 'there is not enough State', while the second find that there is just enough of it, and the third, that there is too much in terms of social and economic intervention.

Figure 1 – *Extract of the Factorial Analysis and Meaning of the Axes*

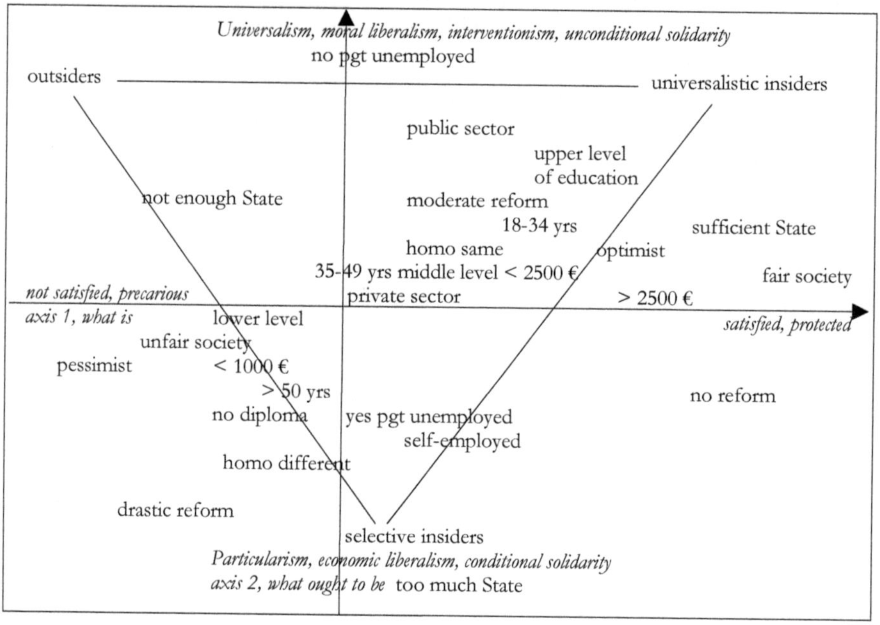


Reading note: Without a high magnifying rate, the figure containing all the points (about a hundred) in this factorial plan is very hard to read. To make up for this problem, only a more restricted number is presented here, without making it impossible to grasp the overall logic of the analysis. The meanings which can be attributed to the axes are represented in italics. Only the points which correspond to some opinions are active in the formation of these axes. The others, which describe sociodemographic positions, correspond to supplementary variables. To spot the three clusters more easily, their positions (in supplementary variables) are connected with lines. Most of the short labels chosen to name the points are quite easy to understand. There may be some exceptions: 'yes pgt unemployed' represents the opinion of those who think the unemployed should be asked to perform a task for the public good in exchange for the benefits they receive; 'homo same' stands for 'homosexuals are not different'; 'level' refers to a scale of diplomas and data in euros correspond to a monthly income.

It is quite easy to find the logic underpinning these three groups. The first one (north-west of figure 1, accounting for 38% of the sample) consider themselves to be ill protected by the State, and wish for both an increase in the State budget and a better-targeted reallocation in its favour. In a way, the second one (north-east, 23%) refuse inequalities, without seeing them. The idea that financial resources can be a hindrance for life plans is strongly rejected. At the same time, this group is not far from thinking that existing benefits are precisely an answer to this principle. Injustices, when acknowledged, are regarded as 'residual', and it would not take much, without many extra expenses, to remedy this. In the last group (south, 39%), individuals see themselves not so much as victims of the economic system in general than as victims of its redistributive pattern, the 'mugs' of the State, to say it crudely. If there is 'too much State', it is essential to make the 'right' selection between outsiders and insiders. Unsurprisingly, they are more likely to claim to be 'willing to accept a decrease in benefits compensated by a reduction of their contributions and taxes'. More surprisingly, however, they also more frequently claim to be 'willing to contribute more to maintain the level of benefits'.[8] It is probably because they have the definite feeling that the social security scheme depends on them and that what they put into it also comes back to them, hence this emphasis on selection.

In brief, north-west of figure 1, we find people living predominantly in a precarious situation, *outsiders* (neither selective nor satisfied) who would like to become insiders. North-east, we find *non-selective or universalistic insiders*, who are satisfied enough with the existing welfare and convinced that everyone gets their share without a major upsetting of the system, so that they do not really quibble. South of the figure are *selective or particularistic insiders* who have no desire to let the outsiders in and are very fussy as to the 'sharing of the cake'. They are rather dissatisfied with the redistributive system and are not far from wanting to overhaul it completely, as are some outsiders too, but in a radically different free-market direction.

These three groups are distinguished not only by their universalistic or particularistic moral stance, or their interventionist or free-market position, but also by their social statuses. The outsider is more usually a woman, aged between 30 and 50 or above 65, living in a middle-sized town or a rural

8 A majority of selective insiders (76%) think that income support should not be abandoned; however it is only in this group that the tendency to call for the cancellation of income support is above the average (21%).

place; she can be a salaried employee or manual worker, and in that case she usually works part-time, but is more frequently in search of a job; the outsider has a low income and few academic credentials. The universalistic insider tends to be a man, is often young, living in Paris or in a large city, with a high level of education and a high income; most often, he works in the public sector as a high executive or even as a middleman. The selective insider also tends to be a man, but usually middle-aged and living in a small town; he is predominantly self-employed without an employee, and, if salaried, he is often a manual worker, mainly in the private sector; he has a low or average level of education. However, differences in income are not meaningful for this group.

It must be underlined that all the *chi-square* corresponding to all the tables crossing clusters with sociodemographic variables are significant. This means that this cluster analysis is not only a good synthetic indicator of the opinions selected for the factor analysis, but also of the social status as measured with the usual variables. Economic opinion, which is already connected with moral opinion, also appears to be strongly influenced by social status, which gives rise to diverging interests and perceptions.

Undoubtedly, these are partial actors, whose judgments are subject to position biases, themselves causing cognitive biases. This does not mean in the least that the actor does not have any good reason to think what he thinks. With respect to the social and cognitive context he belongs to, it is perfectly rational that he should endorse precisely his own economic opinion. It is a rational actor, but whose rationality is situated. In other words, his opinion results from a calculation of his own interest *as he understands it.* It is very much in the outsider's interest that State benefits should be extended, since he can then hope to benefit more from them. There would be no benefit for the universalistic insider either in seeing them increased, or in having them lowered. He is already well-protected. He would not gain much from an increase which, on the reverse, could make him contribute more. A decrease, beyond the fact that it would go against his universalistic morality, could also affect him and turn against him. As for the selective insider, who is often self-employed, he feels (were it only because in this case he himself pays for both his employer's and his workman's share, because he is subject to professional taxes on top of which other taxes are added, etc.) crushed by levies which are detrimental to his professional activity and his final income. Naturally, he wants them to be lowered. It does not necessarily mean that every benefit should be cancelled in order to do so, but it would mean going towards a more selective repartition, which would be at once less lavish and more in keeping with what his moral principles are. This is his own interest, as he perceives it.

### 1.3 *A slight shift towards universalism when immediate economic interest decreases*

Is this sufficient to think there is no room here for a fair spectator? Surely, the universalist, like the particularist, could argue that her economic opinion is beneficial to the common good, and that by adopting it, she cares more about this good than about her own interest. The former may think that the benefits of growth should be submitted to a more egalitarian distribution, that no one should be left out, because benefits of all kinds keep up the demand, which is itself the key to collective economic wealth. As to the particularistic, she can argue that a reduction in spending, debts, taxes, is beneficial to everyone because it encourages economic activity, and therefore employment, wealth, etc. Nevertheless, the use of these theories very much resembles an *a posteriori* rationalisation, which is hardly independent from each actor's own short-term subjective interest. As far as morality is concerned, we find an altruism which is very hard to distinguish from self-help: common interest (or the other's own interests) is all the better satisfied as in both cases alike it amounts to serving one's own interest. It seems there is no room here for impartiality.

Nonetheless, the universalistic insider's position appears a lot more ambivalent. We have seen that her interest lies rather in the *status quo*, but one question remains. How can we explain her rather compassionate opinions on issues which hardly involve her personally? Why is her coordinate on the second factorial axis as high as that of the outsider? Why, for instance, is she favourable to income support with no compensation, or to an extension to the under 25, or still to an increase of its amount (see table 2), while she herself, her children or her friends and relatives are most likely not to benefit from it (see table 3)? And still, if she judges that there is a risk, why does not she settle for the setting up of selection criteria which would be favourable to her alone? The awareness of her particular interest does not seem to be *sufficient* to explain her opinions. Of course, if this interest ran against her moral universalism, the latter would probably be considerably lessened as a result. But this interpretation only justifies negatively her moral convictions on what is fair.

Table 2 – *Clusters and opinion on the level of income support (row % and signs of the significant adjusted residuals)*

| | *Opinion on the level of income support* | | | |
|---|---|---|---|---|
| | *Income support should be increased* | *Income support is at the right level* | *Income support should be lowered* | *Total* |
| Outsider | 80.0 (+***) | 19.1 (–**) | 0.9 (–***) | 100.0 |
| Universalistic insider | 78.7 (+**) | 19.8 | 1.5 (–***) | 100.0 |
| Selective insider | 70.1 (–***) | 23.7 (+***) | 6.2 (+***) | 100.0 |
| Total | 75.9 | 21.0 | 3.1 | 100.0 |

Chi-sq = 94.16, df = 4, p < 0.0001

Reading note: the adjusted residual (or standardised adjusted residual) is a parameter measuring the deviation from the independence hypothesis, applied to the link between two response items, and which follows asymptotically a standardised normal law. Therefore, a value outside the interval [–1.96, +1.96] indicates a deviation from independence which is significant at the 5% level; a value outside the [–2.58, +2.58] interval indicates a deviation from independence which is significant at the 1% level (Haberman, 1973). In this table, as in the next ones, we reproduce the sign of this residual only when it is significant for a two-tailed test at the 1% (***), 5% (**) or 10% (*) level.

Table 3 – *Clusters and personal acquaintance with somebody (including the interviewee) living on income support (row % and signs of the significant adjusted residuals)*

| | *Do you personally know somebody living on income support?* | | |
|---|---|---|---|
| | *Yes* | *No* | *Total* |
| Outsider | 42.5 (+**) | 57.5 (–**) | 100.0 |
| Universalistic insider | 35.6 (–***) | 64.4 (+***) | 100.0 |
| Selective insider | 40.1 (–***) | 59.9 | 100.0 |
| Total | 40.0 | 60.0 | 100.0 |

Chi-sq = 11.23, df = 2, p = 0.004

Three interpretations seem conceivable. Either, since her economic interest is not directly at stake through many of the survey questions, the respondent can give free vent to her 'passion for equality' – the democratic passion according to Tocqueville – without endeavouring to impose it, in order to *motivate her opinion from reasons which are neutral*, that is to say fair. Or, still, this moral judgment is still at work, but biased by the respondent's social status: her proximity and satisfaction with the Welfare State leads her to support its universalistic mission. Or, lastly, it is necessary to revert to a

Marxist interpretation of ideology: universalistic opinions on questions which are of little direct interest to this contented individual are simply part of a rhetorical or cosmetic varnish hiding her particularistic interests. Of course, the factor analysis does not make it possible to decide between these three options. Consequently, it will be necessary to come back to them with other methods.

Let us emphasise, to finish with this descriptive part, that the remarkable macroscopic congruence between moral judgments, economic opinions and social status, which has appeared so far, would probably not be so easily discernible if it did not rest on a steady microsociological reality. If we accept that the threefold logic of opinions to which we have come synthesises correctly the various attitudes towards the Welfare State and its works, it can be inferred that the underlying rationality is not as 'uni-form' in its principle as a theory as restrictive as that of the *homo œconomicus* may suggest. As soon as private interest is strongly involved, there is no doubt that rationality is optimising, as would predict an explanatory utilitarianism. However, if, as one of the options in the preceding paragraph suggests, opinion is founded at least in part on convictions as to what is fair which do not serve the actor's own interests then it is no longer possible to speak of an optimisation. And as this impartial actor's opinion which emerges is not irrational, it is now necessary to understand what justifies it.

## 2. The Explanatory Role of the Moral Dimension

For the time being, we are only at the stage of plausible hypotheses, and, in order to progress, we have to examine the explanatory role of the moral dimension under study. In order to do so, it is necessary to change our statistical method. Technically, it is necessary to use regressions, and since this demands that one focus on a topic, we have selected that of income support – more specifically, opinion as to its amount. Beyond its intrinsic interest, this question has the advantage of calling for judgments on what-is and what-ought-to-be, both documented in the survey. It is then tempting to explore a path not often taken in quantitative studies of opinion: to study the ordering of opinions between themselves and appreciate their power of persuasion beyond the mere sociodemographic determiners – in other words, to attempt to build an interpretation in terms of good reasons.

## 2.1 *The usual interpretations of opinion*

A frequent approach to opinion polls consists in not taking seriously the opinion, and in focusing instead on variables which refer to the context which the actor is supposed to be caught in. What is tested then, at the level of statistics, are a few well-known 'mechanisms'. To explain that individuals should be favourable to an increase of income support, one therefore verifies that the risk of having to rely on it one day tilts the balance rather in favour of wishing for such an increase. It is easy enough to evidence this interest calculation from variables such as one's situation with regard to property or respondent's income level. Of course, this reasoning can be extended to other sociodemographic variables, such as being in the labour force or not.

From this point of view, let us observe that if a distinct majority (76%) of those interviewed is in favour of raising the level of income support,[9] deviations in appreciation between the various sociodemographic categories are rarely very high. A simple 10% deviation is already very high. For instance, 83% of respondents living in households whose income is lower than 381 € a month are in favour of an increase of income support, while only 73% of them are when this income is greater than 5,336 €. Of course, the fact that scatterings should be high or low does not make an interpretation in terms of good reasons impossible *a priori*, but the fact that opinions tend to be rather homogenous reinforces the conviction that one can expect more specifically here that this interpretation will account for the data better than a 'mechanical' deduction based on one's mere belonging to such or such sociodemographic category.[10]

9 More precisely, the question asked in the study was: 'Today, income support amounts to about 400 euros a month for a single person. With which of these opinions do you agree most? It must be raised; it must be lowered; it is at the right level; I don't know.' At the time of the poll, the currency was still the French franc. Here, all the data in francs have been converted into euros.

10 In any case, whether deviations are important or not, in the context of this interpretation, the point is to look for the actors' reasons in making up such or such opinion, especially by statistically setting them against certain categories regarded as biases.

Apart from the mechanisms in terms of interest taken in a broad sense, 'ideological' factors are often considered. Political positioning generally fulfils this function, but this information is not provided in the poll under study. However, it remains possible to partly make up for this lack with the help of a characteristic issue or, if our interpretation of the previous factor analysis is correct, with the help of the second axis, which was a good indicator of a stand for interventionism *v.* economic liberalism. In any case, it is more interesting to highlight the cognitive factors which are usually hastily subsumed under the qualifier 'ideological'. Thus, being located at a certain level of the social ladder leads to quite a good knowledge of this part of the pyramid, and often leads one to generalise it to the rest of society, that is to say to overrate its weight or importance. Similarly, it is necessary to bear in mind that our opinions are made from what we can see and hear around us. The group one belongs to can actually play not only a cognitive but also a normative role. Whether it is close relatives or larger groups, such as civil servants, or the 'right-wing family' *v.* the 'left-wing family', opinion can reflect not a judgment but a form of belonging by which one sets a great importance. Or, inversely, the point can be to distinguish oneself: we saw in the previous section that, apparently, selective insiders are particularly careful to emphasise how they differ from the outsiders, and do their very best for this frontier to be maintained.

The opinion of the caught-in actor is easy enough to modelise from these mechanisms. However, to avoid excluding something arbitrarily, it is necessary to consider that individuals follow moral principles, referring either to an idea of the good life, or to an idea of justice. To highlight this effect empirically, it is necessary to devise some hypotheses about the moral principles which the respondents used to answer the questions they were asked, and then link these hypotheses with the survey variables in order to finally show the explanatory quality of the moral dimension for a question such as the level of income support. In other words, it is first necessary to rebuild the implicit moral argumentation so as to exhibit its efficiency.

Obviously, all these hypotheses to explain opinion are not mutually exclusive. It is even possible to hypothesise that all are at work together. Let us admit this causal pluralism. It is then tempting to appreciate the explanatory weight of each of these hypotheses through a logistic regression. By doing so, we will know whether, in the specific case under study, the moral dimension plays a marginal role by comparison with interest under its many forms and, therefore, if overlooking it is of any consequence; or if, on the contrary, this would mean an important loss in understanding opinion. However, it must be specified that this approach has two limits. First, it makes it necessary to build an *ad hoc* model of the moral reasons implied in the question at stake. To validate the importance of the moral dimension in general, it is impossible to transpose this model as such to another issue. The relevance of this model with regard to this other issue is not guaranteed. In the second place, since we are going to build a very synthetic statistical modelling, certain variables will remain partly equivocal. This model has a heuristic rather than a final virtue, but the hypotheses which it induces, especially with respect to the underlying moral principles, will be the object of a more advanced validation in the next section of this chapter.

### 2.2 *A moral model linking two principles*

The moral model we propose can be summarized in two strong arguments, which individuals will have to link up as they can. What distinguishes this model from an interpretation in terms of ideology is that these arguments are *relevant.* The first principle (P1) consists in saying that people refuse to sacrifice others or to let them live in a situation which is obviously unbearable. It is a *minimum principle* which is strong enough to be clear. For instance, it can be observed in the fact that respondents in opinion polls overwhelmingly condemn poverty, and it is probable that those who accept it simply mean that there will always be rich people and poor people. The second principle (P2) holds that people refuse that others should live at their expense. This principle is less obvious than the previous one. It does not mean that people have no sense of charity at all, but that their will is 'not to get swindled'. This time, it is a *principle of reciprocity* which, in a way, comes to 'balance out' P1. It demands reciprocity, in the sense that if one were in the position of the more deprived individual, one would expect the help one claims to be in favour of, but no more. Getting more would be precisely 'to get swindled'. Interestingly enough, reciprocity imposes a limit on charity, which makes it possible to avoid the pitfall of angelism. If this principle does not seem as immediate, it is precisely because of the increasing role played by the Welfare State against poverty in many western countries, and notably in France, or more accurately because of the transformation of compassion towards the poor which this increasing role entails (Swaan, 1988). It is most probably the reason why P1 is so conspicuous, whereas P2 is increasingly hard to notice. In spite of this, the second principle is still at work, and in the confrontation between P1 and P2, when asked for a clear-cut opinion, individuals are all the more favourable to the first principle as they are convinced that the State fulfils its mission – collectivising charity – in a satisfactory way. The connection between both principles can also be understood through the notion of responsibility: the more the responsibility is regarded as collective, the easier it is to assume P1; inversely, the more individualised the responsibility, the more necessary it becomes to insist on P2, on the limits of charity, not to lose heart.

Table 4 – *Opinion on the level of income support and 'vital' income (row % and signs of the significant adjusted residuals)*

| | *Opinion on the level of income support* | | | |
|---|---|---|---|---|
| | *Income support should be increased* | *Income support is at the right level* | *Income support should be lowered* | *Total* |
| 'Vital' income < 762 € | 67.5 (–***) | 27.6 (+***) | 4.9 (+***) | 100.0 |
| 763 to 914 € | 76.1 | 21.2 | 2.7 | 100.0 |
| 915 to 1,066 € | 78.1 (+*) | 19.4 | 2.5 | 100.0 |
| 'Vital' income ≥ 1,067 € | 78.5 (+***) | 18.6 (–***) | 2.9 | 100.0 |
| Total | 75.8 | 21.1 | 3.1 | 100.0 |

Chi-sq = 37.14, df = 6, $p < 0.0001$

How, now, can these principles be related to the empirical data? P1 must be founded on a judgment of what is at least acceptable to live. Now, respondents were precisely asked their opinion on the minimum income they regard as necessary to live. We will speak of a 'vital' income here.[11] About 99% of the respondents consider that it is impossible to live on less than 381 € a month, and 72%, that the current level of income support is too low. For some, it seems that income support should not be a sufficient income to live on. It is indeed true that income support is sometimes only one benefit among others to help those who live in precarious conditions, but this can only partly account for the important deviation between the desired level of income support and the 'vital' income level actually granted.

11 We use the term 'vital income', but it is clear that strictly speaking, it is rather an income below which people find it is unbearable to live. However, this distinction can seem specious since we are so used to thinking in terms of relative poverty, as opposed to absolute poverty.

In fact, by virtue of the first principle, we can expect those who claim it is impossible to live with less than 762 € to also claim more often that income support is too low, compared with those who claim that it is possible to live with 457 € or even 306 €. If this hypothesis is correct, it can be expected that beyond idiosyncrasies, the ideal income support level will be on average higher with those individuals who also place higher the necessary income to live (decently). A very simple cross-tabulation supports this hypothesis (see table 4).

Nonetheless, 'vital' income is not the only key to understand the making of opinions about the level of income support. If we regard this key as a fact judgment from which P1 can be applied, it is still necessary to find an empirical basis for the second principle. The fact that many French consider that income support should be lower than the 'vital' income implies this principle. The hypothesis here is that individuals pass a judgment on the level of income support which reconciles, as much as this is actually possible, a sense of solidarity, or at least some vague attempt that others should not die – principle P1 –, and the idea that this minimum income should still be hardly decent, or even indecent enough for others not be contented with the situation – principle P2. This interior negotiation leads to a sort of ideal level of income support, which is then compared with the current level, to decide whether income support is too high or too low. It is therefore a search for a satisfactory balance between giving someone a sufficient income to live, and avoiding that this individual should be contented with it. Such arbitration depends on the respondents' convictions, either on the risk that the person benefiting from the help may 'abuse' the situation, or on the 'unconditional' nature of this allowance because it is not his or her 'fault' or still because one gives precedence, as it were, to personal well-being over deserts. It is out of the question here to disentangle all these reasons. However, this dividing line can be located thanks to the variable corresponding to the second axis of our factor analysis (even if, considered in *isolation*, it does not make it possible to distinguish clearly between reason and ideology).

## 2.3 *Estimating the impacts of various interpretations of opinion*

We now have enough elements to carry out an ordinal logistic regression on the level of income support and to judge on the various influences on the making of opinion about this level. We have selected the following explanatory variables: gender, age, level of education, size of community, being or not in the labour force, situation with regard to property, 'vital' income, personal acquaintance with a person on income support among one's entourage, and, lastly, as a continuous variable, the coordinate on the second factorial axis (which we will from now refer to as F2). In order to be able to appreciate the respective merit of each of these effects, a single parameter to estimate is associated with most of the variables.

It results clearly from this regression (which appears in detail in the annex) that 'vital' income and F2 are the most discriminating factors. Our moral model thus seems particularly relevant. It must be underlined that if opinion as to the level of income support was only a matter of ideology, the 'vital' income effect should not appear. In so far as this effect appears, that is in so far as there does exist an argumentation founded on this 'vital' income, we can conclude that F2 is the missing link. Consequently, if, as said above, F2 can be seen as an ideologically oriented arbitration, it appears here that it cannot only have this meaning, since opinion is formed from a *reasoning* which binds together the 'vital' income *and* an argument linked in one way or another with F2.

Before coming back to this fundamental point, let us briefly review the less important effects of the other variables incorporated into the regression. First, we notice an effect of the property situation which can be interpreted in terms of interest or more specifically of risk: those who have a safety net wish less than others for the level of income support to be raised; owners and people with free accommodation less so than people having access to property and even less than tenants. The effect of income is not significant, but the sign of the parameter goes in the same direction and suggests that the wealthiest are more reluctant than others to an increase of income support.

Then there is the impact of age. Most of the opinions in favour of an increase of income support decrease with age. This could be expected: young people are more compassionate with the difficulty of entering the job market. But, once in the market, they become less favourable to such an increase of income support.

Finally, we also note a moderate effect (only significant for a 90% confidence interval) of the size of community and of one's personal acquaintance with somebody on income support. The former of these two effects can be interpreted as a difference in the standard of living: one has greater needs in a city than in the country. Inversely, the impact of one's close social entourage is more complex. If income support earners and those with a person on income support in their families are of course in favour of an increase of income support, the most reluctant are not those who do not know any income support earner, but those who know one outside their family. These income support earners outside the family are less likely to be friends than 'acquaintances' or weak ties, or even mere targets for stigmatisation. However, their importance should not be overestimated: those who wish to bring down the level of income support, even if they are represented in this group, remain actually scant.

Finally, two variables appear to be without effect in our model: the level of education and one's gender. As far as degrees are concerned, even a cross-sectional table does not evidence any effect. However, women strongly favour an increase of income support. This may stem from their over-representation among the economically vulnerable, rather than to genetics or some elaborate psychology (opposing the 'compassionate mother' to the 'warrior father').

## 2.4 *'Vital' income and the aversion to risk*

Nevertheless, all these effects remain less important than those of the 'vital' income and of F2 in accounting for opinions on income support, and this shows the importance of a moral argumentation against interpretations in terms of ideology or individual interest. Still, is it not possible to bring back the judgment on 'vital' income within the field of these interpretations? First, it could be said that this 'vital' income is calculated by individuals from their convictions about the very principle of income support. In this perspective, opinion on income support would therefore be determined by political positioning: right-wing people would rather be against income support, which would lead them to consider that 'vital' income must be low, in order to soothe their 'bad conscience'. And the reverse would apply to left-wing people. In so far as the question of how much an individual should have at the very least to live is asked in the questionnaire, prior to any consideration on income support proper, it would still be necessary to make a rather strong hypothesis as to respondents' capacities of expectation. In fact, it would be necessary to admit that both questions are so intertwined in people's minds in everyday life that they would alter their response on 'vital' income before making any allusion to income support.

'Vital' income can also be brought down to a reasoning in terms of risks: even if the wealthiest are unlikely to resort to income support, they still deem on the one hand that 'vital' income must be increased, since obviously, if the poor can very well imagine how one can get by with very little money, wealthy people find it hard to imagine, and moreover, they are very averse to risk. All in all, therefore, they prefer to increase the safety net. This type of reasoning is unanswerable as long as it does not receive any content, since then the risk can support any empirical result: if the rich wish to lower the level of income support, it is because the risk for them is minor; if the rich wish to increase the level of income support, it is because they do not care whether the risk is low, for what matters in this case is that they were averse to risk. They want to minimise the maximum loss, even if it is unlikely.

How can this idea of an aversion to risk be empirically confirmed or infirmed? It is possible to use our typology distinguishing between outsiders, selective insiders and universalistic insiders (who are better off), and wonder whether the latter are more averse to risk than others. As a matter of fact, there is in this survey a question about the confidence in the future as to the reduction of poverty and exclusion. Are the universalistic insiders, when they are more pessimistic, more inclined to wish for an increase of income support? Table 5 shows this is not the case. Confidence in the future has fewer incidences on opinions as to the level of income support for them than for outsiders and selective insiders; moreover, whether they are optimistic or pessimistic does not change anything to their attitude towards income support. However, it may be objected that this question on confidence is too general, and poorly expresses concern for oneself in the face of poverty risk.

Table 5 – *Opinion on income support and confidence in the future in terms of poverty by clusters (row % and signs of the significant adjusted residuals)*

| | *Poverty and exclusion are more likely to* | *Opinion on income support* | | | | |
|---|---|---|---|---|---|---|
| | | *Income support should be increased* | *Income support should be lowered* | *Income support is at the right level* | *Total* | *Phi* Chi-sq. |
| Outsider | decrease | 77.9 | 2.9 (+**) | 19.2 | 100.0 | |
| | increase | 82.2 (+***) | 0.9 | 16.9 (–***) | 100.0 | *0.12* |
| | remain stable | 68.4 (–***) | 0.0 | 31.6 (+***) | 100.0 | 18.03 (***) |
| | Total | 80.9 | 1.0 | 18.2 | 100.0 | |
| Universalistic insider | decrease | 78.5 | 2.0 | 19.5 | 100.0 | |
| | increase | 79.6 | 1.7 | 18.8 | 100.0 | *0.04* |
| | remain stable | 76.8 | 1.1 | 22.1 | 100.0 | 1.37 (n.s.) |
| | Total | 78.6 | 1.7 | 19.8 | 100.0 | |
| Selective insider | decrease | 69.0 | 7.1 | 23.9 | 100.0 | |
| | increase | 72.4 (+**) | 6.6 | 21.0 (–***) | 100.0 | *0.09* |
| | remain stable | 61.5 (–**) | 4.9 | 33.6 (+***) | 100.0 | 11.67 (**) |
| | Total | 70.7 | 6.5 | 22.8 | 100.0 | |

Another question proves more specific, since the interviewees have also been asked whether they were personally preoccupied with poverty. Table 6 shows that, this time, being worried for oneself does impact on attitudes towards income support. Nonetheless, the link between being preoccupied and one's opinion as to the level of income support is not stronger among universalistic insiders than among particularists, and hardly stronger than among outsiders.

Table 6 – *Opinion on income support and preoccupation about poverty by clusters (row % and signs of the significant adjusted residuals)*

| | *Personally worried about poverty* | *Opinion on income support* | | | | |
|---|---|---|---|---|---|---|
| | | *Income support should be increased* | *Income support should be lowered* | *Income support is at the right level* | *Total* | *Phi* Chi-sq. |
| Outsider | A lot | 82.5 (+***) | 0.7 | 16.8 (–***) | 100.0 | |
| | Rather | 77.7 (–*) | 1.2 | 21.7 | 100.0 | *0.13* |
| | A little | 75.0 | 1.9 | 23.1 | 100.0 | 22.69 (***) |
| | Not at all | 47.6 (–***) | 0.0 | 52.4 (+***) | 100.0 | |
| | Total | 79.9 | 0.9 | 19.2 | 100.0 | |
| Universalistic insider | A lot | 83.4 (+***) | 0.6 (–**) | 16.0 (–***) | 100.0 | |
| | Rather | 74.4 (–**) | 2.2 | 23.4 (+**) | 100.0 | *0.16* |
| | A little | 68.0 (–*) | 6.0 (+***) | 26.0 | 100.0 | 23.03 (***) |
| | Not at all | 55.6 (–*) | 0.0 | 44.4 (+*) | 100.0 | |
| | Total | 78.6 | 1.6 | 19.8 | 100.0 | |
| Selective insider | A lot | 74.2 (+***) | 4.1 (–***) | 21.7 (–*) | 100.0 | |
| | Rather | 68.6 | 7.3 | 24.1 (–***) | 100.0 | *0.17* |
| | A little | 54.6 (–***) | 12.4 (+***) | 33.0 (+**) | 100.0 | 41.08 (***) |
| | Not at all | 42.4 (–***) | 21.2 (+***) | 36.4 (+*) | 100.0 | |
| | Total | 70.2 | 6.2 | 23.6 | 100.0 | |

From then on, the hypothesis that a particularly strong aversion to risk could, among the well-protected, compensate for an objectively low risk is not confirmed. It can be shown even more finely. It turns out that universalistic insiders are, more often than the others, more preoccupied with poverty for themselves than for France in general. This could be construed as a sign of their aversion to risk, but as soon as this deviation in the preoccupation about poverty is crossed with opinion as to the level of income support, it appears that those who are more worried for themselves than for France are over-represented among those who wish for a lowering of income support. If they were that averse to risk, it should be the reverse.

## 2.5 *A moral model which can be read in several ways*

Since the hypothesis 'aversion to risk' can be crossed out, let us come back to our interpretation in terms of 'vital' income. In the end, the hypothesis which resists best consists in combining this variable with P1, and this amounts to carrying out an interpretation which underlines moral arguments. However, it is also necessary to resort to principle P2 to have an operative argumentative model. Variable F2, which is composite and which we used to spot the effect of this second principle, also upholds, as already said, the hypothesis of an ideological conflict between particularists and universalists, but in this conflict each of the protagonists is backed up by good reasons. We will show later that a holistic reading which does not interpret F2 in this way, but rather in terms of constraining superstructures, is not empirically validated. However, it is already very clear that such an interpretation does not make it possible to read correctly what does appear to be a moral model. Moreover, we know that, as the dimension of personal interest has been widely taken into account in the regression, the conflict between particularists and universalists does not rest anymore on springs, but on motives linked to a conception of the good or of fairness. And as a matter of fact, it is not enough to draw directly a conclusion as to the level of income support, since it is only one part of the overall reasoning, and must be interwoven with P1 to lead to such a conclusion. Lastly, at this stage we can conclude that conceptions as to what is moral or fair are clearly far from being negligible by comparison with individual interest in explaining an economic opinion such as that on the level of income support. As a result, the moral model we set forth has the advantage of being the only one which highlights the very significant effect which *combines* 'vital' income and F2.

Nevertheless, at the present stage, we do not know whether P1 and P2 are principles of justice in the deontological sense or whether they are only perfectionist principles. They apply to the whole population, all things being otherwise equal, but precisely, this is only possible because they can be interpreted in varied and diverging ways.

Let us start by crossing out two of these ways, which would consist in assigning, even if for different reasons, some *a priori* orientation to the model. P1 very much resembles Rawls's difference principle and P2 could be turned into a principle of equal liberty or even of equality of opportunity, which are the first two principles of justice according to Rawls. This possible connection must not lead to the conclusion that as a result, P1 and P2 are *ipso facto* deontological principles of justice. As a matter of fact, these principles do not result from a reasoning on the whole income distribution. Only the issue of the minimum income guaranteed by the community is being dealt with here, and the resulting model has no claim to be exportable to a different context. It is not specified in our study whether, beyond a satisfactory ground level (P1), individuals would seek to optimise for instance the average or the standard deviation of the distribution (Boudon, 1995*b*). Anyway, determining whether the deontological interpretation is the right one constitutes the decisive crux of the problem and it will require a solution validated by empirical data. A second reading must also be crossed out. It would consist in making P1 and P2 principles of pure economic efficiency, probably taken from a doctrine, and without any link with the individuals' moral or economic interests. This would bring us back to the *homo œconomicus*, of which we have already said how irrelevant it seemed to interpret the model. Still, let us note that even if P1 can accommodate a moderate economic liberalism, since it advocates little State intervention, it is irreconcilable with both a totally free-market doctrine and classical normative utilitarianism. But there is no reason to exclude an interpretation of P1 and P2 which links arguments of economic efficiency with the actors' moral or economic interests. These arguments are examples of justification aiming at the common good, but which have the specificity of introducing a constraint of reality (such as 'you can't have it all'). In a way, they lead to an intermediary position between two extremes – a highly selective particularistic interpretation and a non-selective universalistic one. Let us consider these three interpretations of P1 and P2 by going up axis F2, without using a justification coming only from the fact that one is involved by income support personally or through someone they are close to, since the moral model applies also when this condition is controlled in the regression. Each time, we will wonder how many equivalence classes are distinguished by a given interpretation.

This is an important question, for if, as shown in the first chapter, justice is a unanimous agreement as to rights and duties, it is truly certain that, *a priori*, this agreement can be achieved by acknowledging that there exists either one or several equivalence classes of individuals who share the same rights and the same duties. More concretely, thinking about the number of equivalence classes here amounts to asking oneself what are the limits of reciprocity which could, from the particular point of view defended, win everyone over.

Thus, at the bottom of axis F2, a 'pure' particularist rejects the plurality of conceptions of the good and applies the moral model by forming (at least) two equivalence classes. She distinguishes, according to her own criterion, the virtuous and the non-virtuous, or the deserving and the undeserving. The criterion may be that individuals show their willingness to work, but it can go as far as to touch on lifestyles. Of course, relatively to P1, the question of knowing what becomes of those excluded, that is of those who, according to the particularist, have no reasonable life plans, is left unanswered. She may think that only the deserving must benefit from a public allowance financed by a compulsory levy and that, for the others, only the emergency cases have to be dealt with, while the charity sector would be entrusted with daily help. In an intermediary position on F2, one finds an individual who admits the plurality of life schemes. But at the same time, she thinks that there should be a limit on reciprocity (P2) in the name of the common good, understood as economic efficiency. She is therefore at one with the 'pure' particularist, as she too forms (at least) two equivalence classes and judges that certain life schemes are unreasonable (such as those which are considered as unproductive). It is true that the selection criterion is less strict, but it remains in keeping with perfectionism. The limits of reciprocity are no longer justified by being 'swindled' by helping those who lead a 'bad' life, but only those who do not make a productive effort. By refusing, in the name of economic efficiency, to ensure those who are economically non-deserving, she may cynically worry about her risk premium. But she can still be convinced this is fair. She is then thinking less about herself than about all the deserving, and 'finds herself obliged' to give precedence to economic efficiency over life plans, so that the latter may be guaranteed. Even if the term is ambiguous, it is 'in everyone's best interest'. It is also in her best interest, since she cannot overlook that this eventually lowers her contribution. In other words, her opinion is a product of compassion: 'it really is a shame, but it is impossible to do more than this'; or, to put it differently: the economic efficiency criterion being regarded as true, an increase in the well-being of the deserving produces as a pure externality an increase of her own well-being. Lastly, at the top of axis F2, we find a universalist who is a pure liberal, in the moral sense. Not only does he admit the plurality of life schemes, but he considers that all of them are equally reasonable to claim the attribution of a minimum income. For him, reasonable life plans cannot be distinguished in the light of a restricted perfection criterion, even if this criterion corresponds to his own idea of happiness, even in the name of economic efficiency. Therefore, he only forms one equivalence class. If, according to him, the principle of reciprocity does not translate into a limitation of one's freedom to choose one's life schemes, this does not mean that he is a pure altruist. Reciprocity simply demands that if one were in the most deprived person's position, one would expect the help (at least superior to the vital income) that one claims to bring to the deprived, but no more. In other words, P2 imposes an upper limit on income support, while still leaving everyone free to give more than the others without reproaching others with not doing the same (supererogation).

In the end, when it comes to applying P1 and P2, the first two type-individuals form, for partly different reasons, *two* equivalence classes. Even if the latter is liberal, she is at one with the particularist on this key point. Inversely, the universalist differs from them by only distinguishing *one single* equivalence class. Now, each of them, the particularist as much as the universalist, can, according to his own reasons, tell himself or herself that his interpretation of the moral model is the right one, that he or she is impartial and that the others are partial, or, which amounts to the same, that his reasonable conception of the good life is just while the others' are not.

To go beyond the mere acknowledgment of a plurality of perfectionisms, it is enough, as we know, to wonder what the position of a spectator would be. We have a moral model, a conception of the good which can be construed in different ways, but the one which is fair, or which makes of P1 and P2 principles of justice, is that of a spectator with no interest relative to the promotion of his material well-being or to his conception of the good life. To make an opinion, he only has to refer to pure practical interest and, thus, to speak as a citizen. The question is therefore 'simple': how can one spot in our data the opinion of such a spectator? Once this opinion has been identified, it will only be necessary to know if it consists in forming one or, on the contrary, several equivalence classes to apply principles P1 and P2 with fairness to the problem of the allocation of minimum resources to the most deprived.

## 3. The Horizon of the Fair Spectator

### 3.1 *The effects of morality and economic interest*

In order to look for the stance of a fair spectator, we are going to re-examine opinions on income support. The previous regression can now be taken up again, with a reduction of the number of variables and, for each one of them, of the number of items. Since we already know the role played by the sociodemographic variables, we will not have to deal with them, and for each variable, whether it is dependent or independent, we only have to group the responses into two items. The opinion on the level of income support will thus be recoded into two categories: it must be increased (76%) *v.* it is at the right level or must be lowered. Similarly, for the compensations that should be asked from the beneficiaries, for which we will only oppose those who are very much or rather in favour of it to the others.

As far as the moral dimension is concerned, this strategy leads us to no longer take into account a continuous and complex variable like F2, but to look for a variable making it possible to distinguish clearly between a universalistic and a particularistic attitude. Any question which is meant to spot a selective orientation, whether in the field of lifestyles or in the economic realm, can be a candidate and, to tell the truth, considering the very strong correlations between all these variables, could be selected without affecting the results very much. We chose the one about homosexuals ('are they like everyone else?') because, at first sight, it seems very far from the issue of income support. We cannot prove that the interpretation of the answers to this question, as indicating a universalistic moral orientation *v.* a particularistic one, is definitely correct, but this is more than likely, because of the very strong correlations just described with the answers to the other questions implying, in the economic field as well as in that of lifestyles, the adoption of a universalistic or particularistic lifestyle. Table 1 gives an example concerning compensations for unemployment benefit, and we can take another one here by noticing the very strong links between the answers to this question and those bearing on the ideal role of women or on immigrants. Cross-tabulations reveal, with no ambiguity, that those who think that homosexuals are not different from other people are also those who think that there are not too many immigrant workers, and that the ideal role of women is not necessarily to stay at home to bring up their children (the chi-square are highly significant). Thus, responses to these three questions are not peculiar to the issue at stake. They are guided by a general moral opinion which opposes a universalistic orientation to a particularistic one, and which can be effectively epitomised by the question on homosexuals.

We already know that F2 has an effect of its own which is highly significant on the opinions on income support. However, because of the particular nature of the question which has just been selected instead of F2, it is important to verify that this is always the case, all things equal. In the field of homophobia, it is especially important to check if the consequences of morality, measured in the light of this new indicator, are maintained for a similar age (it is actually much more generation than age strictly speaking which is at stake here). If this turned out not to be the case, we would have to conclude that answers regarding homosexuality reflect a difference between generations, rather than a moral stance as such, which is likely to occur at every age. But the result is very clear: incorporating the age into a logistical regression does not alter in any way the significance of the link between the attitude towards homosexuals and an opinion on income support.[12] The interaction effect is actually not significant (at the 10% level). In other words, with a roughly similar amplitude, and whatever the age, universalism leads to prefer an increase of income support or an absence of restraining compensations.

Whether in the case of this increase or in that of compensations, those on income support or who know someone living on it among their relatives (13%, and it is then usually one's partner, child, or one's mother or father, as shown by other studies where questions of this kind were asked) are obviously directly involved, and it is not necessary to argue at length that this provides an indication of direct and immediate interest which weighs

12 In a nominal logistical regression where opinion on the level of income support is the variable to be explained, the impact of age, like that of moral opinion, is significant at the level of 1 for 10,000. If income is incorporated into this regression, the impact of moral opinion remains significant; this significance actually becomes stronger than that of age and, even more, than that of income ($p = 0.05$). In an ordinal logistical regression where the effects of the variables household net income, age and attitude towards homosexuals, on the opinions regarding the level of income support are now each modelised by a single parameter, we notice a remaining significant impact of moral attitudes with age and income controlled (the normalised parameters are, in absolute values, 2.98 for the income, 3.28 for age, and 3.22 for the attitude towards homosexuals).

heavily on the answers to these questions.[13] However, it can be argued that living on income support, or knowing someone who does, is too restrictive to judge it. The prospect or the possibility of having to rely directly or indirectly on income support may also intervene in the feeling of being involved. To take this into account, we have built economic interest indicators which also bring in the fact of being unemployed without receiving any benefit, or of being related to someone in this situation, of receiving unemployment benefit, and finally even of being in a precarious situation, either through separate variables, or by gradually cumulating all these situations, since they are not mutually exclusive. Now, since, without being absolutely identical, the meaning of the results which will be presented does not change, in all that follows, we will restrict ourselves to summing up the dimension of direct economic interest by living on income support or of knowing closely someone who lives on it, without it entailing a loss in generality. In this respect, not being involved amounts to being a spectator as far as interest is concerned. Actually, it is only an incomplete spectator, since interests bearing on the conception of the good life have not been controlled yet, but to avoid overloading the expression, we will still use the term 'spectator' to refer to this non-involved individual.

Let us note in passing that individuals who are not directly involved by income support could very well prove indifferent or careless in the face of the various questions on income support. In the first instance, this would be expressed through high no-answer rates or, in the second instance, by random answers. Nevertheless, this is not the case: the universalistic insiders have more often than the others an opinion on the ideal level of income support and, generally, spectators do not show a significant propensity to have no opinion. As to the possibility of them answering randomly, the rest of this study will show that this is absolutely not the case since the deviations on what would be random responses often are – and particularly at key stages of the argument – very significant. The non-involved individual could also prove less well-informed than the others on everything which is linked to basic allowances. However, it is more than likely that it is difficult for anyone to know precisely the meanders of the various administrative dispositions, and anyway, it is hard to see why this relative ignorance should twist the responses in one way or another. It is therefore not these hy-

13 It can be seen in table 8, by comparing, between its higher and lower parts, the rows entitled 'total' (chi-sq = 13.1, $p < 0.0001$).

potheses which need to be addressed in order to find a satisfactory explanation of the opinions of the non-involved, but rather, as will be verified, the idea of a spectator in search of fairness.

Cross-tabulations confirm what can be expected in the light of the previous analyses. Being a spectator as opposed to not being one, just like the difference in moral orientation, has a very significant impact on the opinions on income support. Contrary to those involved or to the particularists, spectators or universalists wish for an increase of income support and are opposed to compensations when they are perceived as coercive for the beneficiary. For both of these questions, logistical regressions show that this very significant effect of morality is maintained when controlled by economic interest, just as the significant effect of individual interest is maintained when controlled by morality (table 7). But the impact of morality is stronger than that of interest (as already appeared in the regression of the previous part).

Table 7 – *Logistical regression on the question 'Asking those on Income Support to accept the jobs they are offered'*

| *Effect* | *Df* | *Chi-sq* | *Prob. of a greater Chi-sq* |
|---|---|---|---|
| Being on IS or knowing someone who is on IS | 1 | 12.3 | 0.0004 |
| Moral opinion | 1 | 22.2 | 0.000002 |
| Interaction between these two effects | 1 | 8.6 | 0.003 |

This very clear effect of morality explains why universalistic insiders are situated higher than one might have thought in the factor analysis previously presented. The outsiders, who are very often in precarious situations, are involved (themselves, or through close friends or relatives) by many of the questions which have been selected to carry out this factorial analysis. It is therefore normal that they appear near the items (at the top of figure 1) implying an improvement on the plight of the most deprived. Morality does not add much to this effect. But the universalistic insiders, not being directly involved, could have been located lower on axis 2 (vertical in figure 1). As already said, these are mainly civil servants or high executives, that is, people who are unlikely to be or to become beneficiaries of income support, or to know closely somebody who is a beneficiary. If they are at the same level as the outsiders, it is because their universalistic moral opinion leads them to prefer answers of the 'solidarist' kind, approximately in the same measure as personal interest does, in the case of the outsiders. But the question remains to know whether this opinion is aimed at fairness, or at the promotion of a conception of the good life.

### 3.2 *A universalistic spectator has a tendency to be committed rather than compassionate*

Among the spectators, on whom we will now focus to answer this question, unsurprisingly, universalists approve very distinctly of an increase of income support or an absence of coercive compensations, while particularists think the reverse. Significantly *and* for a majority, universalism is thus linked to a 'solidarist' opinion (see table 8).

Table 8 – *Asking people living on Income Support to accept the jobs they are offered according to the acquaintance with someone on IS (or being on IS oneself) and the opinion on homosexuals (row % and signs of the significant adjusted residuals)*

| | | | *Asking people on IS to accept the jobs they are offered* | | | |
|---|---|---|---|---|---|---|
| *Acquaintance with someone on IS* | | | *Yes* | *No* | *Row total* | *Column total* |
| Yes | Homosexuals are like other people | Yes | 79.0 | 21.0 | 100.0 | 74.2 |
| | | No | 76.2 | 23.8 | 100.0 | 25.8 |
| | | Total | 78.3 | 21.7 | 100.0 | 100.0 |
| No | Homosexuals are like other people | Yes | 82.8 (–***) | 17.2 (+***) | 100.0 | 72.5 |
| | | No | 90.3 (+***) | 9.7 (–***) | 100.0 | 27.5 |
| | | Total | 84.8 | 15.2 | 100.0 | 100.0 |

Chi-sq of the upper table = 0.44, df = 1, p = 0.51, phi = 0.030, adjusted residuals = |0.7|
Chi-sq of the lower table = 28.32, df = 1, p < 0.001, phi = -0.094, adjusted residuals = |5.3|

However, we have only evacuated the most obvious form of interest (being involved or not). But is it so certain that this solidarist opinion does not conceal a second-degree egoism, whereby the improvement of other people's plight is wished for, because it has a positive impact on one's own well-being? One can also observe that it is hardly expensive to express a solidarist opinion and that there can often be a huge gap between words and actions. The effective action of an individual does not necessarily follow what she claims to think to an interviewer. As for the level of income support, this means that we must wonder whether the costs of the potential increase asked for are really taken into account. If the 'free opinion' were to be verified (among the spectators), what we thought we had identified as a solidarist answer oriented by a universalistic morality would actually be only mere compassion. By a similar movement, we would be brought back to individual interest and we would go further away from the position of a fair spectator.

An individual feels compassion when somebody else's happiness directly affects one's own well-being and we may say with Sen (1977, pp. 326–327) that behaviour based on compassion is 'in an important sense egoistic, for one is oneself pleased at others' pleasure, and pained at others' pain, and the pursuit of one's own utility may thus be helped by sympathetic action.' To go past this stage, it is necessary to go towards what Sen calls commitment. Commitment can indeed be based on individual interest, for instance when an individual commits to a collective action meant to defend or promote his own interests, but it can also be interest-free: 'If the knowledge of torture of others makes you sick, it is a case of sympathy; if it does not make you feel personally worse off, but you think it is wrong and you are ready to do something to stop it, it is a case of commitment.' (Sen, *ibid.*). It must be noted that the economic cost of sympathy or compassion is non-existent. It is a pure externality: it is enough if an individual thinks that somebody else's well-being has increased for his own well-being to improve. But the cost of commitment is not non-existent, because in this case: 'A person choosing an act that he believes will yield a lower level of personal welfare to him than an alternative that is also available to him.' (Sen, *ibid.*). However, commitment can still be guided by two diverging reasons, between which, unfortunately, Sen does not distinguish: altruism or justice. For now, the ambivalence can remain, but of course, it will be essential to unravel it later.

For one to say that she wishes for an increase of income support is not enough to identify the search for fairness. If this opinion is the result either of some direct interest or of compassion, as we can now see, we are in fact dealing with a 'partial spectator'. It must be shown that the non-involved individual holding this opinion is 'committed'. On other words, she is aware that such a step could lead to increase her contributions and she is *willing to contribute more*. She is then in favour of a step which she clearly perceives to run against her immediate 'selfish' economic interest, and we will be more justified in explaining her opinion as the behaviour of a fair spectator.

As they are asked in the poll, the questions linked to this issue do not make possible a total or completely unambiguous verification of this hypothesis. For instance, there is not such question as: 'would you be willing to pay more taxes to finance an increase of income support?' Nevertheless, a few questions can be regarded as good proxies.

The four questions which are directly linked to the cost issue seek to determine whether the respondent is willing to contribute more to make the possible maintenance of: health insurance, retirement pensions, child benefit or unemployment benefit. Between these four items, there is a high correlation. In other words, a majority of interviewees did not seek to distinguish between these four forms of allowance. Actually, it is always more or less the same who favour them – the insiders. The fact they did not frankly wish to orientate their answers in favour of one type of allowance rather than another, suggests they mainly wanted to show they were willing, in one way or another, to commit. Therefore, this validates, at least partly, the choice of one of these questions as a commitment indicator. We have selected the one bearing on unemployment allowances because, just like income support, and contrary to the others which are linked to health, family or retirement, these allowances are no doubt those which are the least likely to involve directly, or in the long term, the universalistic insiders. Moreover, the answers to the various questions on income support are strongly correlated with those asked in similar terms about unemployment (for instance as regards potential compensations); which suggest that, without being identical, these two situations have been treated in a relatively uniform way by the respondents. As with the variable relating to the increase of income support, the one bearing on the increase of subscriptions will be recoded into two categories opposing those who are completely or partly in favour of it (30%) with the others.

As for the raw links for the whole population, let us notice that willing to contribute more, just like thinking homosexuals are like everyone else, leads very blatantly to wish for an increase of income support. Moreover, there is also a very strong link between accepting an increase of contributions and a rejection of homophobia. But the questions we are asking here do not involve the whole population. The aim is to find out whether the universalism of those who are little or not at all involved by social minima is actually at work. For the others, the problem is not relevant. Moreover, even among the non-involved, in order to deal only with the alternative between commitment and compassion, it is necessary to restrict the investigation only to those who wish for an increase of income support. Indeed, for these individuals, and for them only, not being willing to accept an increase in contributions can be seen as an indicator of compassion. They wish to see an improvement in the lot of the most deprived, but they do not want this to have a potential incidence on their own well-being. Inversely, those who are willing to contribute more are committed in the sense they accept the idea that the increase of income support which they call for could turn out to undermine their immediate economic interest. By selecting the sub-sample of non-involved respondents in favour of an increase of income support, we will then be able to determine whether, by comparison with the average of solidarist spectators, the universalist spectator agrees more with commitment than with compassion.

Table 9 – *Commitment and moral opinion among those who wish for an increase of income support without being involved (themselves or through a relative) by income support or unemployment benefit (adjusted residuals)*

| | | *Willing to contribute more* | |
|---|---|---|---|
| | | *Yes* | *No* |
| Homosexuals are | Yes | +3.7 (***) | –3.7 (***) |
| like other people | No | –3.7 (***) | +3.7 (***) |

Chi-sq = 14, df = 1, p = 0.0002; Odds-ratio = 1.6, p < 0.001 (two-tailed test)
*N.B.* – For the definition of the adjusted residual, refer to the reading note of table 2 (here p < 0.001, two-tailed test; number of cases (n) = 1,639)

In order to do so, a contingency table crossing our opinion indicator with our commitment indicator, in the sub-population just defined, is enough. It then appears that particularists, spectators and solidarists, are for a majority compassionate. In the same situation, so are universalists, but to a lesser extent. But it is precisely this difference, or, which amounts to the same here, the deviation from average or from independence, which matters most for us to answer the question asked. From this point of view, the result is perfectly clear: contrary to particularists, universalists favour commitment rather than compassion. This tendency is very significant, from the angle of the chi-square, the adjusted residual or the odds-ratio. In a word, whatever the statistical test we opt for, a non-involved universalist manifests a stronger propensity to commitment than to compassion.

### 3.3 *A universalistic spectator, especially a committed one, is not cynical*

Let us now summarise the situation. The solidarist opinion (wishing for an increase of income support or not wishing for coercive compensations) is that of those who are involved, but it is also very significantly, among the non-involved, that of the universalists; and in this case, they have a tendency to be committed. But then, another form of interest appears, precisely as a result of this tendency. If the non-involved universalist is willing to contribute more to make an increase of income support possible, is it not simply so as to 'buy' social peace? Seeing that the most deprived organise themselves in order to call for an increase of social minima, the universalist could prefer to pay the price to avoid an extension of the conflict, which could for instance mean an occupancy of vacant housing by homeless people or people living in poor conditions, or simply, in order to preserve his psychological tranquillity.

It is important to confute this Hobbesian argument, not only because it goes against the hypothesis which we are trying to verify, but also, more generally, because it leads to a conception of the social contract, seen as binding every citizen to the Welfare State, which is incompatible with the Kantian perspective we adopt. For Hobbes (1651), as for all those who follow the tradition which he inaugurated, the cooperation required by the social contract is rational, in the sense that it only expresses everyone's personal interest. Here, it is rational to consent to a part of my resources being levied and redistributed to the most deprived, because this helps preserve social peace. Everyone makes the same calculation, and clearly sees that they cannot preserve their interest, in the long run, without sacrificing some short-term interests, keeping their income untouched. It is therefore in everyone's interest to consent to the common rule, that is to accept the Welfare State's levies, and even an increase, if it appears that those levies are perceived as not being sufficient anymore to guarantee the absence of any conflict.

Seeing justice as fairness leads, as seen above, to a completely different theory. The fair spectator aims at unanimity through this form of reciprocity which consists, by generalising, in founding the contract on each party's acceptation of the others' perspective. Whereas for the opposing theory, the question is to find out which repartition maximises everyone's interest, here, the question is: which principle of repartition is unanimously satisfactory from the point of view of any actor, and therefore also from that of the most deprived person? In the first case, preferences are already given and fairness only intervenes as an equal weighting of each agent's interests. In the second case, on the contrary, the equal consideration of everyone's interest intervenes as early as during the formulation of preferences, for giving an equal consideration to everyone is to already take into account everyone's legitimate pretensions at the moment of forming one's own point of view or life plan.

Therefore, we still have to show two things: first, of course, that the Hobbesian argument does not stand, in order to evacuate a third form of interest which could be concealed under the guise of the solidarist opinion of the committed universalist, but then, and positively this time, that fairness, as an alternative model, truly is the posture of this universalist.

As presented, the questionnaire does not include any question directly linked to the issue of social peace. It will therefore be necessary to accept to resort to indirect evidence. If the fear of a conflict is a motivation, it may logically be expected that people who accept to contribute more will perceive more than others that poverty or unemployment are preoccupying for themselves or for France in general. Similarly, they should be more inclined to think that inequalities, poverty or exclusion have risen ('over the last five years', in the questions asked) or, at the worst, have remained stable, but surely not that they have diminished. This reasoning should of course be maintained as far as the evaluation of the future of inequalities or poverty is concerned. But this is absolutely not the case, even at the scale of the whole population.

Whether for oneself or for France, being worried about poverty is in no way linked to willing or not to contribute more (chi-square of the corresponding cross-tabulations are entirely non-significant). As for the evolution of inequalities or poverty, the link is significant, but is contrary to what a Hobbesian argument supposes. People accepting to contribute more think that inequalities, poverty and exclusion have receded. This result remains unchanged when, instead of focusing on past evolutions, we deal with future evolutions, as forecast by respondents. Indeed it can be admitted that the Hobbesian argument does not rest so much on a perception of the past as on a fear of the future. But, here again, this is absolutely not the case. Those who accept an increase of their contributions think (significantly) that inequalities, poverty or exclusion will recede.

Nonetheless, these tendencies apply to the whole population and do not answer the question of whether an actor who is not, or little, involved by income support and who wishes for its increase is 'buying' tranquillity when claiming to be willing to contribute more. To know this, it is only necessary to re-examine all the previous crossings in the sub-sample of those favouring an increase of income support, without being involved. These results are actually strictly similar to the previous ones. The solidarism of a spectator who accepts commitment is therefore not explained by the interest he finds in avoiding a situation which is perceived as potentially preoccupying, serious, or even dangerous.

Very logically, these results are maintained if we further restrict the sub-sample, and only retain universalists. Consequently, the commitment of a universalist spectator, which leads him to a solidarist opinion, does not rest on an interest which is cynical in essence. In this perspective, it is actually interesting to wonder whether, among the spectators, committed universalists differs from compassionate universalists. As far as preoccupations are concerned, the link with commitment is just as non-significant among universalists as among particularists. On the contrary, this link differs mostly significantly when questions about past or expected evolutions of inequalities or poverty are at stake. The clearest case is about the future of poverty. In other cases, tendencies are identical, but slightly less marked. As table 10 shows, the judgment about the evolution of poverty has more impact for the universalist than for the particularist. With the latter, the choice of whether to contribute more or not does not rest on an evaluation of the situation in terms of poverty. On the contrary, this evaluation is present in the choice of a universalist, and it leads to a marked difference between the committed and the compassionate. Whereas a compassionate universalistic spectator fears the future and is therefore not willing to contribute more – very logically – a committed universalistic spectator is optimistic. It is with the latter, very specifically, that the Hobbesian argument applies least! Committed spectators, especially if they are universalistic, have a favourable opinion on the increase of income support, which is linked to their optimism rather than to the fear of a future which, as regards poverty, could upset their social or psychological tranquillity. Cynical interest is therefore absent, and this is particularly true among the committed universalistic spectators. Whatever the level of analysis, the Hobbesian argument can therefore be entirely given up.

Table 10 – *Commitment and opinion as to the future of poverty or social exclusion according to the moral opinion among those wishing for an increase of income support, without being involved (either personally or through a relative) by income support or unemployment benefit (adjusted residuals)*

| | | | *Poverty and exclusion in France in the future will tend to...* | | |
|---|---|---|---|---|---|
| *Homosexuals are like other people* | | | *decrease* | *increase* | *remain stable* |
| Yes | Willing to contribute more | Yes | +2.7(***) | –1.7(*) | –0.9 |
| | | No | –2.7(***) | +1.7(*) | +0.9 |
| No | Willing to contribute more | Yes | +0.3 | –0.5 | +0.3 |
| | | No | –0.3 | +0.5 | –0.3 |

Chi-sq of the upper table = 7.7, n = 1,181, df = 2, p = 0.02, phi = 0.081
Chi-sq of the lower table = 0.2, n = 382, df = 2, p = 0.89, phi = 0.025

If we accept these indirect reasonings, for want of some strictly topical questions, there is no doubt that everything that could be evacuated as immediate (being directly involved) or secondary selfish economic interest was taken out to explain the solidarist opinion of a spectator. This opinion is founded on a universalistic conception which is (tendencially) neither compassionate nor cynical. Of course, it could be said that it is advisable to examine other forms of interest in order to reach more certainty. In addition to the fact that we are limited by the questionnaire and that, from this point of view, we have the feeling of having gone as far as possible, it is to be feared that this kind of argument will lead only to an endless quest. Let us come to the positive argumentation, then, as a key question is still to be answered: if the solidarist opinion is that of a spectator whose material well-being is not at stake, why is it fair?

### 3.4 *The fair spectator speaks here in favour of universalism*

Our spectators have no springs and yet, it is not without any motives that they form their opinions. In order to see this, not only conceptions of the good life, but also considerations on justice must be taken into account. A whole group of questions asked in the poll give an idea of the gap between universalistic spectators and particularistic spectators on this issue. We already know that, contrary to the latter, the former think that income support should be increased, and that it should not be conditional upon restrictive compensations. But they also think, and the difference from the particularists remains significant, that it must exist anyway, and be permanent until the beneficiary regains a sufficient income. They are also favouring an extension of income support to the under 25. As regards the causes of poverty, the universalist – once more, in a significantly different way from the particularist – thinks that it can be caused by a lack of luck, and certainly not that the poor refuse to work. It is thus clear that in the universalistic mind, the most deprived must be helped at all costs, and even that one should try to improve it, not out of interest, but because this should be anybody's task. If income support must exist as a sort of permanent right, with no compensation, until the beneficiary is out of trouble, it means that the universalistic spectator refuses to distinguish between the deserving poor and the undeserving ones. In other words, he only forms one equivalence class. He adopts a position which takes into account others' judgments, without lecturing them (whatever his actual thoughts may be).

We can go further and show how far apart particularists and universalists stand on this behaviour. While they are at one on at least one aspect of the good life, they do not draw the same conclusions on justice from it. They do agree on the Aristotelian principle that individuals like (or should like) to exert their talents. Let us say, more simply, that they think it is a good thing to work when one has the opportunity to do so. Thus, a great majority advises those on income support who can work to make some efforts to integrate socially (94.7%) and to look for a job (96.7%). From the way the questions are asked ('if people on income support *can work*, would you find it *normal* if they were asked, *in exchange* for the allowance they receive: [...] (iv) to make some efforts to integrate socially?; (v) to look for a job?'), it is admitted that income support earners only have to want it, which of course makes it easier to ask for a compensation, all the more as it is suggested that income support is part of a deal. Nonetheless, it is characteristic that questions which deal with *advice* meet with approval from both particularists and universalists, while, as soon as one shifts from advice to *coercion* (that is, in exchange for the allowance, beneficiaries should be asked to accept the jobs they are offered), universalists are significantly more reluctant than particularists (see table 11). This means that the former give precedence to the just over the good. What they regard as a good life does not prevail for them. Therefore, it seems it is really with the non-involved universalist that the fair spectator's voice carries most.

Table 11 – *What may be asked to people on Income Support who can work, according to opinions on homosexuality, among those who are not, or hardly, involved by Income Support, directly or through a relative (adjusted residuals)*

| | | *Homosexuals are like other people* | |
|---|---|---|---|
| *Ask people on IS…* | | *Yes* | *No* |
| to accept the job | Yes | –5.3 (***) | +5.3 (***) |
| on offer | No | +5.3 (***) | –5.3 (***) |
| to make efforts to | Yes | –1.4 | +1.4 |
| integrate socially | No | +1.4 | –1.4 |
| to look | Yes | –0.1 | +0.1 |
| for a job | No | +0.1 | –0.1 |

First table: 3,224 individuals, chi-sq = 28.3, df = 1, p < 1 ‰, phi = –0.094
Second table: 3,294 individuals, chi-sq = 1.9, df = 1, p = 16 %, phi = –0.024
Third table: 3,304 individuals, chi-sq = 0.05, df = 1, p = 94 %, phi = –0.01

*N.B.* – In these tables, as in the previous ones, the absence of asterisks means that the adjusted residuals are not significant, even at the low 10% level (two-tailed test). On the contrary, (***) here means that the residuals are significant at the 1‰ level (and even beyond).

To demonstrate this for good, we only have to turn the method backwards and build the fair spectator without using the distinction universalist / particularist. Let us bear in mind that, in order to spot an individual reasoning as a fair spectator, two conditions are sufficient (but not necessary): he should neither have a material interest at stake, nor impose his own conception of the good life. We then face an individual who cannot be suspected of seeking to further non-neutral reasons, in brief, of being partial (since he is *not interested* and he is *not perfectionist*). For us, here, this means that (i) the person who is not involved by income support, whether personally or through a close acquaintance, (ii) who considers that working is a good thing, but (iii) who refuses to impose it on others (therefore not being perfectionist), fills the empirical conditions that make him a fair spectator. The question is then: who is this fair spectator? First of all, we can observe that he is predominantly a universalist (83%, by comparison with 73% for the whole sample). But we can go further by comparing the fair spectator with the perfectionist spectator, that is, therefore, the one who imposes accepting any job. This is what is done in table 12 and the result is totally devoid of ambiguity: a fair spectator is very significantly a universalist.

Table 12 – *Asking people on income support to accept a job, according to opinions on homosexuality among those not involved by income support, directly or through a relative, and who consider that working is a good thing (adjusted residuals)*

| | | *Accepting a job on offer* | |
|---|---|---|---|
| | | *Yes (perfectionist)* | *No (liberal)* |
| Homosexuals are like other people | Yes | –5.3 (***) | +5.3 (***) |
| | No | +5.3 (***) | –5.3 (***) |

*N.B.* – 3,129 individuals, chi-sq = 27.7, df = 1, p < 1 ‰, phi = –0.094, odds-ratio = 0.5, p < 1‰. It is noteworthy that if the spectator is defined more strictly, that is, if those who are also involved by unemployment and precarious living conditions, themselves or through their relatives, the adjusted residual remains highly significant: in absolute value, it amounts to 4.4. The same applies to all the other indicators of significance. In this table, (***) indicates that the adjusted residual is significant at the 1‰ level (and even beyond).

If we now draw a comparison between those involved by income support and those who are not, we can see, firstly, that those involved are obviously less coercive and, secondly, that universalists and particularists are not distinguished anymore (see the higher parts of table 13). It was then important to relax the two biases of individual interest and of perfectionism to locate the position of a fair spectator. As this position appears as soon as both biases have been removed, the precedence of justice as fairness is indeed a horizon.

So far, as we specified from the very start, we have restricted ourselves to presenting the results of the 2000 poll, since those of the polls carried out in 2001 and 2002 are almost identical. But, considering the importance of table 12 for our argumentation, let us make an exception, and see whether the same results are maintained from one year to the next.[14] This is what is done in table 13, and as clearly appears, these results remain unambiguously unchanged when the three samples are compared.

14 Each sample is representative, but not the same individuals are interviewed from one year to the next (it is not a panel). However, there are about 4,000 of them each time.

Table 13 – *Asking people on Income Support to accept a job, according to opinions on homosexuality and the fact of being involved or not by Income Support, directly or through a relative, among those who consider that working is a good thing, in 2000, 2001 and 2002 (adjusted residuals)*

| | | | | *Accepting a job on offer* | |
|---|---|---|---|---|---|
| | | | | *Yes* | *No* |
| 2000 | Involved | Homosexuals are | Yes | +0.6 | –0.6 |
| | by IS | like other people | No | –0.6 | +0.6 |
| | Not involved | Homosexuals are | Yes | –5.3 (***) | +5.3 (***) |
| | By IS | like other people | No | +5.3 (***) | –5.3 (***) |
| 2001 | Involved | Homosexuals are | Yes | –0.1 | +0.1 |
| | by IS | like other people | No | +0.1 | –0.1 |
| | Not involved | Homosexuals are | Yes | –4.8 (***) | +4.8 (***) |
| | By IS | like other people | No | +4.8 (***) | –4.8 (***) |
| 2002 | Involved | Homosexuals are | Yes | +1.1 | –1.1 |
| | by IS | like other people | No | –1.1 | +1.1 |
| | Not involved | Homosexuals are | Yes | –5.6 (***) | +5.6 (***) |
| | By IS | like other people | No | +5.6 (***) | –5.6 (***) |

*N.B.* – In this table, as in the previous one, (***) means that the residual is significant at the 1 ‰ level (and even beyond). The same remarks as those made for table 12 are maintained. The other statistical indicators lead to the same diagnosis. When adjusted residuals are significant, numbers of cases are: 3,129 in 2000, 3,030 in 2001, and 3,049 in 2002. When adjusted residuals are not significant, numbers of cases are: 464 in 2000, 486 in 2001, and 500 in 2002. Even if the interaction between the three variables (except for the date) of this table is significant ($p = 0.0003$), a loglinear model confirms that this interaction does not vary significantly ($p = 0.57$) from one year to the next.

In fact, it has just been established that an individual in the position of a fair spectator has a tendency to decide in favour of a universalistic morality, that is, to refuse to grant different rights and duties to individuals (as far as income support is concerned). This leads her to a solidarist opinion, not out of compassion or cynicism, but because of arguments which are flexible enough to be accepted by a random person. She has her own idea of happiness, but does not seek to impose it. Her arguments are those of justice as fairness, to which she gives priority over the good.

### 3.5 *The holistic interpretation fails to account for these data*

This result – the priority of justice – is out of reach for a theory resting only on a restricted rational choice, but can a holistic interpretation be contemplated? The objection which is most relevant – because it rests on the interpretation of one of the strongest correlations in these data – would consist in holding that, while all the previous reasonings may not be completely uninteresting, they are superfluous, since it is enough to remark the high correlation between one's work sector and an opinion on income support to account for what can be observed empirically. Indeed, a majority of universalists (or of universalistic insiders, if we remember the cluster analysis) are public sector workers, and from then, the *homo ideologicus* thesis (supported by a basic cross-tabulation evidencing the strong significant link between one's sector and an opinion on income support) could find some credit: the fair spectator would only be a public sector worker very much favouring the State's universalistic mission, as a mere by-product of his social status or proximity with the Welfare State. In particular, the result established in table 12 would be twisted because of an over-representation of public sector workers among universalistic fair spectators. Unfortunately for holism, this is not the case. If we take these workers out of table 12, there remains a significant link between universalism and solidarism. The adjusted residual shifts to 4.7 (instead of 5.7) and the chi-square to 22.3 (instead of 27.7), which is still, for 1 degree of freedom, very significant. Moreover, this relative decline in significance is only due to the fact that a smaller number of people is being considered (we go from 3129 to 2643 individuals). To realise this, one only has to compare the *Phi*: it goes from –0.094 to –0.092. It can therefore be concluded that being a public sector worker has no effect of its own on the result of table 12. Moreover, it is strictly the same if we take out high executives and professionals (the adjusted residual shifts to 4.9, the chi-square to 23.5 and the phi to –0.090).

Proximity with the Welfare State, modelised from the statutes of public sector workers, private sector employees and the self-employed, is not enough to absorb a conception of the good life or the horizon of fairness when personal interest is minor. A methodology in terms of good reasons accounts for this perfectly, whereas a holistic interpretation simply fails to do so. The reason is that a quick reading of global correlations, moreover supposing endless black boxes when one comes to the individuals, leads to an overly reductive vision when supported only by the idea of a social position or of an ideology stealing into people's minds to the point of turning them into mere puppets. And, as always when there are exceptions, they must be endowed with a false conscience, if not with irrationality, in order to maintain the explanation. Luckily, as regards the idea that such a reasoning leads to form of the free will of men and women, only the opposite thesis, which only sees one's social status as one bias among many others relatively to the horizon of justice as fairness, is compatible with the empirical data. Without wrestling anymore with the old demons of strong determinism, the results we have reached enable us to underline that even if, to the contrary, the intervention of ideology is explained by the white box of good reasons, this does not mean that the part played by the strictly moral dimension should be understated, as it proves decisive here.

### 3.6 *A universalistic spectator is not an angelist*

However, one final hypothesis could still contradict our interpretation of the result of table 12. The universalistic spectator may well be fair, but is this – as has been said – out of a deontological preoccupation about justice, or out of altruism, for instance out of a love for mankind? We know that she is not selfish, since she is not involved, and is tendencially neither cynical nor compassionate. However, among the three possibilities – egoism, altruism or fairness – only the first one is crossed out. The alternative between the last two remains, since our fair spectator model essentially requires to consider the different conceptions of the good life, the altruistic one as the others, rather than to suppose *a priori* which ones are worth living. This is not the case in other theories, and especially with Rawls (1971), for whom an individual 'behind the veil of ignorance' remains motivated by a selfish interest or an aversion to risk. In this case, the principles of justice can obviously not result from supererogation. But this is a 'coup' in the case of altruism, which turns out to be crossed out by construction. This coup is not without its charms since it makes it possible to turn the rational choice theory against itself. It shows that even if starting from a restricted rationality, behind the veil of ignorance, the answer to the issue raised (by Rawls) cannot avoid bringing about the dimension of justice as fairness. In our case, on the contrary, having done with first- and second-degree egoism, in order to come to a spectator who really is a spectator, we can no longer claim *a priori* that her position cannot be that of an altruist. And there is no point in trying to use the theory of fairness to argue anything here. It could indeed be remarked that fairness implies reciprocity, since by definition it consists in thinking that what is valid for one is valid for the other, and that this is contrary to altruism, which is precisely built without a wish for reciprocity. The sacrifice is consented upon for oneself and is in no way imposed on others. However, this argument does not carry, since, precisely at the point now reached, we are trying to determine whether the reasons of our spectator are the product of a deontological fairness or, on the contrary, of a form of angelism from which, like some sort of a lucky effect, fairness could result.

We could not get out of this dilemma if we did not empirically have an idea of the moral model at work. But we do know it. It has been previously established to explain opinions on the level of income support, and applies of course to the universalists. It includes two principles: a floor one, P1, and one of reciprocity, P2. It is then enough to notice that, whereas P1 can be compatible with altruism, on the contrary, P2 stands in complete contradiction with such altruism. We had actually already noticed this. Consequently, the universalist is fair by virtue of his neutral reasons, rather than out of angelism. All the other possibilities having been excluded, since this is also the stance of a spectator, there is no doubt anymore that the universalist asserts nothing else than the priority of the right over the good.

The moral model associating P1 and P2 is thus strictly a model on justice when only one equivalence class is established, since this is what a fair spectator does for the questions on income support. He also sides with the universalist and refuses to consider two classes with the help of a principle of deserts. As a result, if on average all are based on the same moral model, the interpretation which consists in distinguishing two equivalence classes is only subjectively fair. It cannot be detached from a conception of the good life which always amounts eventually to a greater solicitude for oneself than for the others. This result, far from being normative, is empirically demonstrated: we have only listened to the individuals who are in a position which leaves them no other possibility than to resort to neutral reasons in order to build their opinion. In theory, nothing prevented them from distinguishing two categories, one with the deserving and the other with the non-deserving; and yet, it must be observed that they made the opposite choice, completely freely, since they have no springs which could twist their opinion. To use Rousseau's terminology, they are talking as 'Citizens'; and Kant (1798), as often, goes along with him to sum up their position: 'The opposite of egoism can be only *pluralism*, that is, the attitude of not being preoccupied with oneself as the whole world, but regarding and conducting oneself as a citizen of the whole world.'

## 4. Two Consequences Pertaining to Economics

The fair spectator is therefore not a speculative function and all its implications must be taken in. We will only deal with two examples here, which pertain to economics and make it possible to argue (i) that a theory which only rests on the *homo œconomicus* is *a priori* incomplete and (ii) that an empirical analysis of opinions (i.e. of economic opinions in this case) which does the same takes the risk of not understanding its logic, and therefore of seeing inconsistency in the answers (on the basis of respondents' irrationality), where, on the contrary, it is possible to find its logic again by imagining that interviewees also orientate their answers according to a demand for social justice.

### 4.1 *Amending the Insiders – Outsiders Theory*

The Insiders – Outsiders Theory (Lindbeck and Snower, 1988) is part of a group of middle-range theories aiming at an explanation for the rigidity of prices and wages and eventually, for the maintaining of a high unemployment rate over the last twenty five years in several European countries. Let us briefly go over its principle again. On one side, some insiders enjoy a relatively well-protected job, were it only because of the cost of replacing one employee by an unemployed person in a company (because of difficulties such as finding the right candidate, the time of adaptation for the newcomer, or the legal protection of the employee). On the other side, outsiders are in a precarious condition (unemployment, 'disposable' job) where they have no power of negotiation with an employer. From this imbalance, the theory forecasts the appearance of a *hysteresis* phenomenon, which is going to freeze the existing situation: breaking the Hobbesian social pact (no aversion to risk), the strongest at a given moment decide, in a strategic way, to form a coalition against the weakest in order to maintain for good their prerogative, or even to increase it. In order to do so, insiders use their advantage over outsiders to organise a rise in wages or, more precisely, to get a guaranteed income. This coalition is usually represented by a union in charge of maximising this income without taking into account the lot of the outsiders. The consequence is then obvious: the success of this coalition leads to putting a brake on hiring. The outsider will not be able anymore to work for a lower wage to reach a protected status and the employer will consider his rates to be too high, considering his initial handicaps (lack of immediate adequacy to the job, loss of experience during the period of unemployment, etc.), which are actually not going to improve as long as the outsider remains an outsider. Thus follow a perpetuation of unemployment at a high level and a dualisation of the job market, with, on one side, protected jobs, and on the other, precarious jobs paid at a very low rate.

The Insiders – Outsiders Theory is very general. Even if it is often reduced to a theory of unions, it seems natural to extend its reasoning to the Welfare State, as Olson (1965) already suggested. To establish the analogy, we only need to replace protected employment with a social protection worthy of the name, to imagine that politicians seek above all to please taxpayers and contributors, and to think that the latter could very well form a coalition in order to guarantee a good protection for themselves only.

The criticism we are led to formulate against this theory is not that it is necessarily false. It is perfectly possible that, on a given issue raised by life in common, individuals behave as in the (Hobbesian) state of nature and make the most of their strength to fend for themselves by trampling on others. What we criticise is rather its presupposition, which Olson actually summarises perfectly: 'The union member, like the individual taxpayer, has no incentive to sacrifice any more than he is forced to sacrifice.'

From then on, the theory can only be incomplete, and consequently, it is at risk of resting on some fundamental indeterminacy. What could motivate the stronger individual not to use his strength? For those who subscribes to the rational choice theory, there is only one possibility left: the stronger individual yields to panic and rushes off to sign a pact, even with the weaker one. The reasoning is thus completely dependent on an aversion to risk with which the rational choice theory eventually endows the individuals arbitrarily; and, as if by magic, all moral acts are only consequences of panic, whereas immoral acts result from the absence of such panic.

To deal with the problem seriously and reasonably, the possibility of a fair spectator must be considered, next to the frightened *homo œconomicus* and to the self-assured *homo œconomicus*. The temptation to manipulate the aversion to risk according to the results is thus avoided. The empirical study we have carried out emphasises that the fair spectator is far from being a theoretical case which is negligible in practice. Next to a selective insider, who only wants to form a social pact with a carefully-selected happy few, there is room left for a universalistic insider who still sees in the outsider an equal in dignity. Generally speaking, Simmel (1908) had already developed early in the 20th century some convincing arguments to explain that a social game is always a game played by three people (at least). The monad is a fiction and the dyad has no sociological depth: no coalition can be formed, and therefore no strategy can be devised, etc. (Forsé, 2002). A typology of of opinions or behaviours should therefore be at least ternary. The reduction to a pure duel is not impossible of course, but it is acceptable only if one has explained how the existing conditions and circumstances lead to an empirical disappearance of the third party, unless the notion that the third party has a theoretical status has already been defeated. But we find none of this in the theory of the duel between insiders and outsiders. It is a theory with an incomplete construction.

## 4.2 *The* homo œconomicus*'s opinion*

Such a lack of completeness is not without consequences when it comes to empirical applications. It is rare for economists to dwell on opinion polls. As we are going to see, this is clearly a perilous venture. When commenting on a European poll (Germany, Spain, Italy, France), on the reforms of social security and pensions, Tito Boeri, Axel Börsh-Supan and Guido Tabellini[15] (2001) came across a serious difficulty. It is true their theory is closed off from the very beginning. Opinions in keeping with the rational choice theory are the only serious ones: 'The results [...] are quite consistent with what we would expect. This is encouraging since it provides indirect evidence that respondents understood the questions and answered in a serious manner.' (p. 28) However, as it happens, not any answer proves to be non-serious.

15 The authors are using a poll carried out in March 2000 in France, Italy, Spain and Germany, with questions close to those of the DREES's poll previously studied.

The issue we are going to address, for an illustrative purpose, deals with retirement pensions. The point is to find out whether the Europeans interviewed are willing to leave the system of contributory pension schemes in favour of self-funded retirement plans. It appears that few Europeans accept such an idea. But, if they are asked the same question with the added restriction that everyone would be forced to save part of their income, a majority is now favourable. More exactly, after the future problems of retirement pensions at the national level have been underlined, the following question is asked: 'Suppose that you were offered the following "less contribution – less pension" deal. Namely, you were offered to reduce your contributions to the national public system by one half, and receive this amount in your pay slip. When you retire, you will get a lower pension than if you had worked at 50% of your salary from tomorrow onwards. Would you accept such a deal?' Then, 19% of Spanish, 25% of French, and 47% of Germans and Italians say yes. And, when asked what they will do with the money, most of them say that they will invest all or part of it until they retire. But to the question 'consider a slightly different proposal: the compulsory contributions, rather than being put in your pay slip, would be put in an investment fund of your choice. You would be free to cash money in from that fund only upon retirement. Would you accept such a deal?', positive answers are now as high as 50% for the French, 63% for the Spanish, 67% for the Italians, and 71% for the Germans. For the authors, such a change in opinion is irrational. Why do certain people only accept the restrictive opinion?

Apart from the hypothesis that interviewees did not understand the second question but, surprisingly, perfectly understood the first one, the authors consider several interpretations. The most tempting one makes it possible to maintain the principle of hoped-for utility. The only valid reason to prefer an obligation to a lack of obligation is the wish to abstain from one's future actions: to tie one's hands to avoid doing something stupid. Another hypothesis is that one ties other people's hands because the hard-working part of the population wants to compel the not-so-hardworking part of the population in order not to have to sustain them in the future. However, the authors only moderately defend these hypotheses. A whole group of clues tend to show that respondents are hardly aware of management problems. Their answers tend to be more 'idealistic'.

For instance, we know that one of the hinges in the questions on the pension system is the transition from one system to the other. To shift to a self-funded retirement plan, it will be necessary in one way or another to return the money collected from the previous generations in the old contributory system. Does it justify the gaps between answers to both our questions? Obviously not. Most people are not aware of the problem and those who chose a self-funded system usually change their minds as soon as the difficulties of this passage are mentioned.

In fact, the authors implicitly acknowledge the role of morality. In Germany, the following specification had been added: 'if this would help so that the generation of our children and grandchildren does not have to pay still higher contributions'; but, of course, this orientates the answers. What is surprising is not that respondents take seriously this concern over the next generations, but that the authors only construe this as ideology or political correctness, and that they do not draw from this any conclusion as to the individuals' motivations.

Such deafness is mainly explained by the theoretical framework they have chosen. According to them, only two options are possible: 'Are class and ideological conflicts the key, or is it merely a "neo-corporatist" conflict?' Let us specify that the so-called neo-corporatist thesis simply consists in applying the Insider – Outsider model to the Welfare State (as can be seen by reading their article). But, as it happens, none of these options are convincing. Indeed, the authors point out two crucial points. First, answers very much depend on the respondent's general economic knowledge, and more specifically on his level of knowledge on pensions. Then, the political positioning of the interviewee has no effect of its own, all things equal. Conclusion: respondents do indeed reason from what they know, but this does not lead them to maximise their interest and, moreover, *homo ideologicus* does not step in to make up for the failings of *homo œconomicus*. Our authors are thus caught in the trap of their own presuppositions. They have no other solutions but to offer irrationality as a conclusion – which, to put it clearly, in less politically correct parlance, does not mean anything else than 'people are stupid'.

Of course, if we think that before such a conclusion is reached, it may be preferable to wonder whether the problem does not lie in the interpretative model, it is the fair spectator that is needed to retrieve the consistency and rationality of answers, this is true that in a broader sense than that supposed by the rational choice theory. To do so, we have to formulate the hypothesis that respondents are trying to combine several potentially conflicting reasons in the best possible way. The first reason could be resting on some economic belief. It would be the idea that a self-funded retirement plan pays more than a contributory scheme. We do not have any clear empirical evidence to back up this hypothesis, but the breathtaking skyrocketing of the Stock Exchange rates at the time of the poll (2000) speaks in favour of self-funding in order to guarantee a happy retirement. Moreover, without dwelling on the experts' debates about the relative merits of each system, there may also be a cognitive bias in favour of self-funding. In this system, it is easy to see that the money is invested and therefore multiplies, while the economic merits of the contributor system are more difficult to make out. In one case, the system management is analogous to that of a private individual who dabbles on the Stock Exchange, and benefits, especially at a good time, are clear to everyone; in the other case, the economic merits of the redistribution among generations can hardly be understood without a better knowledge of economic concepts. Therefore, the hypothesis of an *economic* preference for the self-funded system, partly linked to the present economic circumstances, seems plausible. Now, this preference clashes with a second strong reason, which is much more linked to the feeling of justice than to technical considerations as to the passage from one system to the other.

Leaving the contributory scheme has a 'moral cost', so to speak. It breaks the principle of reciprocity, so that it is easy to explain that adding an obligation to shift to self-funding should draw greater support. It makes it possible to combine the conviction that a self-funded system is economically preferable, with the feeling that this is a fair option, since in this case, everybody will benefit from it. On the contrary, choosing the option without any obligation made the interviewees feel that they were the only 'rats to leave the ship'. It is hard to back up this interpretation with the few tables shown by the authors. As the right questions this requires are obviously out of their theoretical framework, they have not been asked. Moreover, the questionnaire is entirely orientated towards personal interest, and presents the Welfare State as a mere company selling insurances. The stumbling points of their approach are thus easy to predict. The authors then come across one last issue which befuddles them, that is: why do a third of the individuals who accept to shift to the self-funded system with an obligation still want the importance of the Welfare State to be maintained, or even extended? How, they wonder, can people who are rational enough to want to leave the contributory system be irrational enough to wish to increase the role of the Welfare State? Obviously, our authors do not understand the idea of the social contract and they cannot see that, throughout their analyses, they are only dealing with a universalistic insider who comes to undermine their theoretical presuppositions. And if they cannot see this, it is precisely because these presuppositions prevent them from conceiving that opinion is not 'irrational' when founded on the moral choice of what is reasonable for everyone.

## Conclusion

This example, added to the previous ones, shows that it is possible to invalidate the idea that the fair spectator could have some theoretical interest, but no practical value. By giving close attention to the empirical data, we actually see the reverse. Not only does the fair spectator theory make it possible to avoid the theoretical pitfalls of utilitarianism (and holism), but without it, it is more than probable that we would fail to reach an understanding of opinions – as long as they are likely to possess a moral dimension, of course.

To work with a simply binary typology, summing up the two terms of a conflict of interest, such as the one which just opposes insiders and outsiders, is not enough. 'Forgetting' the third term means forgetting the position of an individual who seeks a fair solution to the conflict. The error is all the more damaging as this position is not only an opinion which is empirically detectable in certain circumstances, which would be added to those of the two conflicting parties. It constitutes a horizon. There are good reasons, as we have seen, not to put on the same level justice and what is simply derived from this or that person's own interest. But this is not only a question of 'good moral philosophy'. As our analysis of opinions on income support has shown, as soon as individual interest is no longer at stake, or tends to decrease dramatically, opinions tend to adopt the standpoint of a universalistic morality (committed and non-cynical), which happens to be that of a fair spectator, that is, of an individual who seeks to impose neither her rational interest, nor her conception of the good life, thus giving priority to what is just or fair.

Of course, it remains that if the stance of a fair spectator can always be theoretically devised, and if it was empirically observed here, there are situations which hinder its expression, and are thus not conducive to spotting it significantly in statistics. This is certainly the case in the face of very intense and zero-sum conflicts. It can be some interior or exterior war or a pure competition. But precisely, going out of the conflict, or not sticking to the logic of a mere competitive market which sacrifices the most deprived, always consists for the actors in seeking, as journalists put it, a 'political answer', that is, in finding the way to make what everyone can regard as fair come before each of the protagonists' selfish interest. Even if this cannot go without difficulty, of course, it does not follow that the way of the fair spectator ceases *a priori* to be worth considering.

Conversely, as we can see, it is out of the question to deny that an actor may be partial. This stems from many biases, which have been explored abundantly for a long time. Of course, her own interest may be at stake. But, beyond, her knowledge of the facts and her way of considering the solutions can be partial as a result of her place in society; she can take her wishes for realities, if such or such belief boosts her ego, for instance; she may lie, because her opinion is socially looked down upon; her friends and relatives may influence her response, out of loyalty for her community of origin; she can regard her choices of life as the only deserving ones, etc. This is already known. However, as we hope has been shown, these biases are not enough to understand opinion. The usual sociodemographic variables enable us to see these biases at work, but to overlook the fair spectator would make it impossible to understand opinion when these biases vanish.

In the cases where the actor is involved, the expected utility model is formidable. Just as La Rochefoucauld used to say that 'our virtues are usually our vices in disguise', we can imagine with great arbitrariness many utility functions which fit in with the data. The critic quickly gets the impression of playing the game 'tails, I lose, heads, you win'. But, in the cases where the actor is not involved, the model remains fruitless, as it does not have access to the field of neutral reasons. The use of a non-involved actor thus makes it possible to bypass the arbitrariness of explanations of the rational choice theory, and then to re-evaluate even the case of the involved actor when she reasons by putting herself in the (ideal) situation of a spectator.

When an individual reasons in this deontological way, the option she chooses is (or can be), from the narrow point of view of restricted rationality, *under-optimal* (including for a bounded rationality theory); hence the incomprehension of a utilitarian. He may well try to add, next to the preferences on material and moral well-being, some preferences on the right, as long as he will not look for other solutions than what is optimal for this complex preference function, he will only be able to account for the data in a purely contingent way. And yet, it is not hard to see that when an individual gives precedence to the right, she does not maximise anything. As opposed to the perfectionist, she is looking for what could bring about unanimity. But the utilitarian cannot find this solution, for a reason which Kant (1788) already expounded very clearly: 'The principle of happiness may indeed furnish maxims, but never such as would be competent to be laws of the will, even if *universal* happiness were made the object.'[16] The utilitarian will therefore never stop wondering why, in ordinary life, ordinary people do not always behave as they would if they were only these good 'social morons' of game theory he is so passionate about, or these good old 'rational fools'[17] who at every instant are optimising, directly or indirectly, some utility functions. It is high time, then, to consider that the actors' opinions who give priority to justice are not a strange data for an economic or social model. The fact that these actors form their opinions or decide to act by taking some distance from their various springs does not make them ethereal beings, from out of this world, about whom a scientific analysis could not say anything. By putting their own projects in perspective and taking into consideration other people's projects, they do something which is essential for the social sciences and which is perfectly objectivable: they make up a society.

However, this leads us to a more difficult point, which has been glimpsed at in the previous reasonings, but which has not been truly tackled so far. We have observed that the fair spectator is a universalist, but does the preference for universalism is a result of its objective value? Two theories are in direct opposition here. The first one consists in supporting moral relativism. If the choice between the particularistic and the universalistic moral options explains opinion, it is still impossible to overcome the simple fact that this person is a universalist, and that person a particularist. All in all, these are two perfectionist conceptions of the good life in opposition, which cannot be rationally solved. These are only axiological biases. The alternative theory considers that the fair spectator is led for strong reasons

16 In this sentence, 'happiness' may of course be replaced by utility.

17 The two phrases between inverted comas are taken from Sen (1977).

to support one of these two options – universalism in this case, as the other option does not stand an impartial approach. In other words, and as we have been arguing, universalism is a horizon of opinion one gets closer to when any form of interest recedes.

To go beyond this confrontation, we can start by noting that the respective descriptive merits of these two theories are far from being equal. It must be emphasised that in what has been said before, we have distinguished between the impartial and the universalist. We have defined the fair spectator by starting from his non-involvement, and we have interpreted his judgment as founded on neutral reasons. Even if we insisted that the power of conviction of an argument owes to the fact that it can be accepted by everyone, and therefore that an efficient argument aims at universality, we have not used this aspect to say that fairness is intrinsically linked to universalism. In brief, we have avoided the tautology which consists in admitting that the fair spectator is universalistic by definition, and that the particularist is therefore partial. On the contrary, we have *observed* that the fair spectator is a universalist – tendencially committed and non-cynical. We have built the model of a fair spectator, and then observed that this model was congruent *empirically* with our universalist. We can then say that, as the fair spectator is a horizon, it is the neutral reasons which can win over everyone. This model accounts very well for the data, in particular for the strength of neutral reasons when involvement is no longer here. On the contrary, the relativistic model remains silent; at the empirical and explanatory level, it is far less efficient than the fair spectator model.

This point is far from being negligible, but of course, it does not settle all the discrepancies between these two approaches. As it is probably not possible to go much further by sticking to a strictly empirical perspective, it is necessary to come to more theoretical considerations to show that, contrary to what the appearance of a search for a unanimous agreement could suggest, the principle of justice underlying the reasons of a fair spectator invalidates any form of relativism.

# Annex

## Ordinal Logistical Regression on Opinions as to the Level of Income Support

We have carried out an ordinal logistical regression on the variable constituted by ranking opinions as to the level of income support as follows: 1/ it must be lowered, 2/ it is at the right level and 3/ it should be raised. 'Don't know' or 'not answered' are considered as missing values. So as to keep as much information as possible, we have also taken into account the ordinal logic of most of the explanatory variables: household net income, level of education, age, size of community, 'vital' income, and the property situation (1 for owners and non-paying occupants, 2 for people joining the property ladder/first-time buyers, and 3 for paying tenants). We have thus modelised these effects through straight lines in order to judge on a typical tendency. Only in the case of age could this choice be challenged. The age impact has the appearance of a convex curve: opinions in favour of an increase of income support decreases strongly with age to start with, and then subsides. Initially, we had logically modelised this phenomenon with a curve but, as soon as this effect is corrected, with the help of the 'in the labour force / not in the labour force' variable, the curvature disappears, thus justifying our eventual choice. The other explanatory variables taken into account are: being in the labour force or not, gender, and a personal acquaintance with someone on income support. The appearance of the latter variable convinced us to retain its nominal character. Lastly, we have included the coordinate on the second factorial axis (F2) as a covariable, because it encapsulates more information than a single question such as 'Should income support be conditional upon compensations?' and thus increases the quality of the model – its continuous character in this respect actually being an advantage. In any case, both models, either with F2 or with a nominal variable of this type, have been tested, and this does not alter the conclusions.

The model is based on 2,754 individuals. Apart from the two constants, the other parameters must be interpreted as slopes (Agresti, 1984). A positive sign thus indicates a tendency which is increasingly favourable to an increase of income support according to the variable under observation. Inversely, the negative sign of the 'age' parameter shows, for instance, that opinions are increasingly reluctant towards an increase by comparison with a stagnation, and towards a stagnation, by comparison with a lowering of income support, as age increases. We have reported in the table featuring in this annex the value of each parameter, as well as its standard error and the *z-score* of the parameter which follows a standardised normal law. An effect is regarded as significant, all things otherwise equal, with a certainty above 99% when *z* is more than 2.58, above 95% when *z* is superior than 1.96, and 90% when *z* is above 1.65, in absolute values. However, it is important that the parameter is closely observed since, whether significant or not, it provides important information as to the most likely effect. It is also worth noting that the value of the non-standardised parameter for F2 (1.89) is not comparable with the others because it depends on a choice of unit.

Table 14 – *Ordinal Logistical Regression on Opinions as to the Level of Income Support*

| | *Parameter* | *Standard error* | *z-score* |
|---|---|---|---|
| Constant 1 on the level of income support | 2.47 | 0.17 | 14.55 |
| Constant 2 on the level of income support | –0.27 | 0.05 | –4.84 |
| Slope for men (effect coding) | –0.03 | 0.05 | –0.62 |
| Slope for the respondent's age | –0.39 | 0.17 | –2.21 |
| Slope for the size of community | 0.20 | 0.12 | 1.65 |
| Slope for 'vital' income | 0.46 | 0.10 | 4.40 |
| Slope for the household's net income | –0.44 | 0.27 | –1.63 |
| Slope for the level of education | 0.11 | 0.12 | 0.90 |
| Slope for the respondent's property | 0.34 | 0.09 | 3.86 |
| Slope for people acquainted with someone on IS within their family (effect coding) | 0.04 | 0.19 | 0.23 |
| Slope for people acquainted with someone on IS outside their family (effect coding) | –0.28 | 0.17 | –1.68 |
| Slope for people not acquainted with anyone on IS (effect coding) | –0.10 | 0.16 | –0.63 |
| Slope for people in the labour force (effect coding) | –0.15 | 0.06 | –2.42 |
| Slope for covariable F2 | 1.89 | 0.29 | 6.41 |

# Part II

# The Principle of Unanimous Agreement

# Chapter 3

# The Logic of Justice as Unanimous Agreement

It has been shown in the previous chapter that the fair spectator is a method which can be used empirically to identify actors who are trying to form a just opinion. Since this opinion aims at being acceptable by any other individual, the principle of justice referred to is defined by unanimous agreement. Several questions about this definition had already been asked in the first chapter, but we did not have to go beyond the necessary to devise the fair spectator method with a view to its application. However, it is clear that at this stage many aspects still have to be clarified.

In particular, it may seem that if, according to our initial project, the existing social order is not imposed nor presupposed, but rather built, then it is only a human convention and, as such, its value can only be relative. All this second part will be oriented by the confutation of this idea. Leaving it to the actors to build their own social order, not forcing their hands in one way or another, does not necessarily lead to indulging in relativism or subjectivism. On the contrary, unanimous agreement is a principle which, without any ambiguity, makes it possible to distinguish between situations which are objectively just and situations which are not. First – and this is what this chapter will try to prove – because such agreement has a logic, in the formal sense of the term, which cannot be called into question without causing some crippling confusions. It is precisely because they fail to follow it closely that other conceptions or theories overlook social justice. We will see this in this chapter, and come back to it in greater detail for three of these theories in the next chapter. But also because reasonable choice has to do with some practical objectivity which generally speaking has not been sufficiently examined, because of a reductive positivism, and whose ins and outs will consequently have to be set out in the last chapter. All these elements will have to have been examined before seeing fully why this orientation does not lead to formulate a closed theory, which in a way speaks for the actors themselves. On the contrary, it even seems to be the only one which challenges such a substitution, not in a feeble and last-minute way, because of the theorist's intimate conviction, but for reasons which derive from the most fundamental principles of the model it sustains.

## 1. The Free Assent of each Community Member

### 1.1 *There is no justice without a free consent*

Let us start with the most obvious contents in the phrase 'unanimous agreement'. For a principle to be just, it must imperatively result from an agreement between the various actors to whom it will have to apply. It amounts to the same to say that only a free subject's autonomous will to give or not to give his assent to a rule to which he will then have to submit can serve as a foundation of justice for this rule. This first condition shuns the sophism of the 'right' of the strongest. It is indeed certain that a norm imposed on actors by obligation of force or deceit is not a just norm, even if it can be cloaked in the attire of the rationality of a good. If coercion could serve as a foundation, it is clear that almost anything could be regarded as fair. For instance, a rule could enjoin an actor to kill himself just to please somebody else's whim. Moreover, justice would have no stability: remove the gun from the temple of the individual whose 'agreement' had been obtained with it, and it is more than likely that this 'agreement' will be reconsidered. A Hobbesian reasoning is enough to show that the obligation imposed by the strongest one or the strongest few is the lot of a state of nature, from which rights are by definition absent. To break away from nature is precisely what justice demands, and this can only be done with respect for everyone's freedom.

Therefore, speaking of agreement does not make sense unless one assumes everyone's free will, that is, the faculty of being able to give or refuse one's assent. Simultaneously, this freedom cannot be that of a single individual or of a small number of people, since this would mean reverting to what has just been evacuated as being a non-agreement. It must be equal for every subject. In a word, without contradiction, there is no possible agreement if all those who must agree are not *equally free* to do so. It can also be said that before reaching the stage of argumentation, discussion or justification, equal freedom is the transcendental condition of an agreement

(= an *a priori* condition of possibility or 'thinkability' of any experience of an agreement). But of course if it is a necessary condition – as long as agreement is defined as the opposite of coercion – it is not a sufficient one in order to admit the fairness of a principle.

The agreement must also be unanimous. This second condition is about as important as the previous one. As long as everyone does not agree, there simply is no agreement. If a principle which must apply to an equivalence class (the class of all those who will be equally submitted to it) of $n$ individuals, could be said to be fair through the agreement of $n - 1$ on its character of fairness, then the person who did not give his or her consent would be put in the position of being absolutely constrained. We would be back to the situation just avoided by the previous reasoning. Freedom – even that of a single individual – cannot be annihilated if one wants to speak of agreement. As long as this condition is not met, the principle under discussion is only the product of the selfish defence of a good acknowledged as such by the $n - 1$ individuals against one single individual. Now, justice cannot lead to a very small number of people, or even one single individual, forsaking their freedom on the altar of happiness, pleasure, utility, well-being or the good of a majority, were it to be crushing both figuratively and literally, as is the case. It can also be said that if a principle of justice draws the outlines of a community of moral – that is, free and equal – persons, it cannot negate the moral personality of some.

Moreover we can see that if the procedure which reduces the agreement of $n$ individuals to an agreement between $n - 1$ were to be admitted, for instance in the name of efficiency, a recurrence reasoning could lead to complete absurdity. We could gradually come to the idea that an agreement could be said to have been found by a consensus between 0 individual! It is therefore necessary to set a threshold or an imperative stopping limit to such recurrence. But where should this threshold be set? Somewhere near the outlines of a majority, certainly. Which majority? That of 50% plus one of the votes, that of two thirds? And most importantly, as long as this stopping rule has not been established, it is obviously impossible to use it to decide on the threshold. A rule cannot speak about itself (we will encounter this problem again later). Therefore, there is no other solution but to demand unanimity to establish a rule which will then make it possible for a majority to decide.

This enables us to counter the objection of unrealism which is usually formulated each time unanimity is being discussed. Each and everyone can notice that, while it is already difficult to find unanimity in a small group, this seems definitely out of reach in a mass society. This is why democratic regimes opt for a majority government. But this pragmatic principle has no value if it is not immediately paired with the principle that what the majority decides must always be decided with respect for the rights of any minority. In other words, a majority ballot is not a blank check for a majority. Otherwise, it would be tyrannical, and the minority would find itself in the situation of being completely constrained, which is impossible if one wants to speak of justice. We will come back later to the underlying logical contradiction. For now, it may just be remarked that unanimity could not be found pragmatically in a group of individuals on a rule stipulating that the majority is endowed with every right, and the minority, none. In fact, a majority ballot rule only has any value at all if it is based on a consensus, and this imposes to respect the reasonable rights of a minority. Under this condition, unanimity is conceivable and the legitimacy of the majority rule is indeed founded on this unanimity. All in all, there is no contradiction between the principle of unanimity and a rule establishing by unanimous agreement that, from now on, decisions will be taken by majority with a respect for the rights of the minority. Far from being unrealistic, on the contrary, the principle of unanimity is at the foundation of a rule establishing a majority ballot – as long as this ballot has a claim to be just.

It is noteworthy that the reasoning is perfectly consistent with what Arrow's (1951) famous theorem of impossibility demonstrates. The impossibility of founding a collective choice on mere individual preferences, under certain commonly-accepted conditions, has re-stated the importance of unanimous agreement if one wants to avoid dictatorial solutions. In the end, a ballot rule only measures a power struggle between voters. No matter how these votes are aggregated, it will always be a power struggle, even if this struggle varies according to aggregating procedures. Consequently, the main teaching of Arrow's theorem, even more than the re-acknowledgment of Borda's and Condorcet's theses, which had already established that all aggregating procedures do not necessarily lead the same result, is that no aggregating function replaces unanimous agreement.

So far, we have not tried to go beyond what seems most obvious when using the terms 'agreement' and 'unanimity'. We can actually wonder whether we are not on the verge of a tautology. This reproach is only partly valid. Partly so, because the point is only to lay the foundations for the following reasonings and that, from this perspective, tautology, if it exists –

let's say rather the obvious elements which result from the mere application of the principles of identity and non-contradiction – has the merit of providing us with a strong starting-point. But it is still a valid objection in so far as the price to pay for such strength is obviously that, since the concepts are taken in a minimal acceptation, they are not sufficiently specific. It could easily be shown that this for instance is the case of the concept of liberty, a difficult concept if there is one, and which cannot be regarded as simply designating the reverse of any obligation.

Freedom is conceived in the restriction of reasoning, that is, in the limits which reason imposes on itself. This is actually why we have already opposed it to heteronomy in a brief remark. And it is clear that behind the notion of free agreement lies the problem of the passage from infinite freedom (state of nature), first to a rational freedom (from the standpoint of the theoretical reason of a finite subject who as it were still has not come across the question of intersubjectivity) and then, much more fundamentally in our perspective, to a still rational, *but also a reasonable* freedom – that is, one which describes the autonomous will of a finite subject to act with a respect for the moral law (by following a categorical imperative) according to the demands of practical reasons and intersubjectivity. It is actually acceptable here to speak of transcendental freedom, since it is indeed this freedom which both founds *a priori* the possibility of the agreement between autonomous wills but also, as is much more distinctly claimed nowadays, is used by them as a practical project or a horizon or an ideal (Renaut, 1997). From this point of view, Kant's 'kingdom of ends' or Rawls's 'well-ordered society' can be seen mainly as an ideal of practical reason. However, it must be kept in mind that both aspects are closely linked, and that each one is essential. We have already emphasised this when we observed that the fair spectator is both a position and a horizon.

Nonetheless, we must also find out whether this freedom, which is of course formal, is also real, and up to what point, or, to use other categories (MacCallum, 1972; and also Berlin, 1969), whether this is negative freedom as well as positive freedom. This raises arduous questions, since speaking of real or positive freedom never fails to have repercussions on the way equality itself is conceived (which we have claimed to be a necessary condition from the foundation, by using the term 'equal freedom'). These questions will of course not be overlooked, but will be dealt with in order. It is a mistake to want to start with them. For instance, calling for real equality raises the question of the compensations which must be granted in the case of empirical inequalities, of either natural or social origin (Dworkin, 1977). This very quickly leads to the intricate problems of positive discrimination, especially in the case of a liberal theory. But it is pointless to look for some elements of answer without having first firmly established some simple and intangible principles which make it possible to outline without any ambiguity what must be regarded as just.

### 1.2 *The categorical imperative as a principle of legitimacy*

Let us return to the reasoning as we left it. At this stage, we know that justice demands unanimous agreement. First, what is it that must be agreed on? Surely not on something like knowing whether men's umbrellas must be black, and women's, green. In this, the just norm is distinguished from the one which is only a reflection of mores or conventions such as fashion trends. What must be discussed is whether a proposition with a general and universal range is a rule of fairness which may get everyone's assent. 'General' means that the rule under discussion must not be inspired by a singular interest. If we take up again the classic example of the rule which states that debtors must pay for their debts when they have promised to do so, this means that this rule is not moral if formulated as: 'Given that it is in my interest at the moment to pay for my debt, I must do it.' The fact of tying obligation to a singular interest takes us out of the moral sphere, into that of a merely pragmatic decision. The question asked is moral if, on the contrary, as to the issue of interest under its many forms, we reason with a fixed interest, or *ceteris paribus*. Therefore, the question should be: 'Whether it is in my own interest or not, must I pay off my debts, if I can do so and I have promised to do so?' Saying that the rule must moreover have a universal scope means that it cannot be tied to one particular actor or class of actors. The reason for this is that if this rule, as a result of its field of definition, that is, the equivalence class which it constitutes, involves *n* actors, once adopted, it will apply to any of these *n* actors belonging to the equivalence class. Many authors have remarked that the specificity of morality is that it always aims at the universal, and indeed, it is certain that a rule is not moral if it applies to some, and not to those who share the same condition with regard to what this rule aims at. For instance, all those who are able to pay off their debts and have promised to do so. The full question thus becomes: 'Considering that I am able to pay off my debts and that my own interest cannot serve as a motive, should I – just like the others who are in the same situation, but neither more nor less – pay off my debt, and thus keep my promise?' This formulation excludes both the selfish answer (I must do so less than others, because this is me) and the supererogatory answer (I must do so more than others, because this is me, with my sense of honour, my love for mankind, etc.). Determining what the fair answer is, means wondering which one passes the unanimity test, that is, which one is such that *everyone may freely want it to become a law applicable to all.* We have followed the Kantian method closely enough here not to fail to see immediately that this justice defined as a unanimous agreement does indeed amount to the same as what the categorical imperative stipulates (Kant, 1785: 'Act only on that maxim through which you can at the same time will that it should become a universal law.'). Let us also remark again that this imperative corresponds to the motives of a fair spectator.

We could also say, if we wanted to prefer Rousseau's terminology, that justice as a unanimous agreement expresses the general will, or, following Rawls, that it is what a subject desires behind the veil of ignorance, or, following Habermas or Apel, that it is what subjects who share a similar ethics of discussion *(Diskursethik)* want. The point is not to deny that there exist important nuances between all these theories. However, we still think that these differences derive from a shared foundation which the phrase 'justice as unanimous agreement' seems to help one to grasp. There are debates, but these are in some way arguments within the same school of thought while there is no profound disagreement as to the essential, the foundation of the just. This is actually what the protagonists of these debates are keen to re-emphasise when invited to confront their arguments (Habermas and Rawls, 1997). In return, however, it must be acknowledged that some methodological disagreements remain.

### 1.3 *The reciprocity between the subject and intersubjectivity*

Many commentators have remarked that the main difference between Habermas or Apel, on one side, and Rawls or Kant on the other, resides in the way they conceive of the process leading to justice. The former hold that this process is necessarily dialogical. It demands a real, effective, discussion between the protagonists of a conflict. Habermas (1991) thus proposes to complete principle U (for universalisation, which is only a rephrasing of the categorical imperative, to the exception a few nuances)[1] with principle D (for discussion or discourse), which he regards as more economical: 'Only moral rules that could win the assent of all affected as participants in a practical discourse can claim validity.' On the one hand, this must be an important condition to ensure that all the reasonable opinions will be taken into account in the debate which must make it possible for an agreement to appear. On the other hand, however, it does seem quite difficult to deny a subject, possessed with a practical reason – that is, to deny any subject – the faculty of being able to know the moral law. Rawls's notion of reflective equilibrium is there to restate this. It is possible to make out the right for every subject who reflects 'sincerely and honestly' on the reasons which justify what she thinks or does. By a device of abstraction, she must get rid of purely subjective reasons or of those linked to empirical interests, and retain only those which are neutral or objective, which are those on which any other subject reflecting sincerely and honestly would agree. To use our terminology, these reasons are those of a fair spectator (= those which preside over the impartial formation of the judgment) who, by definition, only wonders about the very fact of knowing whether a given norm may correspond to what everyone could wish for. From this point of view, the only fair and valid norm is that which could lead to the consensus of all those to whom it claims to apply. It is true that this supposes that one admits a capacity to abstract mobiles, but it is hard to see in what name one could think that a subject, who is otherwise capable of abstraction in the theoretical field, would *a priori* be deprived of this capacity in the practical domain,[2] all the more as it is *the knowledge* of the moral law or of the just which is at stake here. Or rather, it is just too plain too see. One would have to leave the sphere of an autonomous subject and indulge for instance in some radical empiricism or a total determinism, which, assuredly, is neither Habermas's nor Apel's prospect. Eventually, from this viewpoint of knowledge, this debate refers to the way in which objectivity must be apprehended, and to the question of knowing whether, in order to reach this objectivity, it is possible to start from the subject or if, on the contrary,

1 Its phrasing is: 'Each valid norm must satisfy the condition whereby the consequences and the secondary effects which, predictably, result from its *universal* observance with the intention of satisfying *everyone's* interests can be accepted without any constraint by *all* those involved.'

2 This has actually been confirmed by studies of moral psychology since they were initiated by Piaget (1932).

considering the risk of solipsism which this implies, it is preferable to focus directly on intersubjectivity, which is indeed the main characteristic of a discussion or a public argumentation.

To set up objectivity, as truth or as justice, the subjects must agree on their representations. Objectivity does not consist in the subject's agreement with a thing-in-itself since a finite subject[3] can simply not go out of himself to agree with a thing-in-itself. From then on, understanding how such an agreement is possible demands, according to Kant, to start from the subject and stay within the limits of subjectivity, but in specific and precise terms. To conceive of objectivity within those limits amounts to understanding what the subject can legitimately think of as objective within himself. As we have seen, this implies for him to be able to distinguish between what is peculiar to him (for instance his own empirical interests) and what he shares with any other subject and which, as a result, is universal. Of course, saying that a shared subjectivity is objective, with no further debate, could lead to the pitfalls of epistemological relativism, when one is dealing with truth, or moral relativism, when the right is at stake. Any unanimous agreement could be said to be fair. This is obviously not Kant's position, and this is why all his effort consists in showing that, in both the theoretical and the practical sphere, for every subject, and within himself, there exist some laws, or rather, some universal and necessary rules[4] which are given *a priori*, that is to say, which are constitutive in any possible or conceivable experience of an agreement (= making it possible to synthesise the diversity of representations). Objectivity (which makes it possible to speak of justice or of truth) is thus based on an intersubjectivity which is subject to these rules. Truth or justice are no longer conceived through the relationship with some thing-in-itself, but rather through the way in which a proposition can be claimed to apply universally to a community of subjects. Intersubjectivity is at the root of objectivity, whether the latter is theoretical, practical, or even aesthetic (since, according to Kant, there also exists a universality in judgments of taste).

It is therefore surprising, to say the least, to claim that classical transcendental philosophy has overlooked intersubjectivity. The solipsism of a subject thinking outside any social community on what could be a must-be for him is an extreme which, on the contrary, one can avoid thanks to this

3 The finitude of the subject was established with *The Critique of Pure Reason* (Kant, 1787).

4 These rules apply to the data of intuition.

philosophy. When a subject asks himself whether a given rule (for instance, not to respect the promise to pay off his debts) can have a moral value, he is asking himself whether this rule could be that of any other subject belonging to his community. Without this community, the question is purely and simply devoid of meaning. Universality must be conceived within the framework of one's relationship to a structured community of subjects, and not only in the context of the relationship between the self and the thing-in-itself. Therefore, in no instance can the moral law be interpreted as the product of a pure solipsism. And as a matter of fact, in its very formulation, the categorical imperative implies intersubjectivity, and Kant has not forgotten to draw the consequences of this, for instance by emphasising that the moral law is the medium of communication between reasonable beings, in the context of his ultimate goal, the 'cosmopolitical society'. The same applies to Rawls. To claim that *A Theory of Justice* (Rawls, 1971) ignores social ties is a contradiction. The thinking starts by making out the 'basic structure' of a society (which is actually not any society, but a modern one), to make it possible to draw the list of primary goods which are necessary to every individual, and whose fair distribution – which the theory is actually meant to define – makes a 'well-ordered society' possible. Even the communitarians now seem to have abandoned this critic of a so-called absence of social ties in Rawls's thinking.

As far as Kant is concerned, in any case, because of this way of apprehending objectivity, there is no doubt that intersubjectivity is a condition of possibility of subjectivity. Therefore, starting from the subject does not mean starting from an individual who chooses an ethic because of, for instance, the idea of happiness he has formed for himself, but rather because of an autonomous will to build social ties on social justice. Not only is there no risk of solipsism in such a demand for subjectivity, but such a solipsism would be a contradiction.

This is also Fichte's conviction who, on this issue, reformulates[5] the reasons for a transcendental philosophy to support this theory. *The Science of Knowledge* (Fichte, 1794–1795), which, among other things, was meant to find some answers to the question of representation and self-consciousness, ends up with a still-open interrogation: what are the conditions of possibility of the activity of a non-I which, at the same time, is given as the activity

5 In his own admission, Fichte had no other ambition, in the mid-1790s, than to achieve a 'systematic' reformulation of Kant's philosophy.

of an I? From there, what is the nature of this link between I and Non-I? In general, the link can be thought of according to three categories: substance / accident, cause / effect, and reciprocal action. But the *Science of Knowledge* establishes that if one seeks to conceive of the relation between I and Non-I according to the first two categories, one inevitably stumbles upon the unsolvable difficulties of idealism or realism.[6] The only possible option is then that of reciprocal action, and it will be used in particular in *Foundations of Natural Right*, where Fichte (1796–1797) shows, first, that a rational being 'cannot posit itself without ascribing a free efficacy to itself'. But he cannot attribute it to himself without doing the same for all other reasonable beings. Thinking the relation between I and Non-I only in the category of a reciprocal action necessarily entails as a result considering Non-I as another I, who recognises my free activity, in so far exactly as I recognise his. To put it differently, a mechanical, heteronomous being is not an interlocutor with whom I can really debate. It is necessary that I recognise the other as a free and reasonable being for him to be an interlocutor. And, conversely, I must also acknowledge myself as free and reasonable to make this true communication possible. We can see why, if no status is given to this reciprocity, in opposite ways, idealism and realism end

6 Realism starts from the thing in itself to show that any representation within a subject is only a mere reflection of this in-itself. Thus, for Spinoza, thought is an effect of reality; the rational simply reflects reality. On the contrary, idealism starts from the subject, because there, the real has no existence outside representation (Berkeley). But the real turns out to be in essence in full conformity with the logical principles of the subject, in particular with Leibniz, with the principle of sufficient reason. The real only 'reflects' the rational, one might say, to parallel the previous formulation; hence the possibility, for instance of a doctrine of pre-established harmony. There is actually still another idealistic way of bringing together the subject and the thing-in-itself, if one thinks, with Hegel, that the real *is* the rational, and that a well thought-out system is enough to uncover it, for instance by deciphering the reason's trappings, which, for a moment, could lead to think that there is an ontological distance between the real and the rational, or between the subject and the thing-in-itself, whereas this distance is only 'dialectic'. Let us note that the consequences for morality of such a doctrine (which simply amounts to acknowledging that the good unravels in the world 'in all eternity') are no less devastating than those (probably more fashionable in social sciences today) which will result from Nietzsche's dissolution of the must-be in a will-to-power, or of Heidegger's mere forsaking of rationality (especially of practical reason). For obvious reasons of chronology, neither the Fichte of the early 1790s nor Kant confute the letter of Hegelian idealism, but its spirit is confuted in advance, through the affirmation of the subject's finitude. A finite subject can obviously not experience the totality of the real. The Hegelian system is a venture which is impossible *a priori*.

up condemning mankind to solitude. They do not make it possible to think that, beyond all our idiosyncrasies which make us appear as strangers for one another, we still need a capacity to universalise to be able to find a ground for agreement in order to truly make up a society. On the contrary, by following Fichte, a reasonable I is given in an activity of reciprocal limitation of freedoms. And even if this intersubjectivity must still be guaranteed by the Law,[7] it is well and truly the enabling condition of subjectivity.[8]

Fichte (1794) thus does not hesitate to write in *Some Lectures concerning the Scholar's Vocation*: 'It is man's *destiny* to live in society; he *ought to* live in society. One who lives in isolation is not a complete human being. He contradicts his own self.' This will be repeated, in a different form, in *Foundations of Natural Right*:

> The human being (like all finite beings in general) becomes a human being only among human beings; and since the human being can be nothing other than a human being and would not exist at all if it were not this – it follows that, if there are human beings at all, there must be more than one. [...] The concept of the human being is not the concept of an individual – for an individual human being is unthinkable – but rather the concept of a species.

Let us note in passing that these are almost the very words used by Simmel (1917), and it is hardly surprising that this should have led him to define sociology as the science of the forms of reciprocal action (= of the structures of social interactions). It is therefore legitimate that some should have

7 There probably is a partial divergence between Kant and Fichte on this issue. Kant would no doubt admit that the right cannot be deduced from a strictly individual moral duty, since it supposes intersubjectivity. In return, the fair right (which obviously raises the question of politics) is not – or in any case, not only – an enabling condition of this intersubjectivity. Otherwise, the *Metaphysics of Morals* would only have one part, the *Science of the Right*, whereas, as we know, it has two, with the *Doctrine of Virtue*, which completes that of the right (Kant, 1797). In fact, for Kant, the external constraint which the law exerts upon the will is doubled by the internal, so to speak, constraint of virtue. Nevertheless, the fair right and therefore the political question of the fair constitution are essentially moral (rather than ethical) problems. The social contract is thus only a reformulation of the categorical imperative, reserved exclusively to a legislator. For Fichte, on the contrary, the right is autonomous in the face of morality. Postulating such autonomy, just like refusing it, is far from being obvious, and before we can determine ourselves with respect to this question, other developments will be necessary.

8 This is obviously not the place for synthesizing Fichte's system of the law, but a reader wishing to further explore this aspect may refer to Alain Renaut's (1986) or Luc Ferry's (1984) works.

said that Fichte's philosophy (in the wake of Kant's) heralded more contemporary developments, especially through its insistence on making intersubjectivity the very essence of mankind and, as such, as pointed out by Alexis Philonenko (1996), 'an essential moment in the resolution of the problem of objectivity'. And as a matter of fact, Fichte did not fail to derive a reflection on language from this. Long before Habermas or Apel, he sought to show that if the necessity of communication (already emphasised by Kant) as a 'reciprocal action through signs' is the 'condition of mankind', this is not without its effects upon rationality itself. As Alain Renaut (1997) remarks, this is 'clear evidence that classical transcendental philosophy did not wait for the supposed "linguistic turn" of contemporary philosophy to add to its programme the overcoming of any "methodical solipsism" and the affirmation of the primacy of interaction over self-consciousness'.

In the end, the difference between a monologic and a dialogic approach comes much more from the procedure than from the substance, since all in all its amounts to a divergence as to what must serve as a starting point for a reasoning on justice. Kant starts from the subject. But we have seen that this is in no way an obstacle in conceiving of interaction. Subjectivity contains intersubjectivity as its very condition. This concept of subjectivity is, as Fichte (1796, p. 45) would have said, 'a reciprocal concept', i.e. a concept that can be thought only in relation to another thought. There is no risk, therefore, of lapsing into methodical solipsism.

This does not mean, however, that starting from the interaction is a crippling problem, as long as it remains possible to revert to a morally responsible subject, as is the case with Habermas or Apel, who do not undertake to negate this responsibility in the name of constraints inherent in a practical discussion (even if, in order to follow Apel, it would be better to speak of a community of co-responsible subjects). However, if practical discussions can be seen as a condition of procedure to know whether a fair norm is equitably applied, when the reflection bears upon the foundations or the principles of justice, it is hard to exclude the moment of the subject (as it is understood in the transcendental approach, of course). At the end of the discussion, it remains necessary for every subject to be able to recognise herself as being, just like every other being, at the foundation of the agreement. If the agreement on a principle of justice is the product of a well-argued (public) discussion, it is essential that everyone should be able to own up to it. If not, how could it be a duty for every subject? How could this subject be held responsible if the choices made were not *her* choices relatively to what is fair? By giving her agreement, the subject takes her distance towards her strict individuality (her interests, her conception of the good), and it can be admitted that it is through a well-argued discussion that she constitutes herself as a pure practical subject. But it must also be maintained, as Renaut emphasises (1997), that it is as a practical subject, in the relation between the I and itself, that each person legitimises the principles obtained by discussion, and not in so far as they have been discussed:

> For, at the end of the discussion I must still reinterpret them as if they had been laid down by my own autonomous free will – otherwise I would as it were receive them from outside, I would endure them in a heteronomous way, without this dimension of support and recognition which supposes, no longer a relation to the other, but a relation between me and me, where I can recognise myself in this part of me who took part in the discussion and decided on the law or the principle of justice.

Even if this probably demands a few partial modifications, this idea is not incompatible with an ethics of discussion, and this is why it does not seem to us that on the main the quarrel between the monological and the dialogical approaches within transcendental philosophy conceals some profound divergences. The reason for this is that for everyone, subjectivity and intersubjectivity are *reciprocal* concepts and that, in the context of such an approach, there is no doubt that no one denies that a reasonable subject is also a responsible subject.

### 1.4 *The plurality of agreement procedures*

According to the previous reasoning, unanimous agreement is required in two situations, which do not have the same status. On the one hand, it must lie at the foundation of a norm which is fair *a priori*, serving to the foundation of a 'judicial', and not only social, community – that is, a community which, in political terms, will have the property of resting on the people's sovereignty as a principle. On the other hand, it must serve in problems of application, that is, in order to settle this or that private conflict when actors wonder what could be a reasonable solution. As this solution can obviously not be in contradiction with justice, it must be the object of a unanimous agreement and, from there, the mode or the means through which such an agreement is reached in a given conflict must itself be the object of a unanimous agreement.

There is then no reason to restrict its field in advance. The use of a mediator, of a judge, negotiation, argumentation in a discussion which may be delegated to some representatives, are as many procedures, among others, which are acceptable in so far as nothing in them comes into contradiction *a priori* with the principle of justice as unanimous agreement.

On the contrary, everything which is related to what may be called a 'false consensus' is of course excluded. This is for instance the case of a strategic consensus where the agreement is consented for some time, in a cynical way, with a view to rebuilding one's forces with the firm intention of igniting the conflict again at the most favourable time. This is like the ceasefire one accepts with the hope, not of achieving peace, but to revert to war in better conditions. In order to reach an agreement which may be regarded as fair, on the contrary, it is necessary for every party to endeavour to effectively come out of the conflict by fully and willingly accepting the agreement which makes this possible even if, of course, with the evolutions in everyone's situation, nothing prevents a new conflict from arising later. Situations in the 'lame consensus' category are also excluded, since they consist in believing that things improve spontaneously outside any will to find an agreement. We revert to a sort of *modus vivendi*, whose stability is supposed to become stronger, according to the functionalist belief, because life in society supposedly tends to form or to privilege spontaneously the congruence of the various scales of values. All in all, here, what must be is, or ends up being, for, as Pangloss used to say: 'Things must necessarily be created for the best end.' (Voltaire, *Candide*) All the debate around the notion of 'overlapping consensus', held by Rawls, shows that it is necessary to distinguish between a rationally motivated consensus, which may very well rely on a few common denominators, and a 'lame consensus', where one just waits for it to happen, but is only a way of disguising a non-agreement into an agreement.

In all of this, there is one unchanging element: an empirical procedure is unanimously accepted, because the reasons which justify it are supposedly those of a fair spectator. But all the concrete situations where this reasoning may be applied do not amount to the same. A procedure which is reasonable in one case may not be so in another. For instance, drawing lots is an acceptable procedure when the protagonists' situations in a conflict regarding the attribution of an individual resource are *completely symmetrical*. But it is not always so when this condition of symmetry is not respected. It can be noted that not rejecting *a priori* solutions at random makes it possible to solve reputedly difficult dilemmas. Let us take the dramatic case of two passengers on a plane which is about to crash and in which there is only one parachute.[9] Selfish people will spend their time fighting for this parachute and, by mutually impairing each other, they will destroy each other. If not, it will be the 'law' of the strongest. Pure altruists will hardly do better, by alternately exchanging the parachute. But if the passengers unanimously agree to draw lots for the parachute, this emergency procedure will save one of their lives, without relying on a contingent criterion, such as the strength or the selfishness of one of them, the weakness or the altruistic sacrifice of the other.

## 2. Demands Peculiar to Unanimous Agreement

### 2.1 *Is there an injustice towards those who consent?*

Problems become far more complex when one shifts from these interrogations about the extension of the field of unanimous agreement procedures to those bearing upon the object or the content of this agreement. Outside the fact, which has already been re-emphasised, that the norm for which we are trying to find a legitimacy is a norm of justice, rather than any social convention, is it possible to restrict what the agreement can bear upon and the result, in the name of all that we have so far, that is, the necessity of a unanimous agreement? There is no doubt that such a limitation would be contradictory with actors' freedom, which is a *sine qua non* to speak of agreement. Saying that a given solution in a conflict is forbidden *a priori* amounts to depriving the actors of the right to agree on what they wish for. It would thus seem that nothing can be excluded as long as there exists a unanimous agreement on a solution which, by definition, will be recognised as fair by everyone. But is there no risk of lapsing into the most complete relativism then? The risk is very real, and in order to avoid it, we must be able to answer the following question: is it necessary *and sufficient* that a unanimous agreement is reached on fairness for a norm to be legitimate or

9 This example takes up the Captain's Dilemma introduced by Kohlberg (1981, p. 205 sq.) but modifies its form.

valid from a moral standpoint, or, which amounts to the same, from the standpoint of justice as fairness?

In *Science of the Right*, Kant (1797, § 46) takes up again an old judicial principle: '*Volenti non fit injuria* (there is no injustice when one consents).' Examining the validity of this principle is another way of asking the same question. On the one hand, it is tempting to follow this principle. If an individual gives his assent, it is no longer possible to speak of injustice, especially if only his vote is missing in order to reach unanimity. But on the other hand, what becomes of the objectivity of justice? In particular, what about the case where assent is obtained (freely) on a principle which comes into contradiction with the conception of justice which is, however, accepted by all? Answering that the principle is not fair to us, but is fair for those involved, is not sufficient, for we are confronted to a situation for which the principle cannot be recognised as fair by anyone, even if there is an empirical consensus, that is, to a case where the assent is null and void – which by right is impossible from the perspective of justice. It may happen in fact, but it is tantamount to a self-contradiction. Therefore, it must be admitted that consent in itself does not lead to justice. There is objectively an injustice, even for those who consent. If this situation is not a chimera, the result is that there is no unanimous agreement without restrictions. However, such a limitation can in no way derive from a criterion which is external to the agreement, since this would amount to illegitimately restricting actors' freedom (usually in the name of a conception of the good imposed on everyone). It must therefore result from the very conditions of the agreement, that is to say it should only be the expression of what is imperatively necessary to make it legitimate to speak of agreement.

This restriction can be expressed in many different ways. However, all of them amount to the formulation of the same logical impossibility: it is forbidden that an agreement should consist in a non-agreement. In other words, it is impossible to agree unanimously on the fact that a non-agreement should define a fair principle. This amounts to saying that individuals cannot absolutely alienate their freedom, or that they cannot give up their veto. Indeed, since, in the context of a valid unanimous agreement, every individual enjoys by definition equal liberty, there ensues that they are entitled to a veto – equal to that of every other person since every vote is indispensable for unanimity – which they cannot forsake without negating the very principle of unanimous agreement. If they forsook it, they would simply no longer be able to give their agreement. Consequently, an agreement on the fact that one or several consenting individuals may forsake their veto is not an agreement. This agreement cannot be unanimous, moreover, since those who do not have a veto do not vote. It is an agreement only between those whose vote by not giving up their veto.

This principle is clear; from there, how is it that one can conceive easily and spontaneously enough of the idea of giving up one's veto, without having the impression that this translates immediately into the equation (unanimous agreement) = no (unanimous agreement)? This stems from the fact that the logical impossibility transgressed in order to reach this self-contradiction is akin to the one which is transgressed by Epimenides' paradox (a Cretan who claims that all Cretans are liars) and that, with respect to the characteristic peculiar to the human language, spotting it can prove quite difficult. Let us focus for a moment on what leads to formulating a contradictory proposition with the appearance of sound logic.

## 2.2 *A sentence cannot speak about itself*

Let us start by establishing a writing convention in order to distinguish between propositions, which will be put between inverted comas, and comments upon these propositions. Thus, 'this box is red' is a proposition, but remarking that it is a proposition is a comment on this proposition, just like noticing that this proposition is made of four words. In everyday language, these commas are implicit, which blurs the levels of language. For instance, 'Paul is wrong to say that Annabelle wanted a red box' should be written 'Paul is wrong to say that 'Annabelle wanted 'a red box.''' Now, these commas are crucial to avoid confusions, and forgetting them is a source of paradox. Let us take the case of Epimenides' paradox, which is formulated in the simplest possible way: 'I lie.' This proposition is said to be undecidable or inconsistent or self-contradictory. Whether I hold it to be true or false, it comes into contradiction with what is stated in it. If 'I lie' is true, then I'm not lying, and if 'I lie' is false, then I'm not lying either. In the end, if the proposition is true, then it is false, and if it is false, then it is true. Of course, the paradox is only owed to a sophism, which hinges on us forgetting that a sentence, a proposition, a rule, etc., cannot speak about itself. It cannot be its own commentary. But, by accepting 'I lie', we act as if a sentence could provide its own commentary.

It is necessary to fully see in what respect this error negates the principle of non-contradiction and, consequently, the principle of identity. Formal logic, any logic, whether standard or binary, or whether it is intuitionist or ternary, or whether it is more complex still, must at least admit these two basic principles. According to the principle of identity A = A, or true = true or yes = yes – it does not make a difference, as long as something is fixed. According to the principle of non-contradiction, A is different from non-A. From there, it is possible to evaluate propositions, to produce commentaries on propositions, and these commentaries will have a fixed meaning. This is obviously crucial, since it makes it possible to ensure that when I say that such or such proposition is true, I do say that it is true, and not that it is false, nor that it is neither true nor false. In the same way as if it is true, it is different from any untrue proposition. Otherwise, we would be lost in confusion and meaninglessness: we would have no means of understanding one another. Thus, logic demands that one distinguish between syntax and semantics, between the propositions and their evaluations. Of course, it is possible to lay down rules which modify the values (for instance, to say that true = true except on Sundays, when true will mean false and conversely); this only amounts to shifting to a higher level of language and establishing a meta-meta-language, in order to agree with one another on a meta-language, and, consequently, on language.

Let us note that if a Cretan claiming that 'all Cretans are liars' contradicts himself, on the contrary, a Roman may very well say this of Cretans. The problem is therefore that the proposition 'all Cretans are liars' devaluates any Cretan assertion: the utterance negates the person uttering it. This is a performative contradiction. As such, the utterance is not contradictory at all, but it is impossible that the person uttering it should be the person uttering it. 'There has been a car accident this afternoon, and unfortunately, the driver passed away' is an utterance with nothing dubious about it. But it becomes impossible if, to the question asked to me by the person I'm telling about the accident, 'how do you know this?' I answer: 'because *I* was driving the car.' Similarly, the sentence 'all Cretans are liars', as we have said, raises no difficulty if it is formulated by a Roman (I am free to admit it as true or not); but a Cretan may not say so, since this makes any evaluation impossible. In a more concise way: 'you lie' is possible, but 'I lie' is a performative contradiction. However, contrary to the utterance 'all Cretans are liars', the utterance 'I lie' does not simply negate the very person who says it, but any person who might say it, and whether she is Roman or Cretan does not change anything. From there, it is not simply the subject who is negated, but the possibility of evaluating, or the logic, since we go as far as to debase the rule true ≠ untrue into true = untrue.

In order to highlight this paradox, it is easier to establish a writing convention. We will call V the set of true propositions *p*. If *p* is true, we will write $p \in$ V (which is read as *p* belongs to V or is an element of V). If *p* is not true, we will write $p \notin$ V (*p* does not belong to V), or, in an equivalent form, $p \in$ non-V. Since we admit that whatever *p*, a proposition, is, it is different from non-*p*, its negation, it amounts to the same to say that the intersection between V, the set of true propositions, and non-V, the set of untrue propositions, is null.

Let us briefly digress in order to answer immediately the question: why do we speak of the untrue instead of speaking, more simply, of the false? This is because setting out the equation untrue = false supposes that one admits the principle of the excluded third. But this principle is absolutely not at stake in these reasonings, nor in the following ones. Standard or binary logic admits this principle, which states: '*p* or non-*p*' can be proven without '*p*' or 'non-*p*' being proven. In other words, '*p* or non-*p*' can be held as true, even if I do not know whether *p* is true, or whether it is rather non-*p* which is true. Intuitionist logic refuses the Platonic conception of the truth which underpins this idea. A thing is not true in itself, independently from us, waiting for us to *discover* it as such (after coming a long way to leave the 'cavern'). It is true only if it is proven to be true, it is false only if it is proven to be false and in the meantime it is neither true nor false. The untrue is therefore not the false. Applying this idea, briefly summed up here, to logical reasoning amounts to denying the principle of the excluded third, or to refusing that non-non-*p* should necessarily be identical to *p*. Let us take an example to grasp the difference. A crime has been committed, and the police do not know who the culprit is. For a 'Platonist', the sentence 'Mr Jones is guilty or Mr Jones is innocent' is true. For an intuitionist, this sentence is neither true nor false. Mr Jones is a suspect, like every one of us, as long as the police have not found the culprit. In order not to exaggerate the difference, it can be said that binary logic is a specific instance of ternary logic, and especially that in both cases the principle of non-contradiction (just like the principle of identity) is not challenged at all. The intersection between the true and the false remains null, just like that between the neither true nor false with the true or with the false. Since Epimenides' paradox occurs, as we are going to show, through the negation of the principle of non-contradiction, there remains a paradox whatever stance we adopt towards the excluded third. This was worth emphasizing, since the Kantian perspective we adopt could be seen as rather militating in favour of a rejection of the excluded third, and it could have been wrongly inferred from this that the reasonings which we are going to propose implied such a rejection. But this is absolutely not the case. It is necessary and sufficient to admit what all logics admit, that is, let us repeat it, the principles of identity and non-contradiction. It is therefore not indispensable to settle the debate on the excluded third, and the writing convention proposed below, which does not involve anything with respect to this debate, can therefore be kept.

With this convention, the proposition 'all Cretans are liars' means that whatever '*p*', the proposition of a Cretan, is, it does not belong to V, while the proposition '*p* does not belong to V' always belongs to V. This is written, with the inverted commas, in order to better evidence the three levels of language:

$$\forall \text{`}p\text{'}, \text{``}p\text{'} \notin \text{V'} \Leftrightarrow \text{```}p\text{'} \notin \text{V'} \in \text{V'}$$

Or, more simply, if we only keep the inverted commas whose ulterior removal is going to lead to a paradox:

$$\forall p, p \notin \text{V} \Leftrightarrow \text{`}p \notin \text{V'} \in \text{V}$$

This is absolutely not paradoxical yet. On the contrary, the proposition *p* which does not belong to V is indeed different from '$p \notin$ V', which does belong to V. But if we say that it is a Cretan who is speaking, we set down $p =$ '$p \notin$ V'. The levels of language are blurred, which implies a logical mistake, since it is impossible and forbidden to write such an equality. For two elements to be equal or identical, it must be possible to place them in the same set. But here, we only have one alternative, belonging or not to V, and *p* does not belong to V, whereas '$p \notin$ V' belongs to V. It is therefore impossible that these propositions will ever be identical or equal, unless one considers that there is a non-null intersection between V and non-V or, which amounts to the same, unless the principle of non-contradiction is denied.

Let us stop for a moment on the mechanism of this reasoning. We have a Cretan who utters sentences. But for us to say that he is lying, we need a commentary, a truth test as it is, that is to say a procedure which we acknowledge as valid and 100% reliable (we have noted it '$p \notin$ V' $\in$ V). We have said above that we could ask a Roman for his opinion, but this supposes us to agree that it is a valid testing procedure – in other words, that Romans always tell the truth. In this case, they will tell whether Cretans lie, and we will know that this is the truth. Otherwise, we can imagine a sort of machine, a lie detector, but only if such a detector is reliable. As far as Romans are concerned, it is impossible to give Roman nationality to a Cretan, and as far as the detector is concerned, it is impossible for the individual who is subjected to it to be the detector. But this is indeed the situation of Epimenides' paradox, and there is no wonder that with a lie detector which says itself that it tells lies, everything should be on the blink.[10] It is therefore clear and proven by the above demonstration that a testing procedure cannot prove itself. The metalanguage which defines the evaluation is necessarily external to what it enables us to evaluate (the language it bears upon).

In fact, we have three levels of language, and neither of them must be confused with another. The first level, L1, is that of sentences uttered by a subject. The second level, L2, is that of the detector which classifies these sentences between true or untrue. And the third level, L3, is that of the reliability which we set by this detector, since, for us to accept the detector's classification, and thus for us to eventually be able to tell whether Cretans lie or not, it is indispensable that we hold this detector to be reliable. This last level, owing to which a testing procedure is finally recognised as valid, will from now on be called stopping condition. But why choose this phrase?

At the moment of deciding that a testing procedure is valid, it is easy to see that we find ourselves confronted with the principle of sufficient reason, according to which any reason has its reason, or to the principle of causality, whereby each cause has its cause. Even if we admit that a lie detector is in general a machine providing good results, there remains that *this* machine, the one I am going to use in order to test the Cretans' propositions, must be reliable. It is therefore necessary that an engineer should have come to test it, and declared it 'good for service'. The engineer's certificate is at level L4. But it is also necessary that he should be competent and qualified to issue this certificate. His qualification is level N5. But it remains that those who certify his qualification must be competent them-

10 It is actually clear that whether the detector has only two branches (true or false) or three or four, or more, is not what poses a problem. Whatever the number of branches is, what poses a problem is that the detector is testing itself.

selves. Those who trained him must be recognised by some degree. Their degree is a level N6. But still, was the curriculum of the school where they trained truly in touch with technological evolutions? And so on, *ad infinitum*, for it is hard to see how, even if I question everything, and this is my right, I could not end up going as far as the creation of the school system, and then beyond. Therefore, there must be a stopping condition. The *ad infinitum* regression which the principle of reason (or the principle of causality) undoubtedly allows for must imperatively stop somewhere. No finite subject can deal with this infinite chain. Through which 'miracle' does this stopping condition make it possible to relax my doubts, why do I acknowledge it as valid, and, at the same time, as defining a space of objectivity which, at last, is going to help me decide whether Cretans lie or not, is obviously a question which cannot be ignored, and the least we can say is that it *has not* been ignored in the history of ideas. But, for now, it is enough to remark that such a stopping condition is imperative, that it defines the validity of the evaluation, and that it cannot be mistaken with what it evaluates.

That a paradox after Epimenides's way is not easy to spot is proven since mathematicians themselves (and not the least among them) have often been – very briefly, admittedly – taken in. In order to make up the first set theory, Cantor and Frege proposed close reasonings, but which concealed an unfortunate axiom: whenever we have a property (being a liar, for instance), it is possible to conceive of the corresponding set (the set of liars). In fact, this is impossible unless one admits beforehand that the elements, which might present the property which is constitutive of their set, exist 'before' the set which unites them. Otherwise, and therefore as appears in Cantor's and Frege's theories, the set is an element which can verify the property it is based on. It can thus be one of its own elements. The paradox is not staggering at first, because we do know that the set of liars is not a liar. But such an obvious fact is not enough to take us out of this deadlock for good. For instance, with the property 'being an infinite set', it is possible to build the set of infinite sets. Since this set is itself an infinite set, it is one of its elements. This cannot be a mere peculiarity, and it did not take long for Russel to prove that, as a result, the Cantor/Frege theory was inconsistent. He showed for instance that if we follow this theory, it is possible to build the set of the sets which do not include themselves. It can then be shown, both that this set is one of its elements, and that it is not. Under the name of Russel's paradox, this is a paradox after the manner of

Epimenides's.[11] Just for the anecdote, let us specify that, fortunately, this 'disaster' did not last very long. Two modifications in the Cantor / Frege theory made it possible to make it less sluggish. Zermelo suggested that it should be axiomatically forbidden to form certain sets, such as, precisely, the set of infinite sets, or the set of the sets which are not self-inclusive. As for Russel, along with Whitehead, he proposed establishing a hierarchy between all the objects connected with the set theory. At the first level come basic elements (liars), at the second level, the sets uniting these elements, at the third the sets of these sets, etc. From there, it is only necessary to state that a set can never bring together anything else than objects of a lower level. No paradox can any longer crop up, since it is no longer possible to ask legitimately whether a set can be one of its own elements. This is what we meant by saying that it is impossible to shun admitting that the elements exist 'before' the set which unites those with the same property.

### 2.3 *The impossibility of giving up one's right of veto*

It is indeed a confusion of this kind which is made when one considers that a theory of justice as unanimous agreement could be compatible with giving up one's right of veto, even one single person's right of veto, and even if everyone agrees, including this individual.[12] This would amount to making it an inconsistent theory. Generally speaking, for a theory to be inconsistent, it must include at least one self-contradictory proposition, for in such a theory, just as in the case of Epimenides, it would be possible to prove both one thing and the reverse. Let us see why this is indeed the case if one willingly gives up on their right of veto.

An individual renouncing her right of veto is an individual who, by negating herself, can utter the proposition: 'I agree to disagree.' This is indeed a self-contradiction, but to evidence this, it is necessary that we formalise the logic of justice as unanimous agreement more than we have done so far.

Let there be a community N, with $n$ individuals located by an index $i$ varying from 1 to $n$. These individuals seek to agree on some common rules of life. Let $p$ be a proposition of such a rule. We are at the level of the ob-

11 It can also be found in mathematics, in different forms, for instance with Richard's paradox.

12 It goes without saying that if the individual did not agree, this would be a case of coercion which would place us outside the sphere of justice from the very start.

ject-language, a level we note as L1. Its evaluation is out of the question, since no test has been implemented yet. In order to do this, we must be at the level of meta-language, noted L2, where individuals comment on type-*p* propositions. What we are interested in here is knowing whether the individual *i* agrees to sign *p* and it is then noted: $p_i \in V$ (from the standpoint of *i*, it is true that *p* is fair); or still in knowing whether *i* and *j* agree to sign *p*, which is noted: $p_i \& p_j \in V$. The unanimity test consists in knowing whether all the individuals agree, which is noted:

$$\forall i \in N, p_i \in V$$

The importance of this test has already been abundantly accounted for. We have given it the following meaning: a proposition which gathers unanimity (through everyone's free agreement, as is presupposed here) is a fair proposition. However, two points must be emphasised. First, saying that unanimous agreement means fairness amounts to drawing an evaluation between all the possible tests at level L2. This is therefore an assertion at the level of meta-meta-language, noted L3. This can easily be seen by using inverted commas, which leads to: 'A proposition is fair and it has the status of a law (or a norm or a rule) if, and only if, 'all the individuals sign 'the proposition of the corresponding law *p*'''. In the second place, it is very clear that individuals put freely at the level of L3 the definition of what is from now on called fair. They fix its meaning through a decision taken by every person as a finite, autonomous and reasonable subject. We have indicated what would be the cost of not abiding by this decision, and we will return to this. But, saying this, there is no doubt that we oppose the idea that it could never be necessary to make a decision. Without such a free choice, which is a choice of reason in favour of reason (which makes it a stopping criterion for good), any evaluation should be evaluated too, and this would lead to an infinite regression of the levels of language (L1, L2, L3, L4, etc.) – no risk, no responsibility, but no evaluation either. On the contrary, justice as a unanimous agreement is a stopping condition, at level L3, which is immune to the infinite regression of the levels of language. It is worth noting that, by insisting on this L3-level decision, we are emphasising that the moral point of view is a human point of view, which does not rely on nature or God, or anything at all for which we would not be responsible ourselves.

That said, the basic proposition of justice as unanimous agreement can now be written as follows:

$$p \text{ is fair if and only if } \forall i \in N, p_i \in V$$

It is tautologically the same to enunciate it in the form of its contraposed,[13] and it is striking that the latter simply expresses the right of veto of every individual belonging to N:

$p$ is non fair if and only if $\exists i \in \mathrm{N} : p_i \notin \mathrm{V}$

The fact that it is actually the contraposed of the previous proposition shows, if need be, that 'unanimous agreement' and 'right of veto' are only two ways of expressing *tautologically* the same idea. It will be noted in passing that by writing the contraposed as above, it is not necessary to wonder whether or not it is necessary to apply the principle of the excluded third. We thus conform to what has already been argued above with respect to this question. Here, applying the excluded third amounts to admitting that $p$ is either fair or unfair, and that an individual either signs $p$ or non-$p$. However, nothing prevents us from supposing that $p$ could be neither fair nor unfair, but of an uncertain or indifferent status with respect to justice, nor to suppose that individual $i$ could refrain to sign either for or against. The non-fair is then not necessarily the unfair, and a non-vote is not necessarily a vote against. However, such subtleties leave the previous proposition unchanged.

Let us now suppose a proposition $p'$, for the abandonment of one's right of veto. Such a proposition consists in writing that when a particular individual $i$ does not agree, this is equal to him still agreeing. That is:

$p'$ = '$\exists i \in \mathrm{N}: p_i \notin \mathrm{V}$ & $\forall j \neq i \in \mathrm{N}, p_j \in \mathrm{V}$ means $p$ is fair'

The proposition is invalid in two respects. First, it allows itself to rewrite what has been fixed at the level of meta-meta-language (L3) by turning upside down the meaning of the word fairness. In this confusion, it is hardly surprising that we necessarily end up with the absurdity fair = unfair. Moreover, by bearing upon agreements from L2, in other words upon signatures, the proposition of L1 starts signing instead of the individuals, also causing greater confusion between language and meta-language. We are thus simply confronted with a paradox similar to Epimenides's. Indeed, this paradox amounts to writing $p$ = '$p_i \notin \mathrm{V}$', and then to overlooking the commas; now, individual $i$ can neither sign this proposition, nor sign its negation. In other words, he is made to say 'I lie'.

13 The contraposed is a tautology which is written: $(p \Rightarrow q) \Rightarrow (\text{non-}q \Rightarrow \text{non-}p)$.

It is clear that if the proposition *p'* was incorporated to the theory of justice, in other words if it was accepted for the same reasons as, for instance, the above contraposed proposition, we would end up with a piece of nonsense. The sentence 'I freely agree to give up my right of veto and, since everyone agrees, this is fair', is not a strange paradox in a theory of justice as unanimous agreement, but rather a sheer sophism. A confusion is made, between levels of language which must be carefully distinguished.

## 2.4 *Objective injustices*

It thus appears that there is indeed, in the end, a restriction as to what the *n* individuals can agree on, but this limitation, in conformity with what was required, is not the product of some criterion which is external to the agreement – some good which would be imposed. It simply stems from what must be admitted logically in order to speak of agreement. We have expressed it under the form of the impossibility to renounce one's right of veto, but it can be formulated in many other identical ways.

For instance, as we have already seen, an agreement between *n* individuals cannot be an agreement between *n* – 1 individuals, and from the standpoint of a positive right, this can be formulated as: no individual can be condemned by virtue of a law said to be secret (of course, this applies to any norm which claims to be fair). Indeed, this individual cannot have given her agreement to a law she does not know about. The contraposed of this principle is none other than the famous principle according to which 'no one is supposed not to know the law'. From the point of view of application, however, it may happen that judicial codes have become so thick and complex that only specialists have the possibility to know the texts. If an individual gets prosecuted, it is therefore essential that she is guaranteed the assistance of a lawyer with recognised competence. If this guarantee, for any reason, often political (totalitarian regime) or economic (hiring a 'good' lawyer is too expensive for the convict), should happen to be missing, her potential condemnation would run against the principle of unanimous agreement, and therefore be unfair. This would lead *de facto* to the situation of a secret law. This situation can also be found in many other cases. For instance, when laws are divine injunctions which only a few individuals (such as the priests of the divinity, whatever the form this takes) have the power to know or interpret 'correctly'. Or still, when a law or a norm is so vague that it is impossible for a normally constituted human brain to determine what it allows or forbids in practice. It is also important, for equivalent reasons, that texts or norms within the same group, are not in complete contradiction. By right, this situation is impossible, since an individual cannot give her agreement to contradictory texts without contradicting herself. So, if this situation occurs in practice, it cannot be regarded as fair; it is another disguised abandonment of one's right of veto. In the same way, it is obvious that a retroactive law is a typical instance of a 'secret law'. If an individual is condemned in time *t*2 by virtue of such a law, it means that the action she did in time *t*1 was not an offence. When she resolved to act in *t*1, she could not but ignore a law which did not exist, and condemning her in *t*2 does indeed amount to resorting to a law that was kept secret in *t*1. There is no need to carry this enumeration any further to show that if the right of veto may appear as relatively 'abstract', it nevertheless has concrete judicial counterparts. In all these cases, and in many others as well, it is possible to say, without any ambiguity, that an individual who is prosecuted or convicted would be so in an objective violation of what lies at the foundation of the just or, in other words, for objectively unfair reasons.

The situation would remain equally unfair if she happened to consent. In fact, it would only add to the confusion. To show this, let us revert to the example of the retroactive law, and consider the following textbook case. In *t*1, all the individuals in a community, except one, think that begging must be punished. Therefore, a law banning begging cannot be voted in, and no one can be condemned for such an offence. Let us suppose that the individual who disagrees is a beggar, which is not an offence. In *t*2, he changes his mind and, like everyone else, starts to think that begging is a serious offence. And as it happens, he no longer is a beggar. The law banning begging is now unanimously agreed on. It can be voted in and applied in fairness. But the offence is so serious that everyone, including our individual, agrees that the new law must be retroactive. He is therefore convicted for having begged in *t*1. Without his consent, we already know that his conviction would amount to negating his right of veto. It is clear that his conviction would be unfair, but our individual does not partake in this denial of justice. With his agreement, he does partake in it: he himself negates his right of veto and does so in an absolute way. Indeed, what is under discussion here is a principle, and from this point of view transitivity applies. What has just been accepted as a 'fair' principle for the passage from *t*1 to *t*2 remains fair – unless one admits of a radical change in the definition of justice between two successive moments – for the passage from *t*3 to *t*2, from *t*4 to *t*3, and so on. So that, by accepting the principle of a retroactive law, our individual has in a way completely, definitely and infinitely forsaken his right of veto. We already know that this is paradoxical in the context of justice as unanimous agreement, but there remains another difficulty.

Whatever moment in time is considered, our individual is no longer sure of benefiting from his right of veto, since at the following moment, it may be withdrawn, retroactively and with his own consent. Now, he cannot consent to giving up what he is not certain of possessing. This is actually not only a question of uncertainty, since his consent is self-contradictory. If he gives this consent in *t*2, he admits that in *t*1 his rejection of the law against begging was then illegitimate and illegal, or that a unanimity of $n - 1$ individuals is equal to a unanimity of the $n$ individuals, or that his right of veto is non-existent. He himself thus thinks that he does not have any right of veto in *t*1, that since then he does not have one, at least as far as begging is concerned, and that, as a result, he does not have it at the following moment in *t*2. Therefore, he simply cannot consent to abandoning it in *t*2. But this is what he must do in order to approve of the retroactive law in *t*2. The paradox is well and truly here because the agreement confutes itself. In the self-confuting context of a retroactive law, giving one's agreement amounts to admitting that it is not possible to give it. At the very moment when it is glimpsed at, it becomes impossible.

Of course, our individual may still 'accept' this retroactive law which condemns him, in the same way as the words 'I lie' may still be uttered, or as A may still give B castles in the air which he does not possess, but it is clear that all this is null and void. A retroactive law is objectively unfair, even towards someone who may consent to it.

This closes the debate on knowing whether the precept 'there is no injustice when one consents' is fair or not. This precept is fair, as long as it is added that this subjective consent can in no case contradict objective justice, that is, as we know, the principle of unanimous agreement. In the opposite case, the said consent has no value.

This is the case for contract law, which stipulates that a contract cannot include a clause which contradicts a principle admitted in a contract of a higher level regulating all the agreements of a lower level; for instance, a private contract cannot include a clause which violates a right guaranteed by the constitution. Even if this contract is signed, this clause is null and void.

To put it differently, but still applying the same principle: if an innocent owns up to a crime he did not commit, it is unfair to condemn him.

The same applies when it comes to slavery. Of course, it is usually the outcome of coercion, but it would be just as unfair if it was voluntary. When the candidate for slavery gives his agreement, he excludes himself from the agreement. The point is not to challenge the fact, however strange it may be, that he wishes to be enslaved, nor even to lecture him by saying that such a desire is evil, but to see that the value of the agreement comes from being able to say no. Slavery is a situation of an absolute abandonment of one's right of veto, and this shows that, while there is no justice without a unanimous agreement, justice does not exclusively reside in this empirical agreement. It is not because individuals freely and unanimously decide to become slaves that enslavement in general, and theirs in particular, is fair. The society they have chosen is *objectively* unfair.

This leads us to an aspect of social contract theories which is often neglected, that is, that the social contract is never signed for good, and *must never be* so. The ideal of the social contract is not that it should be signed once, and then imposed as the founding moment of a customary right; the ideal of the social contract is to be signed by everyone at any moment. By rejecting his right of veto, the slave can no longer aim at this ideal because he can no longer freely give his agreement: he has resigned from his reason, and can no longer judge on what is fair. It results that the agreement does not lead anywhere, but on the contrary, leads to a position which is fair as a result of demands which are peculiar to reason and this implies, among many other consequences, that a Kantian contractualism is not a pure conventionalism, in which everything would be allowed, under the cover of a unanimous convention (nevertheless, this crucial problem will be addressed in chapter 5). Since a complete forsaking of one's right of veto is never legitimate, it is never so at any given moment. A contract is therefore a contract at all moments. An individual who wishes to alter a choice he made in the past may do so at any moment. We could also say: 'Any agreement is necessarily revisable.' A non-revisable agreement is an agreement whereby one or several individuals, or even every individual, have forsaken their right of veto. This forsaking is one of the agreement clauses, and this is what makes it non-revisable. Now, as it is established that this clause is impossible, it amounts to the same to say that any agreement is necessarily revisable. It can also be observed that a revisable agreement is by definition temporary. An agreement with a infinite duration would amount to giving up one's right of veto. As soon as an individual wishes to alter her choice, the agreement must be renegotiated, and this is why a contract is never signed for good.

But the objection of unrealism and also of instability reappear. Indeed, it is hard to conceive how this could be made operational, even for a small group. An agreement of every moment seems to hinder action. Let us first point out again that unanimous agreement bears upon rules, and that it is established on the basis of attempts at generalisations and previsions of typical situations. In principle, the agreement remains valid as long as the situations contemplated at the time of the agreement are realised. Everyone agreed with full knowledge of the facts. Therefore, saying that the contract is never signed for good is to underline that what has been granted for predictable cases does not have the value of a law in unpredictable cases. This does not mean however that an unpredicted fact is enough to reject what has been granted, and believe oneself to be free from all the previous commitments. The agreement of every moment replaces a past agreement with a present agreement. But in practice, this remains too demanding, and it is necessary to contemplate solutions of the same type as that of majority ballot previously described. The foundation of this ballot was indeed unanimity, but for reasons of application and efficiency, unanimity could be achieved through the adoption of the majority rule, on the conditions already described. In particular, on the condition that it should always be possible to re-examine this rule, and potentially change it. Here, what is forbidden is a contract with an infinite duration, because an absolute renunciation to one's right of veto is impossible. But a contract with a determined duration is not forbidden. To put it differently, if the foundation of the agreement demands that it can never be signed for good, it may still be signed for a determined duration (through a unanimous agreement between all the parties, needless to say). Since a fixed-duration contract is legitimate, the objection of unrealism or instability collapses. In everyday life, such contracts are often found. Moreover, what we call infinite-duration contracts should not be mistaken with what is called for instance in English law 'a permanent contract'. The indefinite-duration contract is a contract which never ceases to prevail. This means for instance that from the moment when it was signed by our ancestors, it will never cease to apply to all their descendents, whatever generation they belong to. On the contrary, a permanent contract (or any everyday-life contract) can stop for various reasons. In fact, in our terminology, they belong to the category of limited-duration contracts where, on the contrary, the right of veto is not abolished. If one of the parties transgresses the agreement clauses, the other can immediately bring her right to bear, either by forcing him to respect the contract, or by observing that it has become irrelevant. The distinction is clear, but the terminology is undeniably deceiving. The agreement of every moment is indeed the foundation, but application does not proscribe contracts to which we subscribe with problem-less ease.

In the end, if unanimous agreement is demanding, it does not mean that it invalidates the most diverse pragmatic procedures which have been imagined by all societies during their history. In return, as far as principles are concerned, this very demand makes it possible to perceive easily the breaching points between justice as unanimous agreement and other conceptions. For instance, if a just agreement is revisable, it follows that historicism, according to which morality is founded at one point in history, and then imposes itself on everyone, loses all its credit. This will make it possible for us to confute the libertarians' historical theory of the right in the next chapter, but for now, it is possible to come back quickly to utilitarianism by also focusing on its handling of the right of veto and wondering whether, as a result of this treatment, it does not appear straightaway as incapable of attaining the standpoint of justice as unanimous agreement.

Before we address this problem, let us note that a rule of negative discrimination obviously negates the individuals' right of veto in the field where the rule applies. For instance: a citizen fulfilling the conditions which would make it possible to grant her the right to vote (age, nationality, and so on) will be deprived of this right only because she belongs to this or that ethnic minority. For a justice defined as unanimous agreement, such a rule cannot be said to be fair, since, through the negation of the right of veto, it contradicts this agreement in its very principle. In other words, in order to admit a negative discrimination, it is necessary to leave the context of this justice. If we claim to stay within it, it is only through a sheer sophism. Here, negative discrimination is only a self-contradiction leading to a logical paradox similar to Epimedes's: levels of language which must be carefully and scrupulously distinguished are brought back to being the same. It is therefore possible to accept both justice as a unanimous agreement and negative discrimination only if one thinks that it is possible to negate oneself by saying one thing and the reverse.

It is then also possible to hold that normative utilitarianism, which seeks the fair behind the mere maximization of the good, makes a logical mistake.

Let us restate the terms of the debate with the deontological position. For the latter, as a result of the priority of the right, it is not reasonable to take into account all the individuals' preferences, such as they offer themselves, and with no further investigation, under the pretence of an equal consideration for everyone. Preferences which are objectively unfair are excluded from the context of justice as unanimous agreement. On the contrary, for (direct) act-utilitarianism, as for (indirect) rule utilitarianism, only the maximisation of utilities counts. The only deontology which is admitted (by the majority of utilitarians, but inconsistently, for a theory which rejects any form of deontology) is very minimal: every individual counts as one in the calculation of the sum of happiness. It is therefore out of the question to exclude immediately unfair rules or preferences, such as a preference for negative discrimination. Neutrality is indispensable and, according to the utilitarian, it is 'guaranteed' by this acceptation of any preference or, which amounts to the same, the rejection of 'any' deontology (except that of the equal weighting, therefore). It is only because acts or rules turn out to be contrary to the optimisation of happiness that they are eventually, and because of this optimisation, excluded. However, a rule or an act of negative discrimination can perfectly go through the net of optimisation, and since the situation is optimal, it is fair or at least, it is hard to see how it could be any fairer, since the greatest happiness for the greatest number has been reached. The situation is obviously very tricky for the utilitarian candidate himself, since it runs against the deepest-rooted conceptions of justice, starting usually with his own. However, he can still argue that his 'morality-selecting machine' ('neutral' optimisation) will be improved as soon as the necessary alterations will have been found. Rule utilitarianism instead of act-utilitarianism is not the solution, but the theory can still be improved. The project is not doomed. It can be seen here that this is not the case at all, at least for anyone who wishes to keep up the idea of justice as unanimous agreement. Not excluding a rule or a preference for negative discrimination is impossible in the context of this justice. This would amount, as we have just seen, to indulging in logical paradox. As a result, even a perfect optimising 'machine' (which would automatically filter negative discriminations) will only produce nothing else than a situation which cannot be called 'fair' from the point of view of unanimous agreement. The logical mistake is made from the start, and there is nothing the 'machine' can do about this anymore. This 'machine' is only an adding machine (a machine which optimises through calculation) and therefore it absolutely cannot turn the false into the true, as a dialectical machine would. From the start, it has been admitted that justice was not a unanimous agreement by not rejecting the preferences or the rules negating its principle. At the outcome, after optimisation, the same negation still obviously remains. The utilitarian cannot hold that she admits justice as a unanimous agreement, and that she can attain it, by being more 'neutral' as to the preferences or the rules than deontology, through a mere optimisation of the good. She must choose: either she admits that justice demands unanimous agreement, and from then, rules or preferences which negate this agreement can never be fair, or she admits these rules or preferences at some point in her reasoning, but her 'justice' will never consist in a unanimous agreement. Rejecting unanimous agreement, however, has serious consequences, since the worst situations of oppression may then be called 'fair'. The floodgates are open for the 'law' of the strongest and for any coercion. We have no doubt that the utilitarian wishes to close this door, but it will be forever impossible for her to do so in the context of her project.

In the end, the logic of unanimous agreement makes it possible to make out in a rather simple way the many ideas or doctrines which are incompatible with justice, by seeing in which respect they try to force people's hands. To conclude on this chapter, it may be useful to also emphasise that justice as a unanimous agreement avoid the normative *a priori* of other theories, by presenting itself as a pure procedural justice.

## 2.5 *A pure procedural justice*

In the context of this justice, the point is to agree on rules, obviously applied to everyone afterwards, and, as we have seen, this is usually referred to a pure procedural justice. In the case of distributive justice, these procedures are rules for sharing or allocating a rare resource. Overall, there exist three main types of procedure. On this point we follow Rawls (1971), but he takes up a typology which is widely accepted by the specialists of sharing procedures. A justice is simply procedural when it aims at satisfying one or several perfection criteria which are independent from the right and known in advance. This justice is (i) imperfect when its conditions of realisation are such that it is not sure that the result will meet a given criterion. Penal justice is an illustration of this. Even if the Code of penal procedure is highly satisfactory, even if it is perfectly respected, it is never excluded that an innocent person may be condemned, or a culprit let free. A justice that is simply procedural is on the contrary (ii) perfect when it is certain that the correct result will be reached. If every individual having to share a homogeneous cake is a maximiser, a perfect procedure to reach equality consists in having the cake cut by the last person to be served. With (iii) a purely procedural justice, there is no criterion which is independent from the just to satisfy. In the example quoted above of the plane which is about to crash, drawing lots is a fair procedure with respect to the passengers' supposedly symmetrical conditions, but it is correct and fair in its application only by virtue of the passengers' unanimous agreement. Since the procedure is fair, fairness is transferred to the result of its application, and in order to judge on this, the procedure must be applied. To put it in a few words: 'pure procedural justice obtains when there is no independent criterion for the right result: instead there is a correct or fair procedure such that the outcome is likewise correct or fair, whatever it is, provided that the procedure has been properly followed' (Rawls, 1971, § 14). It will be noted that Rawls's method in *A Theory of Justice* consists in searching whether a procedure which is purely procedural in this sense may help to determine the basic principles of a fair society.[14]

Relatively to this ternary typology, it goes without saying that unanimous agreement pertains to a pure procedural justice. Specialists of sharing procedures (Moessinger, 1998) tend to rather describe this as 'satisficing procedure'. Apart from questions of terminology and if we leave aside im-

14 From this point of view, it must be emphasised that, although he is also a contractualist, Scanlon does not give questions of procedure an essential role in founding justice. This is an important divergence – since it touches upon the foundation – between his position and Rawls's or ours. It is true that we often concur when it comes to results in the field of morality or social justice. Nevertheless, by following a Kantian standpoint, it is not necessary to *describe* for each new case all the *substantial* reasons which make it possible to account for what we owe to each other. The principle of unanimous agreement is enough. Because he does not give himself a foundation in pure reason, Scanlon must on the contrary decide for each case which reasonable objections are weighty enough to be accepted and which ones are not. This 'casuistry', which proves very complex in the end, amounts to introducing substantial bonds on what we can agree on. The problem stems from a flaw in the method. In order to establish the principle of legitimacy, one must *start* from an *autonomous subject*, that is to say by granting each other the freedom to think, and not from a 'heteronomous' individual (Scanlon, 1998, p. 6) receiving heaps of reasons whose weights are decided on even before one has had the opportunity to say whether one endorses them or not.

perfect procedures, let us see what distinguishes a perfect sharing procedure from a satisficing procedure.

Perfect procedures have inspired many studies, since some of them, such as 'pragmatic sharing', can be traced down to the Old Testament. In order to share a cake between two people, the principle of 'one cuts it, the other decides' is applied; it guarantees an equal division if both want to maximise their part. This principle is easily generalised to the case of *n* individuals, and perfect procedures can apply to homogenous or heterogeneous, to divisible or indivisible goods. In all cases, the exercise consists in making sure that an individual who maximises his good gets at the end of the procedure an equitable share according to an external criterion given *ex ante*. These procedures basically suppose that individuals pursue the same goal, and that they accept the same perfection criterion. For instance, they accept equity in the sense of 'to each person according to their deserts', but refuse the principle 'to each person according to their desires'. They already agree on the criterion that should be applied and in the end the conflict opposing them is only a false problem since they already know how to put an end to it. In other words, harmony is pre-established. Whether rights are equal or unequal, they are already acknowledged as such by everyone. A perfect procedure does not say anything about them. Let us take the example of an inheritance. Before looking for a perfect sharing procedure, we must know first what the rights of the heirs are. For instance, among the children of the deceased, do the youngest children have the same rights as the oldest ones? In the context of a perfect procedure, actors already agree on the answer and a perfect sharing only makes it operational.

With a satisficing (or a pure) procedure, there is no external criterion. The procedure only guarantees to everyone that no decision can be taken against their will. Everyone has a right of veto and the only criterion is thus that the agreement on the sharing is unanimous. We do not know in advance whether the rights over a sharing are equal or unequal. It is the unanimous agreement which establishes and legitimises these rights, which 'says' in what fairness consists. In this case, the social order is not pre-established by a supposed harmony between everyone's aims, and neither is it imposed (because of the right of veto). It emerges from an impartial consideration by each person of each person's interests. The procedure is founded on the respect of individuals and their autonomy. In those conditions, no one can be sure that at the end of the procedure they will not obtain less than they initially wished for. There is no reason for a sharing to be optimal. But on the contrary, everyone is sure that the sharing will be acceptable for them. They are thus responsible for what they get, and consequently, while it is not guaranteed that envy is totally absent, it is very significantly toned down.

Why are the champions of the rational choice theory still attached to a perfect justice? There are essentially two reasons for this. First, perfect procedures supposedly offer better guaranties of neutrality. Indeed, they do not forbid Pareto optimality. Now, the latter is actually impervious to moral values and in particular to those bearing on rights. The only thing that matters is the increase in well-being. However, there is a high price to pay, since a perfect justice is absolutely useless when it comes to settling arguments on rights, and thus for instance to implement or evaluate a social policy. Moreover, this so-called 'neutrality' is only a sham. The rights and the sharing criteria are always already given, and implementing a perfect justice only means accepting them as they are. The only thing left to do is finding the algorithm which satisfies them, while satisfying also the optimising individual. Far from being neutral, perfect justice turns out to be conservative. Satisficing procedures are reputedly not 'neutral' because they have to do with rights. But it is actually the reverse which is true, if one admits that the only true neutrality is the one which seeks and respects everyone's agreement, and that consequently, no sharing criterion which is independent from the right (from the agreement) should be taken for granted *a priori*. No restriction must be established as to what individuals can agree on, except, as we have seen, what calls into question unanimous agreement itself, by undermining its theoretical consistency (such as an individual giving up his right of veto) or its practical consistency (such as an agreement on a procedure which cannot reach its aim, that is, to solve the conflict or the problem which calls for an agreement).[15] This means for instance that if individuals must agree to split their community into different equivalence classes of rights and duties, no splitting plan is excluded *a priori*, except for the notable exception – let us emphasise it once more – of those which annihilate the very principle of agreement. A second bad reason leads rational choice theorists to give precedence to perfect procedures. They are regarded as easier to apply, while unanimity supposedly leads to blockage. This is a very debatable argument. Mutual agreements, negotia-

15 At this stage, we have not examined this point thoroughly, but we will return to it in chapter 5.

tions in very diverse fields (for interpersonal, social, or international conflicts) are, among many other scenarios, more than common, even though all these procedures rest on unanimity. Blockage is a risk. But most often, everyone perceives it, and uses it as a threat. The art of negotiating consists precisely in overcoming these reciprocal threats in order to find a compromise.

However, the most important difference between a perfect procedure and a satisficing (or a pure) one resides in the fact that in the former case, the social order is already given, while in the latter, it is built. Let us imagine that it is not given or that it is unknown. It immediately appears that no perfect procedure can be applied. Having a cake shared by the last one can only be a good solution if everyone accepts that he has an equal right to a piece of cake. Applying this procedure when everyone thinks that the rights are not equal is pointless. This shows that if the perfection criterion (the definition of fairness in the context at stake) and the harmony of objectives are not supposed to be given in advance, it is indeed necessary to start with a satisficing procedure. The perfect procedure comes only after, and only solves a mere *technical* problem of attribution concerning what has been decided by the unanimous agreement on which it is founded. In other words, there is no perfect justice unless preceded by a pure procedural justice. If, therefore, satisficing procedures are overlooked, it is necessary to find another foundation for the sharing criterion. The most diverse solutions were then considered: divine revelation, pre-established harmony of the maximisation of happiness, natural selection, etc. Different as they may be, though, all these answers rest on the same belief: it is not men who build their destiny together – 'morality-selecting machines' do so for them.

To put a pure procedural justice at the foundation of social justice is to abandon these normative *a priori* on criteria of justice independent from the just, even when it comes to well-being, and accept that in the end, the choice of this foundation is a moral choice. For in turn, what is the foundation of unanimous agreement itself, if not a moral choice? The choice made by everyone, to see in everyone an autonomous and legitimate source of claim, without which unanimous agreement is meaningless, is ultimately a free choice. And, in this sense, it is a moral decision. And yet, this decision does in no way make it impossible to speak of objectivity. We have just seen it throughout this chapter, but, now speaking of an ultimately moral choice, it would seem that the relativistic risk threatens again. In order to show this is absolutely not the case and since this is, no doubt, an essential stake, we will have to return to it in the last chapter.

Chapter 4

# Three Examples of Unsatisfactory Procedures

Admitting a renunciation of the veto amounts to regarding individuals only as means in the name of, or with a view to, a perfection criterion. In the context of justice as unanimous agreement, we have just seen that it is impossible to approve of such a renunciation. But the application of this simple clause leads, among other things, to undermine seriously several theories of justice. It is of course out of the question to deal with each of these. In any case, unanimous agreement cannot be made compatible with what negates its basic characteristics; for instance with the holistic and deterministic position which negates its principle of liberty or with perfectionism which contradicts liberalism (as the acceptation of the plurality of conceptions of the good). On the contrary, some theories, which have actually found contemporary developments in social sciences, are not in principle opposed to any idea of contract, or at least try to account for cooperation and, in this respect, it can be shown that it is precisely because they overlook the principle of unanimous agreement that they stumble upon serious objections.

This is above all the case of libertarianism, which opposes to the right of veto a right of ownership which is then made about as open to discussion as the sacred tables. This doctrine then lapses into historicism by implicitly admitting not only that a social contract was signed at some point – and we are asked to believe that at some point everyone was absolutely fair! – but also that it was signed once and for all, thus negating everyone's right of veto, even those who were not born yet. This is also the case of the utilitarian theory of the social pact, or, more generally, of cooperation. This time, the agreement only results from the maximisation of each of the parties' interests, but, with respect to the conditions of this maximisation, either they reach no agreement and remain in conflict, or they establish some cooperation through the mere play of a reiteration of rounds. However, since this cooperation is not conceived from the viewpoint of the reasonable, it is, in fact and surreptitiously, always presupposed. In other words, we have to pay the high price of believing in a pre-established harmony. Lastly, as for communitarianism, it finds it necessary to introduce a secret clause bearing on the communitarian bond in the social contract, demanding that everyone sign an opaque contract. However, the confrontation of the right of veto with the secret clause is only one approach to discuss communitarianism. Other aspects must be taken into account not to be simplistic. The dead ends of this doctrine are not only of a logical nature. They are also sociological, for instance as a result of the holism which it supports.

## 1. The Failure of Libertarianism in the Face of the Citizen's Priority

The central concept in any libertarian theory is that of ownership, whether it be ownership of oneself or ownership of objects. It is true that one libertarian would insist rather on freedom, and another on equality. One will define freedom above all as the freedom to enjoy one's ownership right; the other will make self-ownership the guarantee of equal dignity. But the essential thing remains to reach as fast as possible the right of ownership since, for a libertarian, freedom or everyone's equal dignity cannot be taken seriously if one does not acknowledge first their imprescriptible right to the ownership of their own person, and therefore to the ownership of the – legitimately acquired – objects which are necessary to their preservation or maintenance. We therefore admit that, in order to avoid the traps of a utilitarian or consequentialist theory of justice, we have to start from the subject's freedom (or equal dignity), and hold it to be intangible, in accordance with a liberal theory, and especially Kant's. But, apart from this starting point, pretty much everything differentiates liberal and libertarian approaches, since for the latter, in the end, it is on the owner, rather than on the citizen, that justice will have to rest. As we are going to show, this is a big mistake of category: the citizen, and only he, should guarantee to the owner that this thing belongs to her, and that one, to someone else. The owner can enjoy only what the citizen grants her, and exchange goods in so far as the citizen consents to it. In other words, unless justice and the market are considered to be identical, the owner cannot replace the citizen.

How do the libertarians[1] still justify an intrinsic link between justice and the market? To do so, they must suppose that, while the owner exerts her freedom to exchange goods on the marketplace, this free action is at the same time an approval on the agora. Three propositions are necessary, and can thus be found under one form or another in any libertarian's works. (i) First, there must be some initial principle for the acquisition of goods which must be legitimate; indeed, without a legitimate property deed to produce on the marketplace, regulated exchanges would only be a huge free-for-all. (ii) There must then be a principle of legitimate transfer; the focus is obviously on voluntary transactions: being the legitimate owner of belongings, my freedom is above all an economic freedom, which consists in being allowed to exchange my goods as I please. It logically follows that any distribution of goods which is the product of voluntary transfers from an initial legitimate distribution is also a legitimate distribution – that is, a fair distribution. Finally (iii) a minimal State is needed to prevent and correct breaches on the preceding rules, that is, the rules of the market, which are at the same time rules of justice. Against mere anarchy, a minimal State guarantees the value of property *deeds*, by defending the legitimate owner against those who are simply the strongest or the most cunning. In the end, these three principles make the market the only possible reference for justice: the first one by avoiding citizen's intrusions, the second by suggesting that the trader-owner easily replaces him, and the third one by avoiding still to relapse into some state of nature where property deeds have no value. It goes without saying that in this context, only the fiscal levies that are meant to compensate an appropriation or an illegitimate transfer are justified.

Robert Nozick (1974) has illustrated this theory most brilliantly through the example of the famous basketball player Wilt Chamberlain. Let us suppose a society where the initial repartition of goods is equitable, and where one basketball player is more gifted than the others. Every individual is free to do whatever they want with their property, and in particular, to let Wilt Chamberlain have part of it, in exchange for a ticket to watch him play. At the end of the basketball season, Chamberlain will have grossed an enormous income and, in the process, the repartition of goods will have become very inequitable. However, can it be said that this final distribution is unfair? And by virtue of what right could this be said? Since the initial situa-

1 On this aspect, the works of David Friedman (1973), Murray Rothbard (1973) or Robert Nozick (1974), among many others, may be consulted.

tion was supposed to be fair, the following actions are visibly legitimate. Challenging the way in which the money was spent amounts to denouncing property rights, as if an owner was not an absolute owner, and could therefore not freely trade with what she owns. The conclusion seems clear: however inequitable a distribution of goods might be, it still remains fair as long as it is the outcome of voluntary transactions. This is why, among other things, any idea of a redistributive taxation is *intrinsically* unfair: taxing the rich in order to sustain the poor is pure and simple robbery – an iniquitous questioning of the rich's property rights. To the 19th-century anarchist, who claimed 'property is robbery',[2] the late-20th-century libertarian, who

2 In this respect, we must remember that, in order to maintain that property is intrinsically unfair, one should be able to show that, whatever the unanimous agreement on a distribution of title deeds, it would be contrary to the very principle of this agreement. Since such a demonstration cannot be provided, it is rather the individual who argues that *any ownership* is unfair *a priori* who, by ignoring the potential agreement between those involved, stands outside the realm of justice. Marx's approach to this problem is different. The point is to find out what to think of the private ownership of the means of production. Private ownership is therefore not unfair in itself (for the worker to be robbed by the capitalist, it must be supposed (Cohen, 1990) that he is the legitimate owner of his working time, of his work force, and of its product – self-ownership in the libertarian way, that is), but in so far as it translates into an exploitation of one man by another. The problem thus becomes twofold. First, one must be able to establish the reasons why this exploitation – defined strictly as an appropriation of part of the yield of work by those who do not work – is intrinsically unfair. But, as Philippe Van Parijs (1991, chap. 4) shows very clearly, this is impossible. Then, it must be established that the collective appropriation of the means of production cancels the injustices which derive from exploitation – or at least the most acute ones. This time – and even the Marxists agree with this – this appropriation does not annihilate as such the injustices suffered by many categories of the population, such as women, the handicapped, the outcasts etc. Hence the idea of defining this exploitation in a different way, not only in terms of transfers of surplus value, but, for instance, of an unequal access to the means of production (Roemer, 1988). However, to do so, one must give up the idea that there is something intrinsically unfair at the heart of salaried work, and, moreover, socialism does not necessarily abolish an exploitation which is redefined in those terms. Marx was probably aware of these difficulties since, if we revert to the letter of his writings, it is very clear that he objects to the idea that his doctrine could be a theory of justice, especially if one intends to link this justice with fairness, and especially if one intends to make it 'the first virtue of social institutions' (Rawls, 1971). If some collectivisation of ownership is called for, in Marx's view, it is precisely because of the impossibility of reaching fairness through a redistribution of resources. Social justice is always *only* corrective, and is therefore essentially a false solution. Communist society, without private property, without classes and therefore without conflicts, makes any justice pointless.

wishes to reduce the State to its simplest expression, retorts: 'taxes are robbery'.

The strength of this example comes from one single intuition: to give someone a property right is to give her the freedom to use it as she likes. As children like to say in French schoolyards: 'To give is to give, to take back is to steal.' For the rest, this example simply masks problems. The citizen is quickly disposed with. Nozick hopes to avoid the issue of the initial distribution by telling the reader that this distribution may be whichever he pleases. However, in the long term, the only essential property is that of Chamberlain's talent: his talent is the only source of income. Therefore, the owners may be as equal as one wishes initially, but there will only be one capitalist. Let us then go to the end of Nozick's demonstration: as he is the only one who accumulates capital, there will be a point when Chamberlain will own everything, and there will ensue a serious problem for the community – in other words, there will be a moment when the citizen will no longer be indifferent to Chamberlain's buying, for instance, all the drinkable water available. If this theory of justice is taken to extremes, it appears that it hurts our deepest-rooted intuitions on justice.

Generally speaking, libertarianism misses the issue of justice, because ownership as such does not give any right to settle a problem of collective life to one's exclusive advantage. The libertarian conception of ownership is simply invalid. What is ownership? A label with a person's name put on material or immaterial objects. As far as justice is concerned, however, there is no point in putting labels onto objects if the other community members do not acknowledge their legitimacy. In this sense, ownership is an institution through which everyone acknowledges that one object does not belong to them, and grant other people the freedom to have it. In other words, ownership is not a 'natural' fact, but the outcome of a unanimous agreement. This can actually be said of any right in general. A right derives its value only from other people's commitment to respect it. Libertarianism simply distributes 'natural' rights (of property) in the same way as others distribute counterfeit currency. But, when it comes to deciding between Chamberlains' property right on water and other people's right to stay alive,

---

Since this society supposes affluence, the true question is not to figure out how to reach a fair(er) distribution, but how to bring about the conditions of affluence. To those who may be desirous to forget so, Marx (1875, I, 3) reminds that notions such as 'equal right', or 'fair distribution' are only 'obsolete verbal rubbish', 'nonsense of some judicial ideology'.

it will obviously appear that all these 'rights' were not worth anything, and the citizen will have to be introduced to avoid coming to blows to settle the conflict.

The problems of libertarianism are then all in keeping. Therefore it seems 'natural' for everyone to be the owner of their talents. Of course, no one will question that Chamberlain's talents are his only, rather than someone else's. However, being the owner of these talents is a wholly different question. And being the owner of their yield is yet another question. It has been regarded as fair for Chamberlain to reap the fruits of his talent. Would the same thing have been said about a handicap? What if, being handicapped, I cannot live on my own income only; does justice impose it on me not to claim anything, and to believe that I am only getting what I deserve? Or still, if I am the only person who is strong enough to draw water from the well, do the others have *absolutely* and *undisputedly* no right as to the product of my talent? It thus appears that things are not that easy and these objections lead us directly to the question of self-ownership and the ownership of objects.

Nozick – to discuss his ideas only – claims to bring the ownership of goods down to self-ownership, and self-ownership, down to the Kantian principle whereby individuals must be treated as ends. However, each of these stages proves problematic. The hinge of his demonstration resides in the notion of self-ownership. Nozick defines it as the ownership of one's abilities, or as the right to put one's abilities into practice. The 'self' in Nozick's sense is already particularly remote, since, in the long term, I will be able to give up this 'self'-ownership. For the time being, however, by guaranteeing self-ownership, Nozick guarantees my independence: I am not a slave, since no master tells me what I must do with my talents. It is already a lot, but it is not enough. A freed slave, I will still have to become a citizen. Independent, I will still need to become autonomous. For now, I have the right to put into practice my talents as a basketball player or a liar, a crook or an inveterate water-drinker. And since the others have the same 'rights', we have in common the right to anarchy – in other words, nothing. What is missing from Nozick's conception of self-ownership is precisely the Kantian principle which demands that the other should be recognised as an end in itself. This requires the other to be acknowledged as a reasonable being, and this stage is essential for an agreement and a common institution of the law to be possible. This can be put differently. Libertarians entrap freedom in the private sphere. Self-ownership guarantees the freedom to put into practice one's abilities, but in private. This is therefore a way of depriving us of citizenship: 'Think freely, but in your own little corner.' But the only true defence of freedom of thought is the one which guarantees us expression on the agora. This is the condition of possibility of a unanimous agreement. In Nozick's theory of justice, self-ownership seems to grant everyone the essential. The only missing thing is the freedom to express oneself in public – that is, each person's right of veto.

The transition from self-ownership to the ownership of objects is also problematic. I may well be the owner of my talents – but does that make me the owner of what derives from them? I am certainly entitled to part of the product of my work, but am I absolutely entitled to all of it, as claimed by Nozick, in the wake of Locke? First, this involves proving that this product is the product of my talents only. It is true that Chamberlain is a gifted player, but what is his talent worth, without his team partners and his opponents? It is also necessary to explain why parents do not own their children. Above all, another difficulty remains to be solved: that we rarely create *ex nihilo*.

Let us stick to the basic case where an individual acquires a right of property on an object, and fashions it alone. The legitimacy of property rights appears to be decided on at the time of the initial acquisition of goods. How must these goods be distributed at time zero? For the libertarian, the question becomes particularly crucial, since the legitimacy of title deeds is decided on then, once and for all. Afterwards, it will be too late. The owner will be substituted to the citizen, and the right of veto will be lost. One can easily see how this conception of justice quickly leads us to a spinning wheel. We are essentially finite beings, led – and misled – by chance; in other words, we are above all lacking in foresight. We buy a ticket to watch Chamberlain play, and the latter does not know any better than to get hold of all the drinkable water. This is a hard blow, to say the least, which could not be foreseen and, had we predicted it, we would not have gone to watch that game. But, according to libertarianism, the accomplished fact (the ticket purchase) implies Chamberlain's right to deprive us of water. By surrendering our right of veto at time zero, we have given up a justice that would rectify fortune's whims: if basketball is fashionable, it is considered fair that Chamberlain can deprive us of water; if basketball is out of fashion, it is thought fair for Chamberlain to die of dehydration. Far from questioning facts on the level of deserts, needs or even equal dignity,

Nozick's justice turns out to be in practice only an appendix serving as a backing of circumstances.

Libertarianism is thus led to mistake the fact (of material exchange) with the right (of the citizen). The importance of the principle of legitimate initial acquisition can thus be taken in. The point is purely and simply to predict everything that will happen, and settle as early as time zero all the collective problems in terms of the initial distribution of goods. It is only on this condition that citizens can give their agreement to this initial acquisition. The simplicity of Nozick's solution (the 'Lockean clause') can therefore only leave one dissatisfied. According to this clause (Locke, 1690), everyone is supposed to be able to appropriate the goods which have no owners, as long as it does not deteriorate other people's conditions of life. This clause seems reasonable only because it guarantees us that we will not suffer from the creation of title deeds. Nevertheless, it guarantees our conditions of life only at time zero, while demanding that we recognise the legitimacy of deeds for future times. Such a demand is not only unreasonable, it is extremely reckless, and one would have to be irrational to sign anything at all at time zero. We are indeed offered the creation of a common law, in the face of which our reason will then have to resign. The right will only depend on an irreproachable genealogy which will have to go back to the origin, and in such a situation, we will have no other choice but to give up our right of veto.

Such a historical theory of the right stumbles upon inescapable dead ends. Thus, some libertarians want an appropriation to remain possible even if the Lockean clause happened not to be observed. In order for instance to allow for the development of an otherwise impossible economic activity, they contemplate the possibility of compensations which, once given, will, through the application of the first occupier's right, bring the degree of well-being of those now deprived of the use of a resource back to the degree that existed before this appropriation. This is typically the case when the appropriation is operated on resources which the members of a community enjoy in common, such as an enclosure trespassing on a communal forest over which everyone has a customary right to help themselves to wood used privately.[3] It is then significant that the libertarian is con-

3 It is worth pointing out that, historically, Locke (1690) formulated the clause which Nozick now makes his own in order to find some legitimacy in the enclosures which affect commoners.

fronted with an inextricable dilemma to calculate the amount of these compensations. Either, in order to remain consistent with his historical theory of the right, he only takes into account the effective use made of the rare resource at the time of appropriation, or he also takes into account its potential use, that is, a use which can become effective under the pressure of climatic or demographic changes, or even of the individuals' preferences. In the first case, it is true that he remains true to his theory, but he falls prey to all the critics which have just been made. He gives his preference to a solution which hurts our deepest-rooted convictions on justice. By occupying a forest or giving a very low compensation, on the grounds that there exist nearby other forests where everyone is free to keep on going to fetch some wood, can it still be regarded as fair if, in the following days, one discovers that these forests are unfortunately being eaten away by some disease, and are going to disappear? The new owner finds himself in the situation of having appropriated all the available wood, and being able to prevent anyone from building or shelter or getting warm. There is *de facto* no difference with the example taken above, of an individual freely getting hold of a water spring, and leaving everyone without water – a situation which was already regarded as unfair. However, taking into account the potential uses of a resource demands that one should be able to reappraise the indemnities with respect to changes in the situation, at any moment *a priori*, which is completely contradictory with a truly historical theory of right. Formally, this amounts simply to admitting a right of veto, whatever generation one belongs to. In the end, either, in order to remain consistent, the libertarian only takes into account the effective uses at time zero, but the situation can be unfair or become so, or he also takes into account the potential uses which individuals can make of an appropriate resource – themselves, or those of a future generation, to whom communal rights can be legitimately transferred – but by doing so, he gives up on what was his initial ambition: a historical theory making it possible to speak of a property right *with no restriction*.

In the end, libertarianism always fails for the same reason: it gives away everyone's right of veto for a random title deed. In the process, not only does it spread 'natural' rights as easily as counterfeit money, since the value of a right stems from the fact that no one has opposed their veto, while everyone was able to do so, but it also relies on an invalid conception of the social contract, by making it a contract which must be really signed, rather than a model of reasoning which must never be abandoned, even for a title deed. Libertarianism thus very logically indulges into historicism. Everything was set at the origin of times, through a supposedly unanimous agreement on the distribution of goods. Then, deprived of a veto, it will be impossible for us to agree on justice, and the right will be dictated by facts. The only thing left for us to do will be to follow facts (the voluntary transfers of title deeds), to return to what the Ancients had regarded as fair. It must be clearly seen that if we unfold all the consequences of such a theory, we come, like Nozick, to the point of justifying slavery in the name of one's freedom to use one's property.[4] The trappings which the logic of libertarianism leads to could not be better illustrated. It is indeed because this theory did not lend enough attention to the necessity of the right of veto that it becomes enmeshed in procedures which end up guaranteeing someone's ownership of someone else's freedom.

To be complete, we would have to add that some have taken good note of the impossibility of trying to hold together the libertarian principle of self ownership, and the Kantian principle whereby individuals should be regarded as ends. They have then tried to make individual property derive from the mutual advantage that one finds in it being guaranteed. We encounter the rational choice theory in this case. But a mutual advantage contract, which is close to a contract of the Hobbesian type (Gauthier, 1986), falls prey to the same criticisms. It is not consistent to think that it could lead us to leave the state of conflict, here called 'state of nature'. Examining the reasons for this will lead us, more broadly, to a critic of the utilitarian explanations of cooperation.

4 That is, 'voluntary' slavery, not the one obtained through force or cunning. Nozick's reasoning (1974, p. 346) goes as follows. I would not be the owner of myself if I was not free to sell title deeds on my own person. However, since self-ownership disappears if I sell myself totally, Nozick immediately adds that there 'exist' some limits to this alienation (1974, p. 283): '[Slaves] are not completely enslaved.' After this contrivance, he concludes: 'Since this very extensive domination of some persons by others arises by a series of legitimate steps, via voluntary exchanges, from an initial situation that is not unjust, it itself is not unjust. But though not unjust, some find it intolerable.' Let us point out again that, on the contrary, in the context of justice as unanimous agreement, it appears clearly (see chapter 3) that the expression 'voluntary slavery' can only be formed at the cost of a pure sophism.

## 2. The Drawbacks of Utilitarian Explanations of Cooperation

### 2.1 *Is it possible to come out of a Hobbesian state of nature?*

According to Hobbes (1651), in the state of nature, if two individuals want the same rare good, they inevitably become enemies fighting for its appropriation. Moreover, this potential appropriation always becomes very precarious, because every individual must constantly be wary of others, who may at any time rob her or take her life away. All in all, the state of nature is a permanent state of wariness, where everyone is everyone else's enemy. In this state of generalised malevolence, it can easily be understood that man derives no pleasure from the company of his fellow human beings. Since he mistrusts them, he tends to avoid them. In this state of war where 'there is no way for any man to secure himself, so reasonable, as anticipation [...]; that is, by force, or wiles' (chap. XIII), there is no room for sociability.

It is not necessary to think that such a state ever existed: 'I believe it never was generally so, over all the word.' (Hobbes, *ibid.*) Empirically, it is not impossible to find situations which resemble it in some respects. But this is not the main point. Hobbes proposes above all a model to understand the emergence of the State, not a historical analysis. He will be followed on this by almost all those who, after him, will postulate a state of nature. This state will be described in very different terms, from Locke to Kant, through Rousseau, but no one will claim to see in it a real historical state. Postulating a natural state is a modelling procedure, a way of building a behavioural model under hypotheses which does not have much to envy to a more contemporary scientific procedure. In the spirit, researches founded on game theory, which we will tackle later, do not proceed any differently. The difference resides in the way hypotheses are validated, rather than in the ambition to build models to understand reality.

This is how for Hobbes, given this state of war, the emergence of the Leviathan State finds a plausible explanation. Since everyone's life is constantly under threat, everyone has an interest in finding the way out of this situation. For it is a law of nature, discovered by reason, 'by which a man is forbidden to do, that, which is destructive of his life, or takes away the means of preserving the same' (chap. XIV). Every man is naturally inclined to seek the safety of peace, and it is only as long as he has not found the way to turn it into a lasting state that 'he may seek, and use, all helps, and advantages of war'. He sees this means very naturally and very rationally. It requires: 'that a man be willing, when others are so too, as far-forth, as for peace and defence of himself he shall think it necessary, to lay down his right to all things; and be contented with so much liberty against other men, as he would allow other men against himself.' To get out of the state of permanent war, everyone eventually concludes a pact with everyone, whereby all give up their unlimited right on every thing, and transfer it to a sovereign (who may be individual or collective), who is *ipso facto* entrusted with the duty of getting this agreement to be respected, that is, to promulgate laws which he regards as useful for civil peace. His primary mission is to guarantee this peace through legal force. Let us note that since the convention which is at the foundation of social ties consists in a transfer of everyone's unlimited right to the sovereign, the latter's right is necessarily unlimited. Everyone recognise as theirs any action of the absolute sovereign, whatever it may be.

Just like previously for the state of nature, this theory of sovereignty does not imply thinking that a social pact must really have been concluded at a given moment, long ago in the past. For, on the contrary, it can be argued that this would lead to a contradiction, for the historical existence of the original contract leads logically to the idea that 'people have the right to free themselves from it as they please' (Kant, 1793, II), which is neither Hobbes's, nor most contractualists' position. In Kant's case, for instance, it will become very clear that the social contract is nothing else than an Idea of reason, that is, a rational principle in the light of which any constitution may be measured. Changing the constitution is one thing, and abolishing the social contract is another. It is true that, by comparison with the absolute power of the Leviathan, Hobbes's people have very little means. But this is another discussion.

Apart from the conviction – which is contrary to the libertarian theory – that no history must be sought here, it remains that almost everything separates the Hobbesian pact from the social contract as it is understood by liberals like Kant or Rawls. For the latter, the contractual procedure is linked to the obligation in which we find ourselves to regard individuals as ends, that is, to treat them *fairly* or with equal considerateness, like reasonable beings, whom we recognise as a legitimate and autonomous source of demands. We might as well say that other people's moral value does not depend on their capacity of nuisance, nor on advantages we could obtain from them. The social contract is an idea which makes it possible to determine the objective contents of our moral obligation, because it requires that everyone should be taken into account in an *impartial* way. On the contrary, for Hobbes, or, in a more contemporary way, for David Gauthier (1986), there is no *a priori* moral equality behind natural inequality. Actions or opinions have no intrinsic moral value; they only express subjective preferences – as demanded by utilitarianism too. Thus, for Gauthier, it is not because a crime is supposedly unfair that it should be avoided, but because everyone finds a mutual advantage in it not being committed. Everyone indeed finds interest in signing a convention which leads them to refrain from committing crimes since they will not need, for instance, to waste a lot of time and energy on their own defence. These conventions are substituted to morality in the traditional sense, even if they are not strictly speaking moral, but rather the mere result of a rational choice based on opinions which are deprived of any moral aspect. In a reasoning of the Hobbesian type, morality, and therefore justice, are thus only artefacts.

In methodological terms, the model is individualistic, and there is no doubt that every actor proves rational – but in a very restrictive way. Everyone is simply defending their selfish interest, by maximising their utility. It cannot be said that this is enough to turn Hobbes into a utilitarian. His actor's psychology is poles apart from the one which the founders of this school of thought will prefer to see in it, partly as a reaction against his ideas actually. It is essentially in reaction to Hobbes (1651) that Shaftesbury (1711) will develop the opposite model of benevolence. And, as we know, this model will be taken up, although in a modified way, by Scottish philosophy – especially, via Hutcheson (1725), by Hume (1739–1740) and Smith (1759), who will support the hypothesis of natural sympathy. Neither is contractualism – to say the least – a characteristic of classical utilitarian thinking. However, Hobbes's reasoning is essentially consequentialist, and his agent's rationality is limited to its instrumental aspect, which, in this case, clearly brings him closer to a utilitarian model. Justice is only the means of self-preservation. It derives from everyone's self-interest, an interest which comes first in the reasoning. No one aims at justice as an end or at some deontological principles. On the contrary, everyone only aims to promote their own good; and the 'strength' of this reasoning, whereby such a promotion is impossible without the use of a central coercive agency, stems from the fact that the hypothesis concerning this good (or this utility) is – or at least seems to be – extraordinarily undemanding. The self-esteem which must be regarded here as natural is indeed not self-love. In more modern terms, we could say that it reflects the preservation instinct; and it is very difficult not to admit that this is not a natural fact. Even Rousseau, who was otherwise so opposed to Hobbes's doctrine, admitted that, contrary to self-love, which supposes an established social state to make sense, self-esteem, as a simple desire of self-preservation, truly characterises man in the state of nature.

However, for this Hobbesian argument to function efficiently, we must add another hypothesis, which is not contradictory with an optimisation of the good, but much stronger, and therefore far less acceptable (as a natural or a universal fact) than mere 'self-esteem'. The hypothesis of an actor who is reluctant to any risk must be made. *A priori*, the idea of an aversion to risk is not unreasonable. It is congruent both with the idea of avoiding what threatens one's self-preservation or one's belongings, and with that of a utility optimisation. The problem is that one must think of such aversion as *absolute*. A risk, however minimal, must always be avoided by an agent of the state of nature. This time, one is allowed to question whether a universal behaviour is being described. Even in the hold of a restricted rationality, on the contrary, aversion is always relative to the nature, the probability or the intensity of the impending risk. Otherwise, one would have to think that living in California, where everyone expects the Big One, or playing the lottery, or smoking, or even investing a small sum of money, in any economic venture would be either impossible, or the decision of a mad man. Aversion to risk must be measured for every case, and empirically. There are configurations where a rational actor turns out to be reluctant and others where he is not (Peretti-Watel, 2000). Every model which supposes a natural, absolute or universal aversion to risk is inapplicable. It takes the risk of being contradicted by the empirical data. However, let us see why this hypothesis must still be added in order to be able to follow Hobbes.

In the Hobbesian state of nature, there is indeed a postulated equality initially, but even Hobbes finds himself obliged to weaken this axiom which hardly corresponds to reality, at least as far as strength is concerned. How can one admit that a handicapped individual is as strong as one who is not? There are thus – and Hobbes admits it – weak people, and strong people. The weak can actually form coalitions in order to threaten a strong person. But the strong ones can also form a coalition in order to compel the weak. Actually, the facts of the state of nature are such (malevolence, defiance, etc.) that the strong necessarily dominate the weak. There is by definition no justice, nor any morality, to protect the weakest against the victorious aggressions of the strongest. And it is actually rational that the strong should tyrannise the weak. If they did not do so, they would take the chance of seeing the weak threaten them. Hobbes (1651, XIII) is as clear as can be on this:

> From this diffidence of one another, there is no way for any man to secure himself, so reasonable, as Anticipation; that is, by force, or wiles, to master the persons of all men he can, so long, till he see no other power great enough to endanger him: and this is no more than his own conservation requires, and is generally allowed.

Logically, then, if one admits the Hobbesian hypotheses, it must be admitted that the state of nature leads to the tyranny of the strongest. It is his interest, whatever meaning is given to the term. How then could he be led to want to sign a non-aggression pact with the weakest? Why would he rationally renounce his unlimited freedom which makes it possible for him to use the weakest and their belongings as suits him? It is very easy to see what the weakest gets from the social pact in terms of protection and safety, but it is hard to see how the selfish interest of the strongest could lead him to agree to the weakest's plea for a pact. Even if, following Gauthier (1986), we give up on basing the social contract on everyone's selfish interest and make it the result of a mutual profit calculation, the paradox remains. The strong have no interest – neither selfish, nor 'mutual' – in signing the pact, and therefore, unless they give up on their (restricted) rationality, they will not sign it.

For them to sign it there is no other solution, but to admit that they are totally and absolutely reluctant to a risk which is yet very minimal. The threat of the weak, even when it is only potential and very unlikely to be put into practice, is abhorrent to them, to the point of making them want to accept the pact they are offered, and give up their freedom on the one condition that everyone should do so. This disproportionate aversion to risk is not inconsistent with the Hobbesian model, since prudence also guides everyone in the state of nature, not as a moral faculty of course, but as a mere result of 'experience'. The problem is that this prudence is here translated into an aversion to risk which has become far too absolute to make it a natural or universal fact. It cannot be an intangible component of a rationality model – assuming that one wants to keep this model in contact with reality at all.

A rational individual is not reluctant to any risk *a priori*. A calculated risk easily dictates a rational behaviour, and from there, the hypothesis of an absolute aversion, which is the only one which, according to us, accounts for the social contract and the emergence of justice in a Hobbesian reasoning, must be rejected. Hobbes's or Gauthier's consequentialist theories, where justice is based on the calculation of everyone's interest, at a first or a second level,[5] eventually fail to explain the emergence of this justice. In the situation they describe, individuals will not find any way of getting out of the tyranny of the strongest. Other solutions will be found by utilitarians in order to keep on ensuring the priority of an optimisation of the good. But, as we shall see, they are hardly better.

### 2.2 *The Prisoner's Dilemma has no general predictive bearing*

The more contemporary reasonings based on a reflection on the Prisoner's Dilemma reinforce this conclusion. The uncountable books or articles which outline the dilemma, which is the most famous case of an application of game theory to a social situation,[6] enable us to be contented with a simplified presentation. First, the number of players can be reduced to two: X and Y. The games with *n* players generalise the results obtained for only two players by making the options more complex on questions which are not of any direct interest for us here. It is also a non-cooperative game. As in a Hobbesian state of nature, players are supposed not to be possessed *a priori* with any will to cooperate with each other at all costs. In concrete terms, this non-cooperation is simulated by a situation which forbids any communication between the players. Two prisoners, isolated in separate cells, will be enough. It means, among other things, that a player has no means of knowing if the other will adopt a rational strategy or not. The situation can also be slightly changed by allowing communication, or even negotiating an agreement. But in this case, the two players have no reason to trust each other and to take seriously the word given by the other. In

5 The search for mutual advantage is only one form of rational altruism: increasing the other's well-being makes it possible to increase one's own well-being. To a first-level egoism (increasing one's well-being without any regard for others), it substitutes a second-level egoism.

6 As for the application of game theory to social situations in general, Martin Shubik's work (1982) is usually regarded as a key reference.

other words, whatever the variation, no player can determine with certainty what a decision eventually made by her partner will be. A player is not co-operative *a priori*, but, obviously, if cooperation is likely to make her increase her profit, she will not be opposed to it in principle. In other words, the prisoner is rational in a restrictive sense. She is only interested in maximising her utility function. In the game theory terminology, this means that if she may choose a dominant strategy (= whatever the game option chosen by the other player, the player under observation will always derive a greater utility by choosing this line of conduct), she will necessarily adopt this strategy.

The dilemma is frequently associated (Tucker, 1950) with the story of a judge confronted with two prisoners suspected of a crime, and who refuse to speak. In the hope of getting them to start talking, the judge offers them the following deal:

1. If one of the prisoners denounces the other and the latter remains silent, the first one will receive 4 tokens, and the latter, 1 token;
2. If both remain silent, they will both receive 3 tokens;
3. If they both denounce each other, they will get 2 tokens each.

The prisoners know that when the game is over, the judge will convert the number of tokens they have into a multiple of a fixed prison remission, if they turn out to be convicted by a jury, which no one can anticipate. It is therefore in their interest to have as many tokens as possible. For greater ease, the possible gains are usually summed up in the form of table 15. In each cell, by convention, on the left of the semi-colon, one usually finds X's gains, and on the right, Y's gains.

Table 15 – *An Example of the Prisoner's Dilemma*

| | *Y tells nothing* | *Y denounces X* |
|---|---|---|
| X tells nothing | 3 ; 3 | 1 ; 4 |
| X denounces Y | 4 ; 1 | 2 ; 2 |

This table operates some simplifications (of symmetry and utility scale) relatively to a more general table which could have been considered. But since these simplifications have no effect on the general conclusion we are interested in, these figures can be retained, all the more as they also have the advantage of expressing directly each player's preferences as to the four solutions of the game. Let us note that two restrictions must always be respected to make it possible to speak of the Prisoner's Dilemma. In table 16, we suppose: D < P < R < T and 2R > D + T (Rapoport and Chammah, 1965). The second inequality is useful mostly to discuss the repetition of the game (which will be tackled later), but it can be set down now with no loss in generality. In the end, we put ourselves here in the simplest situation of a game which is only played *once* and *simultaneously* by each of the players: a prisoner cannot hope to learn anything from a move made by the other.

Table 16 – *Prisoner's Dilemma*

| | *Y cooperates with X* | *Y does not cooperate with X* |
|---|---|---|
| X cooperates with Y | R ; R | D ; T |
| X does not cooperate with Y | T ; D | P ; P |

Let us now consider our prisoners and adopt X's viewpoint. With the values established in table 15, we can notice immediately that if she chooses to denounce Y, she gains more than if she chooses not to say anything – *whatever option Y chooses* (4, as opposed to 3 if Y cooperates, and 2 against 1 if Y does not cooperate). For X, denouncing Y is a dominant strategy. Given the symmetry of X's and Y's positions, it is easy to verify that denouncing X is also a dominant strategy for Y. If each prisoner is rational, even without knowing whether the other is too, there is therefore no other choice but not to cooperate. Therefore, if both players are rational, the game will get solved through the double defection of both players – a situation in which they only get two tokens, as indicated in the south-eastern cell in table 15.[7] Moreover, this solution constitutes an instance of a Nash equilibrium: none of the players has an interest in drawing away from it unilaterally.

Unfortunately, for the players, this Nash equilibrium is not a Pareto-optimality. The situation of a player could improve without deteriorating the other's. If everyone had chosen to cooperate, there would be a Pareto-optimum (north-western cell in table 15), but this optimum cannot be

7 It can be noticed that although each player's individual preference gives precedence to double cooperation over double defection, it is the latter solution which imposes itself as the collective preference.

reached in the conditions of the dilemma. In the end, this dilemma shows that (restricted) rationality leads each individual not to cooperate, even if the resulting collective situation is not the best or the most efficient that may be contemplated.

For an economist, this game translates familiar situations, and especially what happens when everyone seeks to get the best out of the collective good, while contributing to it as little as possible. In this case, everyone behaves as a free rider, but as a result, the collective good does not measure up to what could have been if everyone had chosen to fully contribute to it. And yet, by thinking of the common good, it would have been in every player's interest if everyone did not behave as a free rider, since everyone's situation would have been better. This is one of the basic problems of social cooperation, but whether this problem is examined in the right way is a wholly different question.

Of course, cooperation is not morality, and still less justice, but it nonetheless remains, at the level of generality where this dilemma lies, what seems to represent best its condition of possibility. It seems, at first sight – and, fortunately, at first sight only – that it is a serious blow for a non-Hobbesian orientation, or, more generally, for a non-utilitarian orientation. Rationality draws us away from cooperation, and it can be added, with Hobbes's reasoning in mind, that if actors want to leave this state of nature, they have no other solution but to tie their own hands by resorting to a central agency, a Leviathan State, or more simply, to norms, rules, laws, or whatever, which compel them to opt collectively in favour of the solution which will be optimal for everyone (north-west cell in table 15). This Hobbesian appendix is, however, paradoxical from the strict standpoint of the dilemma, since it implies that actors renounce strictly dominant decisions. They are asked to give up their rationality in the name of rationality! This is why many regard this solution as inconsistent from the perspective of the model's hypotheses. One has to look for other solutions and hope to overcome the dilemma, especially, as we shall see, by reiterating the game an infinite number of times with the same players. For the time being, and without any iteration, nor with any *coup-de-force*, it seems necessary to admit that, unless one denies one's own nature in the name of one's nature, there is no way of leaving the 'state of nature'. Is it that certain, however?

The uncountable experimentations which have been conducted in order to test with real players the Prisoner's Dilemma do not systematically confirm what it predicts (Frank, Gilovich, Reagan, 1993). Observations are sometimes in conformity with predictions, and sometimes, it is the reverse: players spontaneously choose to cooperate. And, as a matter of fact, one single example is enough to show that non-cooperation is very unlikely if the four parameters of the model are given the values shown in table 17.

Table 17 – *A low-risk Prisoner's Dilemma*

| | *Y cooperates* | *Y does not cooperate* |
|---|---|---|
| X cooperates | 20,000 ; 20,000 | 0 ; 20,000.01 |
| X does not cooperate | 20,000.01 ; 0 | 0.01 ; 0.01 |

These expected gains respect what the structure of a Prisoner's Dilemma imposes, and therefore, the dominant strategy has not changed. It is still in X's 'interest' to choose not to cooperate; and the same applies to Y. However, it is such a strange behaviour that it will hardly be adopted. In a real case, everyone clearly sees that by opting for non-cooperation, they refuse to take the chance of losing a cent in order to win 20,000 € (if gains are expressed in this currency). It is not necessary to be an inveterate gambler to accept such a risk. Considering the low sum at stake to obtain a very substantial gain, almost everyone will accept it. The values taken by the parameters thus lead to the opposite result of what was expected following the dilemma model. This time, one would have to be irrational not to try to cooperate.[8]

This example shows that, just as in the case of Hobbes's state of nature, the Prisoner's Dilemma adds another component to rationality, without saying so. In addition to profit maximisation, each player must be assumed to be possessed with a total aversion to risk. In the same way as it had proven necessary in the Hobbesian state of nature to presuppose an absolute aversion to risk in order to explain that everyone did sign the social

8 Imagine that you are a scientist, and that your research centre asks you to organise a series of experiments in order to check that, in real cases, the prediction which the Prisoner's Dilemma allows you to make does indeed come true when the values of the parameters are those which have just been fixed in table 17. Since you are a great scientist and your model enables you to predict that the game will always lead to the double choice of non-cooperation, your laboratory only allocates you 2 cents of research funding for each experiment carried out. In particular, this means that if the players happened to choose to cooperate, you would have to fund the experiment from your own pocket (40,000 € each time). Would you really be willing to organise these experiments?

pact, similarly, here, it is only under this second hypothesis that the dilemma can retain a predictive aspect in every case. Without this hypothesis, it can on the reverse be taken by default. For certain values of the parameters, which respect the inequalities restated above, but which are impossible to determine *a priori*, any actor, without suffering from a random fit of lunacy, will most naturally opt for cooperation. Now, as previously, a *total* aversion to risk is not a plausible and neutral hypothesis to build a rationality model. As we have already said, such an aversion is contrary to the empirical data. Aversion to risk is a matter of degree. It depends on the context and must be empirically judged. Assuming it to be total, natural or universal disqualifies it to be a component of a *general* rationality model. Assuming it to be relative leads to greater realism, but does not help knowledge a lot, since it is impossible to claim to fix *a priori* the exact risk threshold above which a rational individual swings over from non-cooperation to cooperation. This is why, in the end, the Prisoner's Dilemma will never have the hoped-for level of generality.

This internal critic of the dilemma has one advantage and one inconvenient. Its advantage is that it enters the realm of the rational choice theory to show that it leads to a dead end if one claims to provide a general framework of explanation. Its inconvenient is that it does not let the rational choice theorist speechless. First, he may point out that between a situation which is in conformity with the dilemma and one which is not, it is possible to evidence the empirical intervention of the 'aversion to risk' factor. Even if this leads the rational choice theory to only provide *ad hoc* explanations, this is not a small achievement, and after all, it would not be the first time this would be considered sufficient. For many, it would still be a serious drawback, and this is why the rational choice theorist will endeavour to find a consistent retaliation – that is, one which, for the reasons stated above, will not be similar to Hobbes's '*coup-de-force*'.

Indeed, it must be noted that even if the situation of a Prisoner's Dilemma does not necessarily lead to non-cooperation, it remains undeniable that in exchange for a fixation of adequate values to the parameters, the pernicious effect of this dilemma as to the aggregation of preferences can also be observed. As situations of cooperation are plenty, it is therefore necessary to show how the Prisoner's Dilemma can also account for them, without resorting to a low aversion to risk, of course. Some think this is what will be achieved by making the same players play the dilemma an infinite number of times. This strategy will lead us to a second criticism, which is more radical. This type of modelling lacks an essential dimension of social interaction: its fair or unfair character. It can even be said that everything is done, here and also more generally with every restricted rational choice model, to evacuate it. All in all, the point will no longer be to show that the claim to generality is excessive, that the hyperbole cannot be accepted, but rather that the theory is too restrictive anyway not to be condemned to presuppose the harmony which it claims to account for.

### 2.3 *The myth of a spontaneous cooperation*

The project underpinned by searching the effects of mere repetition of rounds is not new. If one wants to confute the deontological approach, since the Hobbesian solution is not consistent, one must show that cooperation can appear either mechanically or spontaneously even while actors are and remain purely consequentialist selfish beings having no other interest than to maximise their utility. Adopting the opposite model of altruists caring only for the other's well-being with no regard for their own would not be very convincing either. There would be a great risk of being drawn back to a platitude which would lead the rational choice model to produce nothing but tautologies: with a fixed risk, if individuals cooperate in a given situation, it is because they are altruistic, and if they do not cooperate, it is because they are selfish or, to be more sophisticated, it is because their level of altruism is not high enough to make up for their level of selfishness. In any case, as we shall see, altruism contains too many paradoxes in connection with its social efficacy to solve cooperation problems. To make sure that the citizen or a fair spectator or an autonomous subject acting out of duty or following an ethics of discussion *(Diskursethik)* play no part, it is necessary to stay within the sphere of selfishness, and show that such selfishness does not prevent efficient social cooperation. Then, morality and justice will appear superfluous, unnecessary or useless to avoid conflict or coercion. Under certain conditions to be specified, a single and simple reiteration of the dilemma must suffice.

For the umpteenth time in science history (Parodi, 2004), we are once more searching for a process without a subject, or for a structuring machine or for a social order as a natural order. Once again, we expect this little boost of Providence, which would make it possible to defy random laws, as if one could revert from disorder to order at no cost (Forsé, 1989), as if some 'invisible hand' was here to help us shift from anarchy to a 'well-ordered society'. All the past failures and all the evidence testifying to the impossibility of such a gamble will not change anything to it. We obviously prefer to be held by the 'invisible hand' than to take our fate in our hands, and be responsible. It is impossible not to gape at the lure of such a phoenix.

In order to clearly show what is at stake, it may be useful to return to the explanation for the passage from the state of nature to the civilised state. When men's interests start clashing, one considers they can choose three solutions: (i) to arm themselves and kill one another, (ii) to surrender out of the fear of death, thus ensuring for themselves the life of a slave, or (iii) to agree by mutually backing down on their claim to the object of the conflict. The latter possibility is of course the civilised response. But for the champion of the rational choice theory, it has the inconvenient of doing away with the postulate of utility maximisation, to the benefit of a civil liberty negotiated between free and reasonable people, just as, for the anarchist, it has the inconvenient of abandoning the natural freedom where everyone help themselves as they please, or rather as they can. This is why the rational choice theory demands that men should only have the choice between solutions (i) and (ii). In the Nietzschean perspective which it inconsiderately abides by, this postulate means that one must know whether they are the master or the slave, and act accordingly; on the contrary, when it comes to becoming a citizen (iii), the question is not even asked.

The Prisoner's Dilemma, as we have seen, deals with the same problem and the same stake, under a different guise. From the formal model of the four skilfully weighted cells, it is easy to tell the story of savages who decide or not to live in peace rather than the story of some prisoners. Not to denounce amounts to wanting peace, with the risk of being enslaved by the bellicose ones. Mutual denunciation corresponds to the state of nature, and this state can be preferable to slavery: the two savages deal each other a few blows, and then each one goes his own way. They will not live together, end of the story. If we look at the Hobbesian version, postulating the impossibility to communicate or trust one another, on which the Prisoner's Dilemma rests, is already present. The point is to refuse a political solution whereby both parties negotiate and decide together which order will be theirs. But is justice as an alternative to selfishness, and to altruism too, as a matter of fact, thereby confuted? It is clear that this is not the case, since it is excluded *a priori*. An individual may well be a free rider or a Good Samaritan, or rather an elaborate mixture of both; but in any case he is forbidden to be or become a citizen. The orientation is all mapped out from the beginning but the conditions in which harmony appears spontaneously have to be explained. Of course, the catch consists in falling into the Leibnizian solution of pre-established harmony (Leibniz, 1710) – a catch which, as we shall see, will not be avoided. This is why, eventually, rational choice theorists will end up believing in miracles: they want to avoid Nietzsche's conclusion, of a permanent state of nature, without going through the idea that each party freely accept not to maximise their utility by virtue of a unanimous agreement.

Attempts to 'solve' the dilemma in such a context are plenty. In particular, we owe to Hume (1740, III, 2, II) the idea that cooperation or respect for the rule could very well be gradually born and become increasingly firm through 'our repeated experience of the inconveniences of transgressing it. [...] This experience assures us still more, that the sense of interest has become common to all our fellows, and gives us confidence of the future regularity of their conduct.' As we have seen, if individuals are absolutely selfish and cannot stand any risk at all, the result is hardly thrilling for each of them. But Hume was far from abiding by such a radical anthropology. On the contrary, he thought that individuals feel sympathy and that it made them at least a little generous towards others; it is true that it amounts to hardly anything at all, and they actually stay predominantly selfish, but if the dilemma reoccurs many and many a time, and individuals start to anticipate it, it could very well be that from this ferment of generosity, a lasting cooperation, worthy of the name, would be born. Or at least, this is the main idea. And yet, does sympathy really change anything to the ins and outs?

We should start by pointing out again that justice is not built on sympathy; how could it be thought that sympathy (or even empathy) is a solution, and not a problem? The preferred person blurs the impartial judgment and introduces the idea of corruption. In small societies, regarded as a large family, it is still possible to be deceived and believe that generosity produces balance; in large ones, sympathy is less at the origin of a fair cooperation than of clans or clienteles which undermine such cooperation. This is actually accounted for by game theory itself. If several groups of individuals each play the Prisoner's Dilemma and there exists in each of them a sufficient dose of altruism to lead to the cooperative solution, it does not necessarily result in an increase of efficiency at the overall level, as long as there are, as economists say, externalities between groups – in other words, as long as the well-being of a group is affected by the decisions made in other groups. As summarised by Pierre Cahuc and Hubert Kempf (2000):

> Local altruism works in favour of a local cooperation which has no reason to reach a socially efficient solution at the global level, since individuals do not control all the consequences of their decisions. Local cooperation is therefore not a panacea. More seriously, local cooperation can have some negative effects. Cooperation within a given group can have an unfavourable impact on the well-being of individuals who belong to other groups. This phenomenon occurs if externalities within the groups and between the groups carry opposite signs. [...] By taking the reasoning further, it is possible to show that local cooperation can accentuate the inefficacy of the non-coordinated individual decisions when inter- and intragroup externalities carry opposite signs. In this case, altruism, by acting in favour of local cooperation, turns out to be globally counter-productive.

The argument is actually not counter-intuitive. If, from a political standpoint, a society is made of separatist groups with different projects, the stronger cooperation between the members of each group is, the weaker the cooperation between groups or the whole of society is. Local altruism may threaten overall social cohesion when it cannot internalise the externalities between groups and the latter turn out to be sufficiently negative to lead to a deterioration of the common well-being. The limited generosity introduced by Hume thus does not change much to the dilemma issue, except by cultivating a zone of darkness in the reasoning. Selfishness is the principle of explanation which is merely counteracted by an altruism which is more or less strong when the real no longer follows. Neither the conflict between the selfish behaviour of each individual, nor the conflict between their altruistic behaviours leads to spontaneous cooperation. How could one believe that an obscure mixture between these two contraries could lead to anything else? Whether selfish or altruistic, it will be necessary to come to an agreement in order to find a way out. That said, can the repetition of the dilemma not lead to modify this diagnosis?

Can it not be imagined that if a certain dose of altruism animates players who are led to meet several times, cooperation will consequently be all the more irretrievably affected than if they were merely selfish? Not necessarily, if we follow B. Douglas Bernheim and Oded Stark (1988). On the one hand, altruism favours immediate cooperation, but with all the reservations already formulated, on the other hand, it plays against sanctions (defection in the terms of the dilemma) which a player may apply in the event of a disregard of cooperation during a previous round. Indeed, it should not be forgotten that an altruist who sanctions a player sanctions herself. Consequently, it is obvious that if this second effect of altruism dominates the first one, the cooperative solution will *de facto* be put at a disadvantage. This paradox of altruism adds to all those already encountered, and leads Cahuc and Kempf conclude that: 'The altruists, incapable of applying sufficiently harsh sanctions, cannot compel one another to honour commitments enabling them to reach socially desirable situations.' Altruism, or a limited generosity, is not more of a panacea with the repetition of rounds, than it is without it.

It is then better to stick to the postulate of utility maximisation between players who remain egoists, while also taking up again Hume's idea that the mere repetition of the dilemma could lead to cooperation. This strategy is the basis of several theoretical speculations, the most famous of them being probably Axelrod's (1984). It is true that in terms of gas factories, Axelrod does innovate: to a lame mathematical demonstration, he prefers the biased computerized tournament. The problem which he seeks to solve is indeed the one we are interested in here: can a common convention naturally emerge from a confrontation of egoisms, through its repetition in time? In other words, can the Prisoner's Dilemma be solved by using iteration, by evidencing through successive adjustments a sort of mutually beneficial convention? For Axelrod, the answer is clearly positive, and actually, adjustment is so natural that, according to his own words, the protagonists do not even need a brain to reach the final 'convention'! Even the most naturalistic of all naturalists had never gone to such an extreme. For many, the human brain remains a natural fact, and one has to accommodate it, while trying to evacuate men and their freedom to explain social life. Axelrod takes the argument to its logical end; if human freedom has nothing to do with fixing a social order, if this order can be obtained mechanically, then mere computerized automates should manage to cooperate.

Not a little is at stake. So far, on the basis among other things of Leibniz's philosophical intuitions and Mandeville's moral fables, brilliantly integrated by Smith (1776) in *The Wealth of Nations*, economics was born by making up for itself the model of a *homo œconomicus* whose actions, though derived from mere selfish interest (or, better still, from rational altruism) end up assembling harmoniously, to the point of forming a balance, under the influence of an invisible hand. However, for many, and of course for the detractors, this invisible hand remained a problem to unravel. To avoid seeing it as the intervention of some Providence, which is obviously hard to admit from a scientific point of view, there remained to prove that it was not a *Deus ex-machina.* It was necessary to show that the umbilical cord could be broken between a monadology and its primary Cause. Consequently, if one can exhibit a model where, through the *mere* mechanical adjustment of egoisms, a socially efficient – or optimal in Pareto's sense – cooperation is eventually established, without, of course, presupposing any pre-established harmony, then the invisible hand will have lost all its mystery and, by repercussion, many reluctances formulated against the *homo œconomicus*, in its claim to provide the fundamental basis of any scientific analysis of social interactions, will collapse. As for justice, it will only have to be a derived product of the good optimised by the *homo œconomicus.* But we will only have gone full circle, according to us, if it can be shown that justice and the market, with no hindrance of any sort, of course, are intrinsically linked. We have seen that this is what libertarians have endeavoured to do, but with the serious confusions already pointed out.

Let us start by examining the principle of the computerized tournaments expounded in Axelrod's book before coming to its application to the dilemma itself. It is hardly possible to go into all the details of these long and tedious tournaments between programmes, but the reader graced with such patience will be able to verify that the following story provides a true summary as far as methodology is concerned. For the man in the street, hours are a convention which makes it possible for people to coordinate themselves. In itself, this convention is arbitrary. It can very well be decided upon at random, the essential being that there should be a unanimous agreement that everyone will adopt the result of this random choice (for instance, $h = 0$ on the Greenwich longitude). However, a small group of people do believe in the existence of 'natural hours', which would be at about 2 hours before what has been the common convention so far. Of course, the further away one draws from this central two-hour value, the less people will believe in it (let us say, without it being imperative, that the distribution is Gaussian). People, enthusiastic about such an idea, decide to organise a tournament in order to find out what the 'best' hour is, which one can be said to be the most 'natural'. The principle is simple. After changing the time on their watches according to their convictions as to what the exact natural time is, each competitor will compare their time with the others'. The time which will guarantee the best coordination is the one which will indicate a time which will most often be close to the others'. This will be the winning watch, and it will give the final natural time. But, now, a common woman finds herself involved in the tournament, without being informed of the new naturalistic theory. She will therefore stick to the notion that time is a convention, and choose it randomly. For her, the essential remains that everyone should agree on the same arbitrary choice. As a result, our common woman obviously loses the tournament. She even comes last (or in any case there is a high probability that she will), whereas the person who put her clock back by two hours *exactly* is delighted: she found the natural time.

How does one end up with such an absurd situation? In order to understand its purpose, we have to keep in mind Leibniz's principle of pre-established harmony. Since individuals have no way of agreeing on a convention ('monads have no windows'), it must be admitted that they each follow their own law (their watches) but that God, as a good watchmaker, has harmoniously adjusted these individual laws from the start, which accounts for their 'natural' coordination. This principle can easily be transposed to the tournament and its 'harmonious' selection of participants. Each watch is one of the programmes taking part in the tournament. All the 'enthusiasts' believe that cooperation comes out of selfishness, allied with a form of 'taming'. The non-cooperator (the person who is too far from natural time) must be punished, the cooperator (the person who is close to natural time or, better still, who changes the time on her watch by exactly two hours) should be rewarded, and the reverse should never occur – this is what a truly 'blind' nature should obviously have considered too. This is why the programme which plays at random, that of our common woman who adopts the only obvious solution because time is a shared convention, comes last in the tournament.

Let us now apply this procedure to the Prisoner's Dilemma and imagine, since we are suggested so, two random decerebrate organisms, which have the choice between denouncing the other and not saying anything. By introducing the threat 'if he denounces me, I will denounce him – if he doesn't say anything, I won't either', one can hope to *tame* the other into not saying anything. This threat corresponds to the 'tit for tat' strategy, or, more classically, to the *lex talionis*: 'an eye for an eye'. It is not through negotiation that the other should be made to understand how to cooperate, but through denunciations. It is thus possible to have the feeling that 'cooperation' is brought about without having to be discussed. The other ends up understanding that if he remains egoist, he will lose in the process; and it is hands in hands, through a reciprocal fear of future revenges, that everyone cooperates. Now, this is a very extraordinary myth, where civil peace emerges spontaneously from a world of brutes.

On a purely technical level, however, this is impossible to demonstrate. Without going into too much detail, let us see why. First, the Prisoner's Dilemma cannot be played by the same participants a finite number of times, known by everyone in advance. In this case, the strategy would settle on what is optimal for the last move, and then on the last-before-one with respect to the last one, and by a regression, the whole game would be determined from the start. The duration must either be random (for instance, the game stops when one of the participants dies) or infinite. *The tit for tat strategy always consists in cooperating in the first move, and then in acting exactly like the other player in the previous round.* The well-being of two players applying this strategy finds itself optimised, since it leads them to cooperate. However, does this mean that defection is thereby completely dismissed? For this to be the case, one of the participants should have an interest in not wandering away from tit for tat unilaterally. In the game theory terminology, the tit for tat strategy must form a Nash equilibrium. Since the game includes an indeterminate series of iterations, a player cannot form an exact idea of the effective total amount of his future gains. However, he can evaluate the gain at a future occurrence by considering the (infinite) series of gains obtained by playing this round and by applying a reduction rate or an interest rate or a current value rate (according to the economic terminology selected). For instance, mutual cooperation yields, if $i$ is this interest rate, and taking up the writing conventions of table 16: $R + iR + i^2R +$ etc.; a series whose sum is worth: $R / (1 - i)$. We may now evaluate the impact of unilateral disregard for tit for tat strategy by a player. The effect of a defection for one single round, knowing that the other cooperates, and then of a return to tit for tat, knowing that the other no longer cooperates, is, on the gain of the player tempted by such a defection, equal to $T + iD$, instead of $R + iR$ if the player had stuck to tit for tat. She is thus deterred from such a defection if $i > (T - R) / (R - D)$. Thus, with a sufficient interest rate, conveying the idea that the future carries enough weight by comparison with the present, this example of deviation does not maximise the utility function of the player who draws away from tit for tat. Consequently, with the added conditions of a sufficiently high interest rate and of an indefinite duration of the game, the tit for tat strategy forms a Nash equilibrium.

Cooperation in the first round, an infinite or uncertain duration of the game and the interest rate are not, however, truly neutral hypotheses. In game theory, the folk theorem is there to remind us of this, since according to this theorem, in a repeated non-cooperative game (such as the Prisoner's Dilemma) there is necessarily a *multiplicity* of equilibriums[9] (Guerrien, 1995). It is therefore only through a partial selection of some hypotheses that it is possible to enhance one given equilibrium rather than another. And, since it is not technique (which is neutral) but this set of hypotheses which is at stake, it is important to grasp in what respect it entails difficulties as to the content.

A calculator is programmed to maximise its gains or minimise its losses when faced with another calculator of the same kind. No one possesses the faculty of negotiation. The hope of the first calculator is to succeed in leading the second to cooperate. It will be noticed that if it really was able to do so, it would be even more beneficial for it to tame the other into submission. But the real difficulty is to make the other understand a 'convention'. Axelrod would like to believe that the second calculator will end up understanding that he will be the winner if he respects the 'cooperative convention' induced by the strategy of the first calculator. And he explains that the first calculator takes risks which will eventually prove paying, since the second will understand that he may get punished if he profits by this. However, the story is arbitrary, and it is consequently very easy to turn it upside down: the first calculator does not take any risk systematically since otherwise, the second will eventually understand that he can profit by this. Given the initial hypotheses, it would irrational for him not to seek to do so: if one of them ends up being convinced that he must cooperate, the other has every interest to subjugate him. Thus, the convention which supposedly emerges is only a sham: those who take it seriously will simply be the gullible of the story.

In any case, there never was in this model any convention between the two calculators. If they maximise their move, they only look at the future, not the past. Rancour, remorse, do not exist for the calculator: everyone acts according to future earnings, not according to past promises. This is why the one who believes that it must respect the contract will be fooled. How could such an obvious fact be forgotten? Calculators do not know how to trust one another. Instead of this, we are told about interest rates: everyone cooperates in the name of the future of cooperation. Yet, this is

9 Systematic defection is also a (perfect) Nash equilibrium in the case of a repeated Prisoner's Dilemma.

quite a strange idea on the part of theorists who, otherwise (Olson, 1965), lay a great store by the problem of the free tickets and free riders. The sacrifice consented here and now by the calculator does not prevent him from maximising his utility, for this sacrifice is an investment in cooperation itself. But, for this, as we have just seen, the return on the investment must be superior to the sacrifice consented. Which return on investment are we then talking about? I do not earn the other's trust, since the other is forgetful of the past. The only way to swell this 'return on investment' consists in turning cooperation into an institution which has a value for itself. Mathematically, this idea is translated by a postponement to an infinite time the moment of the 'return on the investment'. For the poor mortals that we are, this amounts to endowing the institution with a sacred value: cooperation, which one claims to account for, becomes the fruit on an irrational belief in the intangible value of the said cooperation. The announced catch thus closes: in order to explain the final harmony, it is necessary to fall back on a pre-established harmony. The calculators are programmed with the obligation to cooperate. One aims at accounting for the agreement, but *they already agree* to postpone the 'return on the investment' to the infinite. They already agree to sacrifice their finite, present, or even future well-being, in the name of infinite cooperation.

Eventually, this leads us to a tautology. The problem obviously does not reside in this tautology, which in itself is not deceptive, but in the fact that one assumes something has been proven in the process. Axelrod believes he has shown that in the long term some cooperation naturally appears between 'men', without them having to think about it reasonably. He is not the only one who thinks so, and one can only remain speechless in the face of the efforts made by a large community of scientists in order to 'solve' the Prisoner's Dilemma, as if there was anything to solve, once it has been said that prisoners can either decide to cooperate, or not. For indeed, as to contents, intention always remains the same. From Friedrich Hayek to Robert Axelrod, without forgetting John Maynard Smith, all these theorists explain to us that a well-ordered society ends up emerging from unreasonably rational behaviours. Only the painstaking 'technical detour' varies from one author to the next. And we thus end up with theories of self-organisation[10]

10 Researches known 'under various names, such as autopoiesis, cybernetics, homeostasis, spontaneous order, self-organisation, synergetics, systems theory, and so on' reinforce Hayek's belief (Hayek, 1988, p. 9) that: '[...] our values and institutions are determined not simply by preceding causes but as part of a process of unconscious self-organisation

(Hayek, 1976; 1988) or to the theory of repeated games (Axelrod, 1984), or to evolutionistic theories cast of the same league (Maynard Smith, 1982) to hold the hope that 'private vices' will end up being transmuted into 'public virtues'.

The so-called 'evolutionistic' theories thus start from the principle that actors are predetermined and stick to a strategy which they apply indefinitely whatever the circumstances are. The unrealism of such a model has, let us note in passing, nothing disturbing about it for the champions of such an approach (Dosi *et al.*, 1997). These 'strategies' (or rather the programme of these automats) are then set against one another, in order to see which ones give stationary results in time. For anyone, the question is then: 'What is to be made of this result?' And the answer is obvious: simply nothing, except if one believes there is something to be inferred as to rationality, as to the reasons for choosing such or such 'strategy' (under the hypothesis that the other will always stick to one single 'strategy', which is admittedly a heavy hypothesis). In fact, we always witness the same *coup de force*. It consists in defining a Nash equilibrium or a 'fixed point', and regarding it as an *attractor*. This amounts to convincing oneself that individuals have no real choice if they rely on 'true' rationality, then to claiming to impose this unilateral redefinition of rationality to all. Rationality is first supposed to be alluring, attractive of the choice in favour of the point which, precisely, is called attractive, but then, it must still be imposed, as if its real attraction

---

of a structure or pattern.' He (Hayek, 1976, p. 39) infers from this that justice is not a well thought-out agreement on rules, but a blind adhesion to the rules 'secreted' by the spontaneous order: 'Justice is thus emphatically not a balancing of particular interests at stake in a concrete case, or even the interests of determinable classes of persons, nor does it aim at bringing about a particular state of affairs which regarded as just. It is not concerned with the results that a particular action will in fact bring about. The observation of a rule of just conduct will often have unintended consequences which, if they were deliberately brought about, would be regarded as unjust. And the preservation of a spontaneous order often requires changes which would be unjust if they were determined by human will.' It is therefore necessary to have faith in the spontaneous order, which supposedly self-produces justice without people having to give their agreement. Because the social world is complex, the effort to follow the categorical imperative is simply pointless (Hayek, 1976, p. 120), illusory: 'Men can be allowed to act on their own knowledge and for their own purposes only if the reward they obtain is dependent in part on circumstances which they can neither control nor foresee. And if they are to be allowed to be guided in their actions by their own moral beliefs, it cannot also be morally required that the aggregate effects of their respective actions on the different people should correspond to some ideal of distributive justice.'

was not enough. If one is not cautious enough, one ends up believing that individual rationality (for me) and collective rationality (for us) are the very same thing.

Formally, behind all these attempts at evacuating the reasonable, there is nothing less than a return to an explanation congruent with the wishes of a theology, since all of them call in one way or another for a Providence, against the common and simply human effort to live together. Naturalism and theology, though through opposed paths, meet in their anti-humanism.[11] The aim is to deny any model putting human freedom at the foundation to explain social behaviour. One then lapses very logically into determinism and a whole series of machines to select morality are invented.

Nonetheless, all of this should not hide the true morality of the dilemma. The prisoners are free to denounce each other, and it is not by looking for a hidden constraint, or any hidden determinism which would magically favour the right option that they can disentangle themselves. The cooperative solution implies trust. Each person must take the bet that the other will freely make the choice not to be detrimental to them. Now, this is a reasonable gamble, so much so that prisoners can come to this agreement only tacitly. It is easy for everyone to see that one of the choices can be accounted for with one's accomplice, while the other will remain unjustifiable.

But there is more, since the so-called cooperative solution is not necessarily the fair solution. So far, we have not taken into account crime and the rest of society. By playing the Prisoner's Dilemma against each other, the judge has encouraged mutual denunciation without enquiring any further about real culpabilities. In other words, with the hypotheses of this model we are in the position of not having to judge crimes or unmask culprits. The players do not have to look for what can be justified publicly, and therefore be justified on the basis of neutral or objective reasons. Apart from the hypothesis of an absolute aversion to risk, this is probably the reason why this model has little empirical value. It forces actors to put on

11 The theological claim to come before morality and found it in truth is here obviously at stake, and not the claim to follow it, in order to give it meaning. Luc Ferry and Jean-Didier Vincent (2000) develop this idea, among others, in their work: *Qu'est-ce que l'homme? Sur les fondamentaux de la biologie et de la philosophie.* It goes without saying that historicism – that is, the theory which consists in seeing in history the foundation or the code of morality – proceeds from the same deterministic search.

glasses which are not theirs, or at least not in every occasion. And, as we have seen, this is not an isolated case.

When it comes to explaining the most elementary and ordinary civic or civil behaviours, such as going to vote or waiting for one's turn in a queue, the reiteration of rounds is actually of little use. People vote just as well in a large urban metropolis as in a small village. Waiting lines are formed between individuals who are and will remain strangers, just as they are formed between people who know each other well. To account for these situations, or more generally, for the social order, in the end, all the problem of utilitarianism is to succeed in managing to bring utility for us down to utility for me, or the production of a collective good to personal interest; or still, as we have just seen, cooperation to a strictly dominating strategy. But, in the way the problem is presented, restricted morality must grant its favours only to one of the terms of the alternative, to the exclusion of the other. As a result, there is no solution, unless *my* interests are dissolved into *our* interests, and pre-established harmony is assumed. We have come across an example of this reasoning in the first chapter when examining the 'logic' of collective action according to Olson, and we have just found its analogous in Axelrod's theory. They aim at showing us that free riders can follow cooperative norms, but it appears that these norms always *already prevail.* They aim at making us understand that positive or negative sanctions which accompany any norm make it possible to find selfish reasons to cooperate, but they fail to explain why there are still some free riders. Pretending that these sanctions are not perceived as sufficiently inciting or deterring by those free riders would only lead to a pure circularity. One would eventually be simply led to hold that when norms apply, it is because they apply, and when they do not apply, it is because they do not apply. Let us note actually that by replacing the under-socialised individual by an over-socialised individual, the symmetrical (holistic) explanation does hardly better. This time the cooperative norms of a group are *inculcated* thanks to socialisation, and we apply them without even thinking about it, or pretty much so. There should therefore be no free riders. If there are some, it is because the socialisation process did not function well. We are thus brought back to a tautology of the same type as the previous one. In the end, if the fear of negative sanctions or the valorisation of positive ones or a mere 'reflex' lead to the respect of the law or of norms, it is because at the end of the day there is only egoism or coercion, and the 'rest' is a question of angelism. It is a strange sort of moral psychology, admittedly, since it is not even in accordance with the works of psychologists on morality – or rather, it is accordance with them only to stay at the first stages of moral development, those of infancy. The idea that someone may want to abide by a norm to which they have given their consent for good reasons is crossed out without even having been closely examined.

To 'validate' this exclusion, while hoping to remain explicative, it is necessary to invent a clock mechanism which guarantees in the long term the congruence of my preferences with our preferences. In this domain, as we have underlined, there is a vast literature. And yet, there is nothing to do about it, as soon as a preference for some negative discrimination is introduced in these 'clocks', everything gets jammed. The clock is supposed to warrant impartiality by making no discrimination between everyone's claims, by the grace of a spontaneous composition of these claims. But such neutrality is clearly illusory as soon as *ego* claims the pure and simple negation of the pretensions which *alter* brings under discussion. Such a negation can only remain incongruous or conflicting. This is a fundamental difficulty, which actually summarises most of those against which all the elaborate mechanics which do not contemplate that justice could not be derived from the good stumble upon. Regarding a negative discrimination as fair is one way among others of regarding as valid the argument: 'I must not do this, simply because it is me', in other words, 'it is fair for me to exempt myself – me and no one else – from the rules of justice'. *Alter* cannot recognise such an argument without negating itself as an end in itself. If there is a reasonable egoism (self-esteem) which simply consists in everyone granting oneself the preference, it must be distinguished from pathological egoism (self-love), which is being discussed here, and which leads *ego* to demand from others to care for it more than themselves. Utilitarianism really cannot disentangle this dilemma. Either the pathological claim of *ego* is legitimate, because it is rational, and free riding becomes the (paradoxical) rule. Or it is not, and it is necessary to understand why, by giving reasons which visibly exceed *ego*'s own utility.

## 3. Communitarianism and the Dead Ends of an Embedded Subject

The communitarian approach to justice is opposed in almost every respect to utilitarian theses, and actually, to libertarian ones too, and at first sight, one could think it represents a way of overcoming these difficulties. It is true that it does not reject in principle the idea of unanimous agreement. And yet, because of its basic postulate, relative to the actors' embedment in their community, we will see that it is led to give a vision of it which is nonetheless objectionable. Once more, a hidden harmony prevails. True, it no longer presides over the interest composition, but since it proceeds from communitarian bonds, it is still very present.

Before we come to this, it must be underlined that, contrary to the previous two cases, it is tricky to grant a true unity to what is called communitarianism. We are dealing with a group of very disparate authors, among whom we can count, among others, Alasdair MacIntyre (1981), Michaël Sandel (1982) or Charles Taylor (1989). And finally, we are confronted with a series of arguments, whose overall coherence is far from being certain, either philosophically or sociologically or politically. Compared with the lifelessness of debates of political philosophy in the heyday of utilitarianism, at least in the Anglo-Saxon world, however, such diversity is not necessarily damaging. It has provided an opportunity to broaden these debates to important questions, such as the right of cultural minorities, triggering new thoughts, including among liberals. They will be discussed at the end of this section.

In order to propose a typical ideal reconstruction of communitarianism, in spite of this and without too much danger of making a mistake, the following two propositions can be regarded as constitutive:

(C1) The I and the good are inextricably linked; or still, the I is always embedded in a context and in roles from which it cannot establish any critical distance.

(C2) The good is a true good only if it is inscribed in a 'horizon of shared meanings', that is, in a community; or still, in its critical version, political liberalism cautions and favours an atomisation of society by negating any idea of 'common good' and, therefore, any authentic life-plan.

A few general considerations are necessary before these propositions are examined in detail. First, each of them is a frontal questioning of the liberal idea of the priority of justice over the good. According to the first proposition, the priority of justice is simply impossible, since it demands an effort of abstraction which is 'unrealistic'. According to the second proposition, even if this turned out to be possible, it would not be desirable, since the (vain) attempt at abstraction leads to negating social bonds, as well as any principle of the 'common good'. The priority of justice would feed individualism and eat away society.

We thus come across the two facets selected by André Berten, Pablo Da Silveira and Hervé Pourtois (1997) in the work they edited with a view to bringing together the main texts of the debate between liberals and communitarians. The critic of liberalism which results from this debate can be found for instance in Sandel's writings (1988, p. 61), one of the initiators of communitarian theses:

> Recalling the arguments of Hegel against Kant, the communitarian critics of modern liberalism question the claim for the priority of the right over the good, and the picture of the freely choosing individual it embodies. Following Aristotle, they argue that we cannot justify political arrangements without reference to common purposes and ends, and that we cannot conceive our personhood without reference to our role as citizens, and as participants in a common life.

At least, this is clear. But we still have to find out whether it is really possible to reach a relevant theory of justice when giving up both liberty and the priority of justice.

So far, we have only taken up the two characteristic propositions of communitarianism, and already, difficulties are piling up. Each of these propositions develops an argumentative course which clashes with the other. The consistency of communitarianism is therefore rather dubious, from the very start. To put it briefly, before we come back to it in greater detail, this doctrine stipulates that the individual is not capable of taking distance in order to agree with someone different – this is proposition C1. The embedment theory thus makes differences 'natural' and 'insurmountable'. Men, caught up in the sound and the fury of history, deprived of any hold on history in return, get closer or become estranged, to the whim of circumstances. The idea that they make up society *in spite of all* is absent here. From this point of view, communitarianism rejects any principle of cohesion between individuals which would imply an attempt to overcome their differences. It relies on 'nature' or 'history'. Then, *a contrario*, it goes on to claim that cohesion is always already granted, since happiness only happens to those who take root in their community – this is proposition C2. In doing so, the community takes precedence over everyone's life plans. Against the supposedly atomising position of political liberalism, and against the pluralisation/ dispersion involved by C1, cohesion is not only wished for, but enforced through notions such as authenticity or 'freedom-in-situation' which, in the end, amount to one form or other of fideism towards tradition. The second proposition thus puts an arbitrary stop to the first one, and conversely. From then, the only truly relevant question is who decides that when facing one problem, it will be necessary to rely on C1, while in the face of another, C2 will be used – in other words, when should pluralism be the answer, and when should it be unity?

It turns out that this is not a new difficulty, and that the two propositions which we have said to be constitutive of communitarianism strongly invite one to only see in this movement a *repetition of romanticism*. Here, we join a good many commentators (cf. Renaut, 1998, p. 211), and Taylor himself, since he owns up having 'a very strong affinity' with Herder, the distinguished philosopher of the Romantic Movement. However, let us first see why propositions C1 and C2, thus taken up by both communitarians and romantics, lead to an invalid interpretation of justice as a unanimous agreement, before coming back to the detail of each one.

### 3.1 *A unanimous agreement with a secret clause*

The first proposition (C1) attaches to each individual a conception of the good life whose value cannot be discussed at the moment of forming an agreement with others. She cannot say no to this conception of the good life; therefore, she cannot say yes either. In this perspective, this conception accompanies any unanimous agreement without being itself an object of reflection. One way of translating this situation consists in saying that the conception of the good life invites itself in the unanimous agreement just like a secret clause. It is presented without being subject to criticism. Of course, the idea of a unanimous agreement containing some secret clauses is absurd. As we have established in the previous chapter, such an idea amounts to negating everyone's right of veto and, eventually, to negating the meaning of the agreement. Logically, one cannot hope to develop from

C1 a theory of justice which would be compatible with the principle of justice as unanimous agreement.

However, let us suppose that the communitarian is convinced of the reverse, and has the strong intention to develop a theory which, overriding that of the unanimous agreement, could decide what the 'true' or the 'good' unanimous agreement would be. According to her, the 'good' unanimous agreement is the one which would not be inconsistent for an observer reading the secret clause of each contractor. This is essentially the case for communities where everyone shares the same conception of the good life, or compatible conceptions. Inversely, the 'bad' unanimous agreement is that which is inconsistent, with respect to the secret clauses, and which is unduly perceived as fair by the liberal, who cannot see the said clauses.

The difficulty comes from this ideal observer, who judges on the consistency of the secret clauses. We quickly end up lapsing into theological or tyrannical clauses, as was often the case of romanticism. Indeed, either one thinks that a genius is capable of holding this ideal position, but in this case the legitimacy of the agreement only stems from the charisma of this genius. A tyrant legislates 'on behalf of everyone' and subjects do not have the freedom to think that these laws may not be made 'on their behalf'. Or we consider that this ideal observer is God, and that 'the ways of God are unfathomable'. The guarantee of a 'good' unanimous agreement then involves religious faith as well as the community of believers in the same god. It is in this sense that some romantics have laid the stress on the religious community.

If we want to avoid both flaws, we must find the way of making the unanimous agreement less prominent, with the help of another form of guarantee, which would be superior to it. The second proposition (C2) partakes in such an attempt. The principle of the agreement can be presented as follows: the community is seen as a mode of production of subjects sharing the same conception of the good life, or whose entanglement of conceptions does not imply any inconsistency. The latter formulation, which is more subtle, encapsulates Taylor's idea of horizons of shared meanings. But, since one cannot judge by oneself this implicit consistency, the mode of production of the conceptions of the good life is now the object of an undisputable enhancement. The evaluation is imperceptibly turned into a forced enhancement of the existing community. The 'common good', which we are supposed to discuss publicly, is degraded into a secret clause whose sole manifestation is the communitarian bond which can no longer be refused. There follows a most peculiar conception of the 'common good', which boils down to this secret order which gives meaning to our lives and which cannot be evacuated without taking the risk of being dehumanised.

By starting from a clear idea of justice as unanimous agreement, the communitarian method can thus be reconstructed as a theory which never finds the right distance. First, it denies any possibility of distance, which amounts to negating the capacity to use one's right of veto and, equally but implicitly, to negating the other's right of veto by denying at the same time the intellectual capacity which consists in recognising *alter* as an *alter ego*. Imperceptibly, a unanimous agreement can only exist anymore between the same individuals. Different people differ absolutely, to such an extent that they can neither be understood, nor, consequently, be agreed with. The individual, too stuck in her roles and her conception of the good, mistakes the just with her conception of the good, a conception which, however, she shares with those who are like her. Then, communitarianism radically changes its course, and takes too much distance by denying the individual her capacity to recognise what is good for her – that is, by denying the right of veto, this time in the name of 'happiness'. Abstraction, which was previously regarded as impossible, is now rejected as non-desirable. Happiness is in one form or another of entrenchment. But this judgment conceals a far more formidable abstraction than the one which was denounced. In order to find out what is 'truly' desirable, in spite of what the subject could say about it, or still to find a principle of cohesion beyond everyone's will of cohesion, someone must overhang everyone's 'embedment', and say: 'everything is for the best in the best possible world'.

### 3.2 *Holistic flaws*

The presupposition of these reasonings – that individuals are embedded in a context, and carry values which they have not chosen – will not surprise any sociologist. We define daily the identity of an individual from the social roles he takes on, and his belonging to various social circles (family, association, ethnic, cultural, religious, political groups etc.). It is then tempting to reduce identity to this empirical apprehension of the individual, a temptation which can go as far as to regard this individual as a 'second nature', and thus mistake him for his roles and the stereotypes derived from his social circles. By claiming that the I and the good are inextricably linked, communitarians mostly revert to the idea that the individual is a 'soft clay', modelled from his birth (through various mechanisms of subordination) by social and cultural structures imposed on him. In other words, communitarianism reverts, in one form or another, to holism. We find the same emphasis on the inherited, received, or prescribed nature of identity: the I is always associated with an idea of the good and with ends which have not been chosen.

Such a perspective obviously stands in complete contradiction with the liberal idea of the priority of the just over the good. This priority supposes that we are free to assent or to reject an existing social practice and that, from this point of view, the I comes prior to the ends it stands for. In other words, in a liberal perspective, the essence of men, what makes them human, does not consist so much in pursuing such or such end, in adhering to such or such value, but rather in choosing their ends and values. The perspective is clearly humanistic, since the emphasis on this choice, that is, on free will, goes hand in hand with the rejection of 'natural' or prescribed ends, or of the idea that everyone has a 'natural' or assigned place in the world order. Man is nothing by nature. It is the subject who evaluates the world and, precisely because he is the evaluator, no evaluation is imposed on him, nor decides for him.

And yet, in the start, the communitarian criticism seems well-inspired. In the wake of the critics of 'abstract humanism', (Hegel), it sees in the liberal emphasis on the capacity to choose an instrument for a potential distance and even according to it, for destruction – as if at every moment the point was to *effectively* do away with the past in order to sever all past links. This is for instance what MacIntyre writes (1984, p. 215):

> According to the liberal account of morality, *where* and *from whom* I learn the principles and precepts of morality are and must be irrelevant both to the question of what the content of morality is and to that of the nature of my commitment to it […]. By contrast on the alternative account of morality which I am going to sketch, the questions of *where* and *from whom* I learn my morality turn out to be crucial for both the content and the nature of moral commitment.

One could believe that the emphasis on the *where* and *from whom* simply serves here to re-establish the importance of socialisation, in order not to deny that we make up a society with others. And yet, this would miss the point. As has just been recalled, the liberal conception claims that eventually it is always the subject who evaluates. Whether he evaluates this custom rather than that one as a random result of his birthplace, or whether he evaluates this proposition rather than that one because he is educated, or advised by some person or other, is an obvious fact which no one challenges. That it is the context or the others who start evaluating in his place is a wholly different matter. But, as opposed to the liberals, MacIntyre confuses both aspects.

The complexity of the world as well as natural and historical determinations can be endlessly underlined, but it remains that morality starts with freedom; it starts when the question of a well-thought-out orientation in the world is asked. Theorists, led to describe the state of the world, sometimes think that they can infer from it what is to be done. But in order to do so, it is necessary to decide (together) on a goal. As soon as this goal is put between brackets, some ends are supposed to be in one way or other 'natural'. This is why the communitarian position is highly delicate. It can deprive the individual of his right of veto by giving the priority to the community. It can say: 'Here is the good you inherited, be true to it as you are true to yourself.'

This is a displacement which is typical of holism, since it turns the individual into a mere support for a structure. Actuated by this structure, the individual ends up drowned in the whole, so that the parties' agreement on justice is at risk of ending up in them being absorbed into the engulfing totality – the risk of lapsing into totalitarianism not being excluded then. It is important to grasp what leads to such a mistake. The theoretical reason is always in search of what makes a given situation absolutely determining for the actor. In other words, the theorist is only satisfied with his explanation when the actor no longer seems to have a choice. But such an ideal – especially when one believes they have reached it – no longer leaves any space for the practical reason, that is, to the fact of trying to orientate oneself in the world, a fact which necessarily supposes a capacity for self-determination on the part of the subject. Therefore, it is necessary to distinguish carefully between the actor who is simply *situated* (the context is an initial fact for action) and the completely *determined* actor (the individual is 'actuated' by the context).

However, this is not the end of the critic. It is not enough to hold that the actor has the choice to escape the holistic failing. The theorist can still believe that, when it is not determined, the actor's choice is arbitrary. As a result, self-determination is reduced to being only, in theory, a partial blurring of the superstructures. This time, it is necessary to distinguish between the actor who orientates herself blindly, and the actor who orientates herself knowingly. Undeniably, every actor has her reasons, as some communitarians never fail to point out when they insist on self-comprehension and call for depth-psychology. However, if the idea of blindness is restricted to acting independently from others, without caring about what they do or what is done to them, then, this blind orientation can only be avoided by resorting to a public use of reason and relying on intersubjectivity. Instead of considering a heap of individuals who orientate themselves blindly (even if each of them, separately, displays efforts of self-comprehension), it is necessary to start from a community of subjects where everyone attempts to account for their orientation in the world.

Without going back to the necessary link between the subject and intersubjectivity, one of its key moments can be recalled, by focusing on the right of veto and unanimous agreement. Stipulating that *ego* has a right of veto as to its choices of orientation only has any content if this right is aimed at founding an agreement with an *alter ego*. *Ego*'s right of veto is nothing as long as it does not *set down* that an *alter* is also free and reasonable. Without the acknowledgment that *alter* is an *alter ego*, without the acknowledgment of *alter*'s right of veto, there is no true agreement. Insisting on freedom against the radical embedment theory of the I thus does not only signify that an actor can be wrong because there is some play in superstructures, but, more importantly, that he can orientate himself in a reasonable way, that is, act in a direction which would gather everyone's assent.

Thus, in spite of what the majority of communitarians claim, political liberalism rests on this essential acknowledgment which turns *alter* into an *alter ego* by giving it *a priori* a right of veto. Such an acknowledgment *does not demand* the other to have a *specific content* to be acknowledged and welcomed. Acknowledging that others are ends in themselves with whom I can agree in reason does not demand that others should be like me, that they should be the same as me, or that they should have the same culture or a similar conception of the good.[12] The importance of recognising that man is noth-

12 This is the crux of the discourses on tolerance which have been developed in the West between Catholics and Protestants, and which is explained either as the result of obscure reciprocal evolutionary adaptations, or as the acknowledgement of two minor variations on the same Christian religion, without seeing that, in order to stop slaughtering one another, everyone must have acknowledged the other as another I. It was necessary to decide to live together by considering that this new (fair) norm had the priority over every-

ing by nature can now be measured (this has obviously nothing to do with physiology). It can now be seen that this translates into the idea that a conception of the good is never so different from mine that I can infer from it that others are no longer ends in themselves. Seeing in others 'a second nature', in which I cannot recognise myself, never constitutes a valid reason not to recognise them as being reasonable.

We must therefore be clear. If it is important to assert the priority of the I over her ends, it is above all in order to avoid that the subject should lose her right of veto by becoming the mere representative of a whole which surpasses her. In particular, the right of the individual has the priority over the possible rights of the community. In good logic, even though not everyone owns up to this point, communitarians should claim the reverse. But they do not see that the capacity to evaluate not only makes the rejection of the community possible, but also makes living together possible. The right of veto goes with unanimous agreement like the subject goes with intersubjectivity. It seems that communitarians want one without the other, whereas they must choose: either they reject the subject and end up with a totalitarian affirmation of the community, or they logically reach political liberalism. It goes without saying that this choice, like all those which have just been discussed, more generally involves any holistic doctrine claiming that a totality to which an individual belongs determines her in a strong way.[13]

## 3.3 *Life plans and freedom of choice*

However, a communitarian like Taylor is far from challenging the importance of individual rights to guarantee the individual's freedom against the

---

thing that separated each community. In order to do so, there was no possible middle way between transubstantiation and consubstantiation. Therefore, it was indispensable that everyone, while retaining their conception of the good, accepted freely to put justice at the basis of social ties. Without claiming to speak as historians, we think that this must have represented a decisive turn in the advent of modern societies. Contrary to what had happened between Catholics and Orthodox, who had simply separated, here, it was necessary for reason – that is to say, the reasonable – to take precedence over trials for heresy. The movement towards the Enlightenment had started.

13 According to Marx (1859, preface), for instance, 'in the social production of their existence, men inevitably enter into definite relations, which are independent of their will'; in other words, the conditions of the individuals' activity eventually part away from them, becoming reified outside them, and determining them.

coercive claims and actions of a group. On the contrary, he accepts the liberal thesis whereby individual rights are part of the conditions of possibility of self-achievement. Some communitarians thus only claim they are trying to complete liberalism with socio-psychological elements which account for the constitution of the I and make its self-comprehension possible. In other words, the capacity to choose is not questioned, on the condition that there really should be something to choose from. In this frame of mind, communitarians insist on the conception of the good life and restate that this is what counts. They reproach liberalism with insisting too much on free will, when it is the freedom to have a well-filled life that counts. But political liberalism does not say anything different. Saying that man is nothing by nature makes it possible to welcome *a priori* all the conceptions of the good life (which, however, will have to be reasonable *a posteriori*); this does not mean that an actor does not have to choose between these conceptions, that he does not have to use his capacity to evaluate (this would mean falling into the existentialist trap of an individual who, being fascinated by so many possibilities, remains *incapable of acting*). For a liberal theory, life plans, far from being secondary, are essential. This is why it seeks to preserve for each actor the right to call them into question and change them if they turn out to have lost their interest to the extent that he cannot recognise himself in them. It is precisely because life plans are important that we must not abandon the right to evaluate them whenever we please. It is also for this reason, actually, that the social contract must never be signed for good.

But beyond the importance given to life plans, the disagreement remains between liberals and communitarians. The latter's insistence on self-understanding for a theory of justice always leads to the conviction that life plans which individuals assume are less *taken up* than *given*. The communitarians want to think that life plans have meaning because they are received and cannot be abandoned, because one cannot say no. But it is actually the reverse which is true. It is fundamentally because one could say no but keeps on saying yes, that the project makes sense. Will Kymlicka (1990, p. 209) points out, very relevantly, that in the liberal perspective: 'Freedom of choice is not pursued for its own sake, but as a precondition for pursuing those projects that are valued for their own sake.' The liberal theory of justice does not deny that many life plans are received and that groups (were it only the family) orientate the individual in such or such direction. It sees no difficulty at all in this. On the contrary, it refuses to found justice on the eviction of the critical moment where what is received is deliberately taken back. Rejecting this perspective would amount to accepting to call 'fair' an agreement where some individuals have been made not to say anything.

If only modifying one's choice counted, if the capacity to choose effectively took the lead over what is chosen, then it would be for each different second that choices should be modified; one would have to exert one's capacity to choose as much as possible, with no regard for what is chosen and what is already about to be dismissed. But the image which is then adumbrated is not that of a free individual attempting to live her life to the full, but rather the existentialist image of Antoine Roquentin (Sartre, *Nausea*) or still, that of fashion victims who, deep down, cultivate indifference for what they set their eyes on. Communitarians and liberals concur quite extensively on this point. What creates stability (of life plans as well as of unanimous agreement), is precisely that, on second thoughts, the plan which is selected is picked up for good reasons. But the communitarian pushes the argument too far by denying the right of veto at this precise moment: he sets once and for all the 'good reasons' which eventually prove detrimental to the subject; he forces stability by denying that one may have good reasons to change one's mind and plans. In passing, the *critical* mind and the *will* to reach out for improvement and adapt *intelligently* to change (both within and outside oneself) bear the brunt of the operation. The communitarian goes through a form of depth-psychology which obscurely tells the subject what her good is. Now, it is one thing to give much thought to the matter of what one wants to do with one's life, and to acknowledge that it is difficult, but it is another thing to ask the subject to commit for a good which she does not recognise as being *hers*. The liberal conception of identity demands that the subject should recognise her good as being effectively hers (and not someone else's).

These arguments make it possible to add a few extra specifications as to the nature of unanimous agreement. The actor can take her distances from the ends and the roles she assumes; this is why she can welcome the other without setting down *indisputable* conditions as to the substantial conception of the good life of this other; however, this does not prevent her from becoming involved in life plans and enhancing *for herself* one conception of the good rather than another. Once these two ideas have been clearly distinguished – (i) the subject recognises that the other has the capacity to evaluate and (ii) the subject does not make the mistake of simply enhancing the capacity to evaluate, but uses this capacity to become involved in a well-filled life without losing her veto in the process –, everything is in place for the agreement to be the fruit of a true confrontation of viewpoints rather than, as communitarians believe, an empty agreement which no one could possibly want. *Agreement is a well-thought-out integration of various conceptions of the good life and in this sense it is legitimate to say that the just has the priority over these different conceptions.* People agree on the way to live together with different conceptions of the good life, and tolerance is guaranteed from the start because I set down that *alter* is equally free and reasonable. The shift from a communitarian conception is manifest. For the communitarian, it seems necessary to agree on what the true good is, and it is hard to see how such perfectionism could avoid drifting imperceptibly towards intolerance, especially in the case of societies which are *de facto* pluralist.

The sometimes heated debates which have unfolded over the Rawlsian method of the veil of ignorance illustrate these ideas perfectly. Rawls's *Theory of Justice* (1971) is a difficult book, since it breaks away from utilitarianism, while retaining (to a large extent) its language. Habermas (1995, p. 111) underlines this point very aptly: 'This construction of an original position that *frames* the freedom of choice of rational actors in a reasonable fashion is explained by Rawls's initial intention of representing the theory of justice as part of the general theory of choice.' Also, on the one hand, there is a debate which is internal to political liberalism, on the merits of the *original position model* developed by Rawls. On the other, there is the justification of political liberalism which can only be understood in Rawls's theory by taking into account the Kantian dimension through the notions of reflective equilibrium and the reasonable (as opposed to what is only rational).

Historically, Rawls's objective was to prove to utilitarians that a plurality of conceptions of the good does not rule out finding rules for life in common. In the end, utilitarianism could not avoid perfectionism. The idea of the veil of ignorance or of the original position thus serves above all to make the idea that everyone has of their good at the moment of the agreement *relative*, and to underline everyone's tolerance towards the others' conceptions of the good. It is a way of introducing a plurality of conceptions of the good against perfectionism – conceptions which are all equally reasonable. If, as to the contents of the debate with utilitarianism, Rawls is definitely right and has made this doctrine largely outdated, however, one may question, especially in the wake of Habermas, the internal coherence of his model. It is difficult to know to what extent Rawls's attachment to the rational choice theory was purely tactical; it remains that this attachment does not go without difficulties. The individual behind the veil of ignorance is put in the position of reasoning with fairness, because she does not know what her position in society is. In Kantian terms, this ignorance prevents her from resorting to the imperative of skill, which in this case is replaced with the imperative of prudence. It can also be said that the individual is forced, because of the device of the veil of ignorance, to accept rationally the all-important Golden Rule ('do not do to other people what you would not want them to do to you').[14] The gap with the categorical imperative is then eloquent. Kant (1785, II) had already noticed that the Golden Rule is in no way to be mistaken with the categorical imperative and that at best it is 'only a deduction [from the latter] though with several limitations',[15] and Rawls does not ignore this point, since he himself restates it in his teaching (Rawls, 2000). The Golden Rule supposes that *alter* necessarily has the same conception of the good as *ego*. It negates the plurality of reasonable goods. This is actually why Rawls will be led in the second part of his *Theory of Justice* to develop a theory of primary goods which everyone is supposed to have a share in. And yet, he was far from supporting the perfectionism inherent in utilitarianism: it is even the crux of his criticism. This is the reason why he adds that an individual in the original position not only ignores his position in society, but also his own conception of the good. Consequently, one may question, along with the communitarians, the impact of such ignorance for if, contrary to what we have said initially, Rawls not only makes the conceptions of the good relative, but really leaves aside these conceptions, then his theory of justice as fairness could very well boil down to only being an empty agreement. If individuals can neither discuss their ends, nor discuss what could hinder the fulfilment of their ends, there remains nothing important to agree on. According to us, such an interpretation does not account for Rawls's intention, however, unless one is convinced that he confused the Golden Rule and the categorical imperative, or that his critic of perfectionism was, if not factitious, at least superficial; which seems rather unlikely. In Rawls's mind, the veil hypothesis does not amount to ignoring any conception of the good, but to ignoring *among a number of reasonable conceptions of the good* which is one's own. It is very differ-

14 Or in its positive formulation: 'Treat other people as you would like to be treated.'

15 By application of the negative formula, a convict could tell the judge who punishes him that he should not do so, since if he was in his place, he would not want to bear such a punishment. Moreover, what about duties towards oneself?

ent, and this is why the original position model is indeed a modelling of the categorical imperative, rather than of the Golden Rule. At the same time, the limits of this modelling appear clearly: at the moral level, everything is brought into play at the moment of deciding what it is reasonable to ignore behind the veil. In other words, political liberalism may well discuss, internally, whether the procedure imagined by Rawls is relevant or not for western societies or for such or such question about a fair distribution, but it remains that this procedure is only legitimate if it is the object of a unanimous agreement. This is what must be understood through the emphasis on the reflective equilibrium and the reasonable.

In the end, the example of this debate shows that the priority of justice is not a way of evacuating any idea of the good, to the benefit of some abstract duty. The priority of the just refers to the effort to integrate intelligently several reasonable conceptions of the good. We have already seen that this amounts to making the truth of one's own conception of the good relative (were it only to the benefit of doubt) and accepting the search for a compromise with individuals with whom one does not share the same values.

### 3.4 *Social ties and the evaluating subject*

Moreover, communitarianism is also a theory on social ties, a theory which once more will not surprise any sociologist. To put it briefly, using Tönnies's categories (1887), the idea of the community in this doctrine resembles more *Gemeinschaft* than *Gesellschaft.* Social bonds are prescribed and strong (in the sense that they are affectively charged and hardly specialised); they are not chosen and weak. One's assigned belonging conceals one's chosen belonging, as if there was no capacity to become linked. The theory of the embedded I implies that individuals can only reproduce what nature and history have bestowed upon them. Once more, only the passive character of individuals is emphasised, not their active character. In other words, individuals are not creators; they are incapable of acting out of their mere will, since everything is about habits and inclinations. As a result, inherited social bonds acquire a singular value. They are (along with love bonds) everything that one can hope to receive from society (this is the reason why these bonds cannot be specialised). Their rejection or their destruction is dramatic since individuals cannot choose between faithfulness and de-socialisation. This is why the communitarian is tempted to enhance social bonds to the point of making them betray the actors' will to be together. Even if such a theory can entice readers concerned about the future of 'social bonds', it raises heavy difficulties and has consequences – clearly unappealing, this time.

In ecological terms, the communitarian conception amounts more or less to regarding the collectivity as an endangered species. Men, not being able to create anything, are reduced to animals of a species which must be protected in priority, before such or such 'animal' in particular. Hence the necessity of creating collective rights, in other words, rights for the protection of the community understood as a species. The problem is of course that men do not belong to their community in the same sense as animals belong to their species. Will individuals be forbidden to leave their community of origin, or forced to take up *in the name of the community* cultural practices which, in their heart of hearts, they are opposed to? Once more, the totalitarian danger is far from being non-existent.

However, it would be necessary to start by giving more thought to what is commonly called 'social bonds' before calling for collective rights against the individual, and extracting oneself from a spontaneous sociology which, undeniably, recurs as unfalteringly as flu every winter. We have seen that (truly) making up a society demands that one recognise the other as reasonable. For such a recognition to be more than just words, this means that I am willing to acknowledge the other to be right, and therefore that *I am willing to believe and act out of a motive which goes neither in the direction of what I have an interest to believe, nor in the direction of my conception of the good life.* This argument is obviously crucial if one aims to focus on the reasons of the fair spectator. And yet, it is a delicate point since many 'spontaneous sociologists' think that the only method to study individuals consists in seeing in them a (second) nature. Admittedly, this is an understandable presupposition in the course of a police inquiry, where suspects are seen as mere heaps of springs: the inspector must set down that some *nature* actuated the criminal, and made him or her act in a predictable way, which can be reproduced by thought – and this nature can moreover also be described in material terms (utilitiarianism) or in terms of individual passion (communitarianism). Nonetheless, one dimension escapes the inspector, no matter how suspicious she may be – that is, the free act which is a pure product of the will; in this instance, the crime committed out of sheer malice.

Consequently, if we wish to avoid crossing out anything *a priori*, we must take seriously the 'anti-natural' dimension of society; it must be emphasised that, against the natural temptations which may bring individuals together or apart to the whim of circumstances, individuals *want* to live together. In his famous critique of Rawls, Sandel (1982) makes the will the mark of the subject closure over himself. As we have already underlined, this is a logical mistake, since intersubjectivity cannot be separated from the subject. But moreover, his theory amounts to denying the will to live together. Implicitly, like the police inspector, like the utilitarian and like any 'spontaneous sociologist', he only swears by springs. But there is at least another motive for acting. It can be supposed, reasonably enough, that crimes without reasons are quite rare, and that it is normal that not every criminal makes his will public. He acts without claiming to account for his action. But, nothing allows thinking that the will to make up a society is rare. Moreover, such a will has no reason not to be publicly expressed.

It is most likely that only a few people seriously consider living in the state of nature. Individuals generally wish for a life full of relations; they also want to live in a society where their dignity (as free and reasonable beings) will be acknowledged. This does not mean that such or such relation is a good that the subject cannot call into question, or that he is rooted in such or such society, which has become good for him by force of circumstance. Recognising that an individual is an evaluator means accepting that he may wish to go away. Typically, an emigrant is someone who uproots himself in order to go and settle down, take root, somewhere else, where he considers that he will have a better life. As a matter of fact, experience shows that most often an individual emigrates from a society where he is denied the right to evaluate; it is for this reason that this society is no longer good for him.

### 3.5 *A liberal solution to the rights of cultural minorities*

If communitarianism is often ambiguous, it nonetheless has the merit of restating that some goods are intrinsically social. Most cultural goods, such as one's language or the school system, only exist because they are kept up by a community of individuals. The liberal claims to neutrality can therefore only be deceiving. We are in a field where a cultural good (for instance, the one backed by a majority) prevails over competing cultural goods (for instance, those supported by minorities). In economic terms, under the guise of a free cultural market, it could be a case of cultural monopoly. The problem is not internal to a community sharing the same conception of the good. On the contrary, it affects societies which are usually referred to as 'multicultural'. In this respect, people speak of discussions on multiculturalism, but it is in fact a continuation of the debate between liberals and communitarians.

So far, we have defended the priority of the individual over the community. Because the individual is the evaluator, one cannot rightfully silence him in the name of a higher evaluation (the one which is traditional in a society). We have also underlined that the liberal principle did in no way forbid individuals to associate. This has actually led us to insist on the desire to live together. But, as Kymlicka (1995) points out, this liberal approach is not hostile *a priori* to any form of multiculturalism. On the contrary, the priority of justice over the good allows conceiving of the coexistence of different cultures. This priority forbids neither valuating a particular idea of the good, nor forming particular associations in the midst of the overall society, since freedom of association allows individuals to gather around a particular conception of the common good. If the unanimous agreement is a well-thought-out integration of the various conceptions of the good, it follows that nothing prevents this association from being aimed at conceptions of the individual good just as well as conceptions of the good common to a sub-group.

But, in the name of cultural diversity, multiculturalism is often tempted to go well beyond this minimal sense. Instead of enhancing a culture, multiculturalism enhances *the difference between cultures*. This time, it is legitimate to wonder what sense there is in claiming that difference is a value *in itself*. For instance, should one think that a one-eyed horse is of great value because it is different from two-eyed horses? Will it then be necessary to blind a horse in one eye, the day such 'diversity' will be lacking? Rather than coming to such extremities, it is preferable to restrict oneself to observing that *in fact*, individuals evaluate differently. This difference is neither good nor bad; it is only a fact[16] – which is possible in a liberal context, which precisely consists

16 It is therefore self-obvious – but why not repeat it – that the critique of the *valuation* of difference does in no way imply either the rejection of difference or the adherence to the discriminatory politics connected with it.

in not going over the individuals' heads, by acknowledging that it is they who evaluate.

It is therefore not possible to claim with some multiculturalists that since one should be able to make a real choice between various forms of life (or cultures, or conceptions of the good life, all of this here amounting to the same), the latter should be kept alive at all costs, to the point of compelling an individual to keep up a culture she comes from, but which she no longer wants. Moreover, implicitly, such a conception divides humanity into two parts: one where it is possible to really choose one's culture and the other where, in the name of the protection of culture, one cannot choose. In the end, by laying the emphasis on cultural diversity against everyone's right of veto, multiculturalism relapses into the same mistakes as communitarianism.

That said, we should be careful not to make mistakes about the liberal critique of collective rights. It essentially aims at refusing that a community should be able to exert internal constraints over its members. Any individual has an inalienable right to leave his community for another. But, if we remain firm on the right of veto and the impossibility to grant a community coercive rights over its own members, we can very well grant external rights to a community in order to protect it against a neighbouring and assimilating culture. The preventions of liberalism against these rights have no reason to be, in this instance. As a matter of fact, during its history, as Kymlicka reminds us (1995), liberalism has said the most diverse things on the rights of cultural minorities. The most recent speeches, which claim that liberalism must fundamentally stay blind to the claims of these minorities as such, are thus largely fabricated.

Acknowledging the rights of a cultural minority which sees its practices jeopardised by a cultural majority is not incompatible with the principles of justice as unanimous agreement. Nothing forbids in logic that compensations be given to a minority which sees its culture bounced about by the cultural practices of the majority. Refusing these compensations *a priori*, in the name of the 'benevolent neutrality' of a State in the face of the various cultural ties, has nothing neutral about it. However, it is hardly possible here to do otherwise than leave generalities. The questions asked no longer aim at a frontal questioning of the principle of unanimous agreement. They only involve the procedural problems of reaching such an agreement. They must therefore be discussed one after another. As for us, we will only deal with two examples: that of electoral borders, and that of regional languages.

Let us first consider the issue of procedures for political representation. It is common and largely accepted to choose deputies during elections taking place on a local basis. However, since every voter counts for one and chooses freely, it seems completely unjustified to make distinctions between voters. Neutrality consists precisely in not discriminating between the vote of a man and that of a woman, between those who can pay the franchise and those who cannot, etc. However, the will to always remain blind to differences between voters is not always a guarantee of neutrality. It is still necessary to divide the national territory into constituencies in order to organise elections on a local basis. If there were no difference between the voters, this division would not matter and neutrality would always be already granted. But, as any politologist knows very well, there is nothing neutral about such divisions. Thus, in Canada, the Inuits formed a minority within the North West territory, but as soon as this territory was cut in two, the Inuit became a majority in the eastern part (which became Nunavut). Canadians thus deemed fair to rebuild the voting procedures by taking into account the fact of being or not Inuit, without hiding behind some 'benevolent neutrality'.

Such a redefinition of electoral borders is indisputably a measure of positive discrimination. The point was to unanimously agree on a redefinition of rules in order to live with the Inuit minority as a group. Far from being only a testimony of pragmatism, this example shows on the contrary that it is always the unanimous agreement which founds the legitimacy of a procedure. Just as a unanimous agreement is needed on the fact of choosing one's representative with a pure majority ballot, a unanimous agreement is needed on the borders of local elections. The principle of 'benevolent neutrality' hides away a little too quickly behind imperfect procedures of justice which have nothing else to speak for them than their having been historically established. If procedures are needed, even imperfect ones, nothing forbids criticising their biases without denying that, for some problems, there will always be biases. The main thing remains to settle conflicts fairly, and procedures of election are aimed precisely at organising a reasonable debate between conflicting groups.

Nevertheless, one should avoid two pitfalls, which lead to negating the unanimous agreement in the name of an imperfect and particular procedure, erected to the rank of first principle. The first pitfall is that of the 'mirroring' representation where, at the national level, every deputy is only the mere representative of a specific category of individuals from which she came. First, it is impossible that a small number of men and women making up a parliamentary assembly could really mirror the social diversity of a mass society. Since the criteria cross one another almost infinitely, the stopping point is necessarily arbitrary. Moreover, there is then a great risk of building the debate from identity stereotypes and thus of giving up on the attempt to neutralise differences. *Alter* is no longer an *alter ego*. Those elected are no longer the representatives of the nation, that is, of the whole of the citizens, but simply of corporations or various categories. And if representatives stick to this role, there is no longer any manifest will to live together or any priority of justice over the good of these groups. The second pitfall is the one which consists in regarding as legitimate a procedure for the settlement of conflicts which, because of obvious biases, leads to one of the groups involved having any mouthpiece. This can happen for instance when people think that, whatever may happen, the majority ballot always leads to legitimate decisions. But a majority can prove tyrannical, and those elected, out of ignorance or contempt for the mores and the conception of the good life of the minority, can produce laws which are unreasonable as far as the latter are concerned. However, the example of the Inuits shows that such a mistake is not ineluctable. The Canadian majority managed to avoid this pitfall by regarding as reasonable an act of positive discrimination in favour of the Inuits.

Let us come to the example of regional languages. In a society made up of several linguistic communities, several factors contribute to impose a *lingua franca*. The main factor is obviously the coordination of all with each person, and of each person with all. It can be shown that, from the moment a central administration imposes its language, not only do the local elites have an obvious interest in learning it in order to perform their role as bilingual mediators between central power and their local 'clientele', who remain monolingual, but also that members of minorities have an interest in doing so precisely in order to acquire their autonomy from their traditional elites (Swaan, 1988). If any minority has an interest in bilingualism, on the contrary, the language of the central administration has a monopolistic advantage over each of the minority languages. And as a matter of fact, all the great nations have developed a standardised educational system in order to make coordination and mobility in the whole of society possible. However, justice as a unanimous agreement has no reason not to acknowledge the frailty of minority languages in the name of a so-called 'benevolent neutrality', or of a misplaced defence of the 'republican tradition'.

This would be tantamount to ignoring that standardised education, the demand on the job market for mobile and literate elements, and the common links with the various administrations pertaining to the Welfare State do not only stand in favour of bilingualism, but also, frequently, of the pure and simple abandonment of minority languages, which find themselves 'emptied' of any public use and reduced to 'folkloric' uses.

Of course, and we have relentlessly insisted on this, every person should decide on which inherited practices deserve to be taken up and which ones they are willing to give up. This remains valid for languages. However, one should distinguish between cases of willing abandonment and the cases where the central administration maintains coercive means against a minority language. A linguistic minority can very well consider that the majority pushes their advantage too far, and ask for specific rights in order to keep up and develop their language. In compensation for the disadvantages experienced, a minority may ask for instance for a logistical support for cultural creation. Of course, one may legitimately worry that such support, which is a form of positive discrimination, could turn into an undeserved pension. But there is a reasonable margin for positive discrimination. The construction of the European community shows very well that problems of translation can be (at least partly) handled by the administration, in the name of the equity between national languages that no one wishes to give up on. The European administration has thus been led to be flexible against the 'efficient' solution which seemed to impose English.

It is not by virtue of communitarian arguments, such as the valuation of differences, that such or such measure of positive discrimination can be supported fairly. In return, if the liberal claim of justice as unanimous agreement is not in principle opposed to any such measure, it remains that the problems raised here are too complex to hope to find a general or comprehensive answer. Some rules must not be breached. This is the case of all those which would lead to transgress the right of veto. For instance, criteria must be relevant.[17] Beyond, in order to judge on a debated proposal,

17 If, in order to restore a certain degree of social equity, the aim is to extend the intake of students in a higher education institution (with a limited number of places) to disadvantaged categories of population, the general criterion for entry being academic merit, the *mere* fixation of social, ethnic, racial or other quotas is not relevant. On the contrary, welcoming students who are academically deserving but who, because they belong to disadvantaged categories, do not even try to enter the said institution, seems relevant to us.

cases should be dealt with individually, and with no other *a priori* than the principle of unanimous agreement.

In the end, and in order to bring to a close this study of three examples of unsatisfactory procedures which we have just conducted, it should be noticed that, though very different from one another, these procedures fail each time for the same reason – that is, purely for their refusal to give the priority to justice as a unanimous agreement. This rejection always leads to erasing the citizen in the face of a hidden harmony, whether it is the product of history, of particular interests or of communities, whether it is presupposed or imposed. In return, if social order is not given, but built freely around common conventions, the danger of some relativism undermining the very bases of these conventions is real. There thus remains to rule it out for good by establishing the objectivity of reasonable choice.

# Chapter 5

# The Objectivity of Reasonable Choice

If communitarianism encounters some success in North America, and increasingly so in Europe, it is not only because it seeks to legitimise the irreprehensible right which any community supposedly has *a priori* to enhance its difference in a given society, it is also because it provides the champions of relativism with new arguments. If one accepts principles C1 and C2, which have been set out in the previous chapter, values and norms derive from communities which exist concretely here or there, at some point or other in history, and consequently, no value, no norm, could have any claim to universality; and of course, justice is no exception. To quote from the title of a book by Michaël Walzer, there are *several* spheres of justice, and they are regarded as relative to the communities.

Communitarianism thus gives a new basis to what is probably one of the most widespread intuitions of social sciences. For it is precisely these very social sciences, first among which stands ethnology, which have taught us how much values and norms differ from one society to the next. At first sight, with this great variety, pretending to universality or objectivity of justice is nothing else than badly-disguised ethnocentrism. Without even going as far as to compare the social organisation of the Zulus with that of the Americans or that of the Romans with that of the Saxons, it is also within modern societies that this argument has a pretension to prevail. Many of these societies are multicultural and multicommunitarian, and these cultures and communities are just as incommensurable as the ones just mentioned. It thus seems that the only way to be objective, insofar as this is possible, consists in taking good note of this extraordinary diversity and considering that values and norms derived from each community are all equal and provide good reasons to legitimise the claims (any claim) for the recognition of ethnic – or merely social – minorities. The formula is well-known: anything goes. Everything is good, and it is all the same. No one could say the contrary without passing a value judgment and consequently leaving the field of science or, to put it differently, without abandoning the ethics of responsibility to the benefit of an ethics of conviction. Of course, like any citizen, the scientist may deem that some values or norms are preferable to others, but it is only as a citizen that he expresses himself then.

We already have strong objections to emphasise against the 'anything goes' argument since we have shown (in chapter 3) that, in the context of justice as unanimous agreement, some situations are objectively unfair. But we also ended on a question mark. In the end, is not the choice to resort to a unanimous agreement a moral decision, and consequently, is it not ultimately arbitrary? Should we not admit, then, that in fact, it is impossible to get out of relativism? There thus remains to establish for good that even if the unanimous agreement is a human convention and the reasonable decision to use this convention as a foundation is freely taken by each member of a community, there is no reason to draw a relativist conclusion from this.

## 1. The Plurality of Values and Conflicts between Norms

### 1.1 *Plurality does not lead to relativity*

Moral relativism, the spearhead of 'postmodern' thinking, finds all the more vigour as it encounters most often an epistemological which, in turn, claims that anyway, in the first place, truth is only relative – or even, following Auguste Comte's famous phrase,[1] that 'everything is relative', and that this is indeed 'the one absolute thing'. Science history, where the truths of the past are constantly given up for those of the present, and the social construction of scientific truths (which are therefore relative to a given society), are supposedly there to testify to this.[2] A lot could be said about these questions. Without devoting too much time to it, let us still point out that two and two make four, whatever the network of relations between scientists taking part in 'normal science' is, and that, while it is clear and certain that

1 It is true that Comte often uses paradoxes. He also claimed that altruism (a word he created) is a duty for everyone and, after singling out the main characteristics of a positive rationalism, he turned it into a catechism.

2 One example – among many others – of this position can be found in *Against Method* (Feyerabend, 1975).

some truths of the past can be called into question through new discoveries, in fact, this does not lead to any relativism. Very often, the new 'paradigms' consist not so much in showing that the old ones are false, but rather that they are more particular than previously thought. It is one thing to say that truths are relative to scientific models which are increasingly refined – that is, that science progresses – and another to 'infer' from this that there is no truth. What is striking in both cases, that of moral relativism as well as that of epistemological relativism, is that they rest on a *non sequitur* and that they can be formulated in the form of a logical paradox. Behind a phrase like 'any truth is relative', we can recognise a variation on the theme of Epimenides' paradox. This is a very good example of a sentence which provides its own commentary and, as always in such a case, while it is true, it is at the same time false.

Similarly, if 'anything goes' in moral terms, then this morality, which can be said to be lax, is worth as much as any other. Therefore, it has nothing to oppose to the morality which claims that 'not anything goes'. In brief, if anything goes, then not anything goes. To overcome this paradox, 'anything goes' would have to give itself an objectivity which it denies to any moral discourse, which would be contradictory, except if we admit that lax morality is not a morality but a truth, and not a relative one of course, which can be opposed to all those who do not agree and which are mistaken. Whether we want it or not, this is nothing less than a perfectionism, which functions like any other perfectionism by resorting to normativity, that is, miles away from the so-called objectivity which the phrase 'anything goes' was supposed to reflect.

Moreover, as in the case of epistemological relativism, there is a *non sequitur* between facts, which form the basis of the relativistic principle, and this principle. Fact cannot be challenged. The 'polytheism of values' can hardly be contradicted. Nonetheless, these facts do not contain any premise which makes it possible logically to infer *ipso facto* that there is no room for some objectivity in the moral sphere. It is impossible to infer from the mere and simple existence of a plurality of norms that none of these could be claimed to be objective. This would require this plurality to forbid any objective reasoning by itself and *a priori*, which can obviously not be proven. The fact that there exists a plurality of colours, and that each one is about as inexplicable to a born blind that values aiming at the good are incommensurable from one community to the next, does not lead to us not being able to recognise together what is yellow or to understand that what is yellow is not blue and not being able, moreover, to give ourselves a definition of it without any ambiguity (even for a blind person) by remarking that yellow in the spectral analysis of light is comprised between such and such frequency, which are not those of the blue. To shift directly from the fact of moral plurality to the necessary absence of any objectivity, or to the necessary absence of 'the fact of reason', to take up Kant's phrase, there is nothing, except the crude sophism of 'anything goes'. If we want to establish this link, we must admit a series of intermediary propositions consisting in a very idiosyncratic theory of morality and objectivity – for instance communitarianism which, as we have seen, leads to think that since norms are embedded in concrete human communities, they can always only be subjective. Consequently, the 'spontaneous' relativistic argument no longer holds, since another theory, liberalism in this instance, which starts from the same observation of a *de facto* plurality of reasonable conceptions of the good in modern societies, and which sets itself the task of precisely not seeking to reduce it, reaches a radically opposed conclusion as far as objectivity is concerned. The background arguments of these different theories must be set against one another in order to form an opinion. And, in this debate, communitarianism cannot derive any advantage from a social reality which is supposed to prove by itself or lead ineluctably to relativism. If there is any relativism, it is entirely the product of the doctrine which serves as its support.

### 1.2 *The principle of non-contradiction and the conflict of norms*

We have already seen all the reasons which lead to reject communitarianism if one wishes to maintain the principle of justice as a unanimous agreement; therefore we will not return to this. But this is not the only doctrine which supports relativism. If we brush over these 'postmodern' reflections which do not have the same consistency, other authors and other movements go in the direction of a sceptical relativism. Hume's radical empiricism is an example of this, and so is nihilism too, of course, and more recently some jurists specialised in norms have also taken up relativistic ideas. Hanz Kelsen is no doubt the best illustration of this. He is the author of a bulky *General Theory of Norms* (Kelsen, 1979) which often serves as a reference. And as a matter of fact, it is to an extremely detailed and minute examination of the question of norms that he devoted himself. It is worth turning our attention to it for a moment since this shows that relativism is not an affair of expeditious thinking allowing itself to deduce, with no further questioning, and with an acute sense for paradox, moral relativism from value diversity. But there is another reason. Kelsen denies that the principle of non-contradiction can be used to examine practical questions. Since this goes against some of the reasonings suggested in chapter 3, it is quite useful to take a closer look at his arguments.

Kelsen starts by distinguishing between the norm and the statement on a norm and, in particular, on the validity of a norm. The norm deals with what ought to be, while the statement has to do with what is. However, and contrary to what could be expected, this distinction does not aim at discovering the levels of language which overlap in a proposition bearing on the validity of a norm. The point is only to distinguish clearly between a norm, such as 'Thou shalt not kill' (unauthentic must-be, subjective and prescriptive, which cannot be verified objectively), and an utterance like 'in such country, there exists a law banning murder, and therefore in this country, "thou shalt not kill" is a valid norm' (true must-be, descriptive, whose truthfulness can be established by the conformity to facts). The sentence 'one should not kill', deprived of any other specification as to its context, is ambiguous since it can either express the norm as such, the moral command, or express the fact that the norm is valid (objectively), that is, that there *exists* in a given community a norm which commands not to kill and to which every individual in this community is subjected (cf. chap. 38 and 41). Whereas a norm is neither true nor false, when one says a norm is valid one means that it is a fact that it should be observed. In other words, 'an utterance as to the validity of a norm is true' is a sentence which means that the norm is valid in the context described by the utterance. This logic applies to utterances without any difficulty, since they can be either true or non-true, but it does not apply to norms. No analogy is possible between the fair character of a behaviour (when it is conform to a norm), which is a practical value, and the true character of an utterance, which is a theoretical value. Having set down these premises, Kelsen comes to what constitutes one of the most significant results of his *Theory*: the principle of non-contradiction does not apply to conflicts of norms (chap. 57).

'It is beyond any doubt, Kelsen tells us, that the one and same person can say "Do this!" and "Don't do this!"', as a result of which whoever has to abide by these two imperatives will be faced with a conflict of norms. But knowing whether the principle of non-contradiction can be applied to this conflict amounts to wondering whether two contradictory norms can be valid at the same time. If the principle of non-contradiction was applied, we would have to infer that the same norm cannot be both violated and observed. Which is contradictory with the most ordinary observation. The very fact that there are normative conflicts, or that a person may observe and breach the same rule, or that the latter may be violated by some persons and observed by others, shows that the principle of non-contradiction does not apply to norms. One could think that it applies to two utterances, one of which bears upon the validity of the norm and the other upon its non-validity. Or, in a given normative conflict, the two conflicting norms are by definition valid, otherwise there would not be any conflict of norms. There is therefore no logical contradiction between these two valid norms, nor between the utterances on the validity of these two norms, which are not contrary to each other, since they are both true. To summarise: 'There is no logical contradiction between two utterances on the validity of two conflicting norms, just as there is no contradiction between the two conflicting norms.' To put it briefly, Kelsen would like to apply the Humian principle whereby what ought-to-be cannot be deduced from what is, but he does not really manage to do so and in the end his reasoning leads him either to a commonplace or to an unarguable position for a reason already clearly indicated by Popper (1945, II, p. 392): 'Thus – so argues the relativist or moral positivist – we never have to transcend the realm of facts, if only we include in it social or political or historical facts: there is no dualism of facts and standards.' Let us see, then, what appears to be refutable in Kelsen's reasoning from this perspective.

There is no doubt that there may *exist* two contradictory norms, but Kelsen forgets that it does not follow that this situation is right or morally *legitimate*. And, according to us, it is not so, especially because the principle of non-contradiction finds itself violated. Let us take the same example as Kelsen (1979, p. 220). Let there be a norm such as: 'Go to church every Sunday.' Some Sundays, Paul observes this command, whereas on other Sundays, he does not. Or still: some people can observe it and others violate it. For Kelsen, everything goes as if there were two valid norms in conflict, 'go to church every Sunday' and 'do not go to church every Sunday', not abiding by the principle of non-contradiction according to which two utterances cannot be true together, for instance for Paul. But, in fact, even from Kelsen's point of view, it is wrong to pretend that these two norms are 'valid'. Since Paul does not go to Church every Sunday, he *never* respects a norm which says: 'go to church every Sunday'. Even in Kelsen's sense, there is only one valid norm here, 'do not go to church every Sunday', and by sometimes going to mass on Sundays, Paul respects it in full.

With this example, Kelsen makes a logical mistake, but of course it is not so much on this mistake than on what is at its origin that he should be corrected. If two contradictory principles can be contemplated by the same individual or by the same community, it is either because no norm imposes itself (the reason why 'you must wear a red hat' is as valid as 'you must not wear a red hat' is because it is merely indifferent, when an individual wears a hat, whether the latter is red or not) or they are logically in contradiction. If we admit that 'A must be' is a valid norm, the non-respect of A does not form another valid norm. This is simply a deviating behaviour with regard to a valid norm. Contrary to Kelsen's position, we do not think that it is possible to hold that any behaviour, as soon as it is a recognised fact, reveals the existence of a *valid* norm. Without this, it would no longer even be possible to speak of deviance, nor even of crime or offence. If 'one must not kill, except in self-defence' is a valid norm, murderers do not follow another valid norm as a mere result of the fact that they commit murders. A deviating behaviour may spread to the point of tending to impose itself as a new norm. But precisely, there is then a conflict with the still prevailing norm. It is actually precisely because of the contradiction between the two norms that the conflict must be solved, since this contradiction itself – and this is what Kelsen neglects a little too quickly – is legitimate neither for the champions of A nor for the champions of non-A. But, as we know, there are essentially two different ways of solving the conflict: either through justice (with a potential ritualisation of the conflict), or through force. Either the Catholics conceive that there is a more fundamental norm than what separates them from the Protestants, and in order to put an end to massacres and live in the same community in the respect of everyone's beliefs, they promulgate the edict of Nantes, or they repeal it and start chasing Protestants again.[3] We take this example purposely, to emphasise again that a conflict between norms can go as far as war. This is not a simple ethereal confrontation of different ideas. But, with Kelsen's, as with all those who think that 'it is all the same', the conflict with no contradiction

3 Translator's note: In 1598, Henri IV signed an Edict in Nantes, which granted religious freedom to the Protestants. Louis XIV repealed it in 1685, and not until the French Revolution was the freedom of worship guaranteed for good to any citizen.

no longer truly is one. And actually, it is hard to really see what its driving force could be. After all, if any existing norm is valid, all is for the best in the best possible world. By wanting to evacuate contradiction at all costs, the notion of conflict between norms finds itself emptied of its meaning, so much so that it is not a true situation of conflict which is described, but rather a simple juxtaposition of different norms.

It is true that the principle of non-contradiction does not apply in practical life as a diktat coming from who knows which transcending logical universe to prevent *a priori* any conflict of norms. If this is what Kelsen means, he is very right. However, this is a very old and well-known critic. The project of a dogmatic rationalism which would claim to found practical reason almost entirely on theoretical reason is, as we know especially since Kant, impossible. This would necessarily amount to denying the freedom of the subject at one point or another in the reasoning. The principle of non-contradiction does not apply because moral problems could find solutions forming the object of mathematical demonstrations. It applies for practical reasons, not only without denying everyone's freedom, but probably even more because not applying it would eventually end up precisely calling into question this freedom. It applies, not because the universe from which it would be absent is impossible, but because it would be impossible to live in, as would be a universe where a subject could hold one thing and its contrary in a public argumentation, or a universe in which incompatible norms would permanently rule over everyone's behaviour.

### 1.3 *The demand for practical consistency*

Relativists like Kelsen content themselves with emphasising the diversity of norms to the point of forgetting that these norms have a *practical interest.* But all the value of a norm comes precisely from the fact that it settles a conflict in a way which gathers everyone's assent. By forgetting this dimension, Kelsen may well not be constrained by the rejection of the principle of non-contradiction since, for him, norms do not fulfil any practical goal. Norms become a gratuitous game and there is indeed no reason to worry about them forming a heap of contradictory utterances. Against the relativistic mistake, the practical interest of norms must therefore be emphasised:

individuals agree on rules for living together and in order to do so they must solve the conflicts[4] which oppose them.

As a result, and more generally, despite the large choice of norms, methods, or even procedures to solve a problem or a conflict, an obligation to be coherent is necessary to enable everyone to certify that these rules meet their goal. Let us take an example. Let us imagine a couple, Emmanuelle and Frederic, in a supermarket. They contemplate going each their own way to do their respective shopping but decide to agree on a meeting point so that they can leave together. The supermarket is large and there can be no question of relying on chance. At the same time, it is totally indifferent whether this couple meets at cash desk no. 1 or at cash desk no. 30. In fact, as Frederic, as a good relativist, notes, any cash desk will do. He thus suggests to Emmanuelle, as a rule for the meeting, that in half an hour she goes to cash desk no. 30, while he will go to cash desk no. 1. Emmanuelle, who is full of good sense, is surprised by such a rule, but Frederic is sure of himself: since anything goes and since cash desk *x* is not any better than cash desk *y* this rule will be just as satisfactory as any other! He does not understand the insistence of Emmanuelle, who suggests that they meet rather in half an hour at cash desk no. 8 – as if cash desk no. 8 was better *in itself*, as if the cash desk number was not arbitrary. Frederic is even shocked: 'Now, this is clearly an indication of ethnocentrism! Would you claim to compel this other couple to meet in half an hour at cash desk no. 8? Don't forget that everyone is free to choose.' This is of course out of the question, and Emmanuelle could reply to any relativist that she does not impose her conception of the good life. Here, actually, she feels nothing but indifference as to the choice of the cash desk, and she does not care whether to impose cash desk no. 1 rather than cash desk no. 8. If she challenges Frederic's proposal, it is not out of a lack of good will (which would consist in denying Frederic's right of veto) but so that the meeting point rule should translate accurately their *common will*. From the moment Frederic really wants to meet up with Emmanuelle, *the latter does not impose anything on him but to manage to reach his goal.* Of course, if Frederic did not wish to meet up with Emmanuelle, if, for instance, he wanted to leave her for good, then the meeting point rule would be authoritarian. Emmanuelle would impose

4 Conflicts which are solved by themselves, with absolutely no will from the protagonists, because of the modifications in their global environment (such as a natural catastrophe) do not interest us as long as actors are supposed not to have any hold over the evolution of this environment.

it on Frederic to do something which he does not want to do. Inversely, as soon as the will to meet up is verified, there is no longer anything authoritarian in demanding that the procedure should effectively reach its goal. The point is to verify that the agreement is a true one, no longer in the moral sense that everyone should have a say, but in the sense that the procedure should reach the objective which the agreement gave itself. In this respect, Frederic's proposal is symptomatic of Kelsen's difficulties. All the norm utterances may well be accepted ('I go to cash desk no. 1', 'you go to cash desk no. 30') for there is obviously no True cash desk, in the Platonician sense, to meet up at. However, it remains that the contradiction between the rule planned for Emmanuelle and the one which Frederic plans for himself is in itself a problem. It is actually not so much that the rule to follow should be the same for both of them which matters (an asymmetrical procedure could be contemplated: Frederic would go to cash desk no. 8 by reaching it from the left, while Emmanuelle would reach it from the right), as the fact that, in the end, Frederic and Emmanuelle should effectively meet up. The agreement must be an agreement on a consistent proposal and an inconsistent proposal *is not worth* a consistent proposal, because the former betrays the common will.

In the end, one of the main discrepancies between our claim and the relativistic proposal, of which Kelsen only provides an illustration, stems from the fact that we hold justice as a unanimous agreement to be a stopping condition which must be *applied* to a conflict (or a problem) and that consequently it is false to say that, since unanimous agreement is a free convention between free subjects, it may consist in pretty much anything. For a unanimous agreement to be valid, it must define a consistent procedure in order to reach the hoped-for result. From this viewpoint, the principle of non-contradiction, and not only it, applies. An argumentation or a justification is publicly acceptable only if it puts together its reasons in a consistent way, and it will be the object of a unanimous agreement only if everyone realises that it has the power to effectively solve the conflict or the problem encountered by all.

We had already seen a first reason why a fair unanimous agreement is not any agreement. It cannot be in contradiction with the transcendental conditions of this agreement; otherwise an agreement would be a non-agreement. We can see a second reason here. The reasons presiding over the choice of the procedure must be consistent with the problem posed; that is to say that when it is applied the procedure must solve the conflict by expressing the general will. In a word, the 'choice of reason' must be made.

## 2. The Choice of the Reasonable

In the example of the supermarket, it is not hard to see that the choice of reason consists in coming to an agreement on Emmanuelle's proposal, even if it could imply that Frederic may persuade her to choose rather cash desk no. 1, because it is closer to the exit. But this question of the choice of reason, understood as the choice 'to become involved in a process of argumentative discussion in order to solve a conflict over norms' (Mesure and Renaut, 1996, p. 136) is an extremely delicate and debated question. The theoretical dilemma is as follows: either this choice is not free, it is determined by some exteriority (nature, history, community, class, etc.), but it can no longer be said that justice as a unanimous agreement has its roots in the principle of freedom or in the autonomy of the will. Or this choice is free, it is a final decision made by an actor, whom nothing nor anyone could compel, and as a result, it seems that one cannot avoid lapsing into relativism or decisionism, which had just been challenged. Our position will consist in holding that this element of final decision, which can be made explicit in many ways (the choice to reason and not only to rationalise, the choice of a stopping condition for the principle of sufficient reason which is found in unanimous agreement, etc.), cannot be crossed out without a loss of coherence, but that this does not lead to any relativism. But before we argue in favour of this, and in order to take in every aspect of this problem, a short summary of the history of this debate is needed.

### 2.1 *The confrontation between the rational and freedom*

The problem can be summed up as follows. In so far as man is the evaluator, it cannot be said that some orientations, some choices, are better than others before he evaluates for himself. We then touch upon a fundamental opposition between the rational (or the theoretical reason) and freedom (or the practical reason). In a non-Kantian perspective, the contradiction can be solved by choosing between the two terms of the alternative which opposes relativism to dogmatism. Either man is free to say what is (morally) worthy, but values which result from this evaluation are only subjective, for objectively, everything is arbitrary, 'it is all good'. Or a good choice awaits him, and his rationality leads him to choose it, and freedom is nothing else than the freedom to be irrational, mad or dumb.

Let us acknowledge that this is a crucial question in which many theorists have ensnared themselves. It can even be said that only transcendental philosophy (or critical rationalism, as it can also be called) has really taken in the whole extent of the problem. To stick to two major schools of thought, it must be emphasised that neither Leibnizian monadology and the economic theory of rational choice on the one hand, nor Nietzschean genealogy and Weberian sociology on the other, are left unscathed. Rational choice theorists always conclude a little too fast that Reason is on their side and that the others are irrational: they cannot see how to introduce freedom otherwise. We have already made sufficient objections to this orientation not to need to go back over it.

Weber proceeds in a very different way. The famous 'polytheism of values' which he stands for does not boil down to the mere statement of cultural diversity. By claiming that this polytheism is irreducible, Weber unfolds down to their very end the consequences of Hume's (1740, III, 1) ban (from 'is', one cannot infer 'ought') and draws the same conclusion as him: there is no practical reason (or, if there is, it is merely empirical). Contrary to what Kant thinks, reason is not capable of defining ends which can prevail universally, and consequently, practical questions cannot receive any answer pretending to any objectivity. In the end, everyone stands firmly on their values and as a result, no one reasons anymore, and everyone is rationalising. But this is far from being the same thing. While those who reason utter synthetic judgments on the world, those who rationalise simply unfold analytically (logically) the implications of their final decisions. While the former seek a *relevant* rule in a given situation, the latter merely apply a rule which is *already given*. In other words, some think, the others calculate. The fact that this calculation is merely logical, that is, that it only seeks to verify the coherence, without caring at the same time about the consequences which the theoretical reason can predict, must not conceal that it still is a calculation. This amounts to saying, in passing, that a calculation may be non-consequentialist. Those who follow an ethics of conviction must only ensure the coherence of their actions with their final convictions (or decisions).

The vocabulary chosen by Weber betrays blatantly this intention to evacuate the (pure) practical reason from sociological analysis. What Kant used to call the 'imperative of skill' is renamed 'instrumental rationality'[5] *(Zweckrationalität)* and, however, refers to exactly the same type of action. Of course, the point is not to give the impression of turning the old into new. The point is to erase the reference to moral choice by no longer talking about the hypothetical imperative when an actor chooses to implement the means which are best-suited to the realisation of an objective which she has set herself. Where it used to be very clear that such an action could imply not to follow the categorical imperative and that one thus had to take a moral decision, with good reasons, this is no longer the main question at all. The skilful action is a sheer affair of rationality. One can no longer see that it may possibly consist in choosing to give precedence to the reasons of a partial actor over those of a fair spectator – for instance when the principle 'whoever wants the end, wants the means' clashes with the fact that it would lead, in a given circumstance, to regard some individuals or justice only as means, and that this principle is still chosen. As for axiological rationality *(Wertrationalität)*, it offers us to put all values at the same level, in particular the right and the good. Choosing the right or choosing the good is one and the same thing: a mere rational choice in value (where, according to Weber (1922, I, § 2), the motivations of action rest on 'the belief in the value for its own sake of some ethical, aesthetic, religious, or other form of behaviour, independently of its prospects of success'). Such a reduction is legitimate only if one thinks that anyway, the decision is ultimately arbitrary, since it is founded on values and reasons which are purely subjective. The reasonable is at best one value among others. And since there can be no objectivity (other than factual) of moral values, there can be no question of giving a different status to the reasonable. But we must see clearly where this leads us. If, like Weber (1919), we draw all the consequences of this, we

5 Other translations are also used: rationality of the means, rationality in finality, teleological rationality, etc. Whichever phrase is chosen, this form of rationality confuses the possible ends with the given ends, contrary to a Kantian analysis, which distinguishes between skill and prudence.

find ourselves in the end ineluctably confronted to an unsurpassable war of the gods.[6]

Weber's axiological rationality deals with a decision which cannot be justified *for a random other*. It is a subjective decision which implies final values and as a result it is a commitment in the strongest sense, for what can be made relative before the decision (it is only a possible choice whose value stems from free will) becomes absolute after it, all the more as this commitment is subscribed by the actor by virtue of reasons which are strong for her. For, as Boudon (1995*a*) emphasises, prescriptive beliefs, in the wake of descriptive beliefs, must make sense for the subject who adopts them, and this supposes that she has strong reasons to make up her mind or commit in favour of such or such belief. But if we take Weber's reasoning to its end, this subjective decision or this commitment is equivalent to a revelation and it cannot be formally distinguished from an act of faith for a God (resting on strong subjective reasons too). Since all decisions are ultimately and objectively arbitrary, there results that individuals will not choose the same gods: there will be a war of the gods. In other words, the practical reason degrades here into a practical decisionism which sets an *arbitrary* bound to our capacity to agree: humanity is divided into as many humanities as there are 'final decisions' to be made, and there is *by principle* no means of coming to an end. Maybe some sort of *modus vivendi* can be contemplated, but it is only a precarious balance between powers which remain in conflict as long as no decision has been made in favour of either of them. For in the end, each group may have *its own* fundamental and substantial conception of the good life; each group may have *its own* final principles of justification and legitimacy; each group may have *its own* reasons which are different from others' and which can make them Martians or inhuman animals (barbarians for the Romans, slaves for the masters, etc.).[7]

6 Weber (1919, p. 152) used this metaphor in a conference in order to refer more specifically to instances where: 'The ultimately possible attitudes towards life are irreconcilable and hence their struggle can never be brought to a final conclusion. Thus it is necessary to make a decisive choice.' A reader wishing to further investigate this question may consult, among others, the essay which Mesure and Renaut (1996) devoted to it. More recently, Pierre Bouretz (1998) showed how, with this issue of the war of the gods, Weber oscillated between nihilism and scepticism.

7 We can actually understand why Kant has devoted so many efforts to building and maintaining the unity of reason (on the basis of the practical reason). This is not a question of purely 'speculative' philosophy or simply of settling the quarrel with Hume's radical empiricism. As long as one does not set down for oneself the unity of reason, the

Relativism is not avoided – unless one supposes arbitrarily a single God and/or denies freedom, as do Leibniz and, after him but without knowing it, rational choice theorists.

### 2.2 *Recognising* alter *as* alter ego

If one wants to avoid relativistic or dogmatic 'solutions', or those which mix both, one must take the 'Copernican revolution' carried out by Kant to its end. One must therefore rely on the idea of a community of subjects or of intersubjectivity – without which the practical reason could not give to the will the law of its action. As we have already seen, there can be no subject without intersubjectivity and, inversely, no intersubjectivity without any subject. It is around this central point that the seeming contradiction between the rational and freedom may be solved. For, in the end, this intersubjectivity can only start making sense and be effective – outside coercion or conflict, since they do not ensure *a priori* an impartial or fair foundation for morality – if there is an autonomous subject acknowledging that another subject is autonomous. In other words, there is no intersubjectivity without a full and complete recognition of the other and in this respect recognising the other always consists in the end in seeing *alter* as an *alter ego*. It does not result that the other is the same. It is the I which *sets down* that a non-I is equally free and reasonable. By doing so, reason and freedom are no longer opposed in an absolute way. The rational, free to evaluate, seemed to depend only on my free will, and therefore to be arbitrary, unless one believed in God and/or one was no longer free. But, from now on, since I no longer am the only one possessed of reason, I can be free without my evaluation being reasonable as a result; this can happen if *alter* does not regard my reasons as admissible. There is therefore really an other who, being endowed with reason, forbids that free will and reason should be confused. Relativism is more than denied – it is made impossible or incoherent. Moreover, this other is not absolutely other, as a result of which *ego* is not deprived of his reason when *alter* contradicts him. And it is precisely

unity of mankind is not guaranteed, or only empirically so, which amounts to pretty much the same. And all the logical deviances, denying some people's humanity, remain possible.

because this dispossession does not occur, it is precisely because the right of veto is retained, that one does not sink into dogmatism.

Recognition, understood in this sense, is thus the nodal point of the reasoning, the one which allows (critical) rationalism to become one with (universalistic) humanism. In passing, it should be noted that it is not tolerance, or any other feeling of the same type, which represents the first, central or driving element of a liberal morality. Tolerance supposes in the first place, and much more fundamentally, the recognition of *alter* as *alter ego*. What is at stake is to understand that *alter*, with whom I share my reason, is not only someone who belongs to the same community, race, class, religion, etc., as me, but truly any woman, any man. That this did not happen in one day is very certain. That significant regressions remain possible is just as certain. There remains that if something must characterise modernity, it has to be this will to take mankind to the very boundaries of *homo sapiens*. As Popper (1945, II, p. 238) says: 'Faith in reason is not only a faith in our own reason, but also – and even more – in that of others.' And it is from this idea that his argumentation in favour of the *free* choice of reason stems.

### 2.3 *An ultimately free choice*

Weber's theory left us with a series of arbitrary final decisions. Popper, just like Kant or Weber, accepts the Humian ban and he too is thus obliged to conclude that there is a dualism of what is and what ought to be or of fact judgments and value judgments. However, he asks, does this mean that no principle brings them closer? He sees this principle in the fact that both types of judgment are subject to the same regulating procedure. With both science and morality, judgments are not worth anything if they cannot be submitted to a publicly argued critical discussion. It can be objected that the criterion of truth for an experimental science, conformity to facts, is not the criterion of justice for a moral and political science where, according to Popper (who leaves there the Kantian field and meets intuitionism, except if one sees in his reasoning some sort of premise of Rawls's reflective equilibrium), we can only rely on our conscience. However, holding one thing to be true or holding one thing to be fair hinge identically on a *reasonable decision*. There is nothing true or fair which may not be the object of a (temporary) unanimous agreement at the outcome of a well-argued discussion. In the end, behind all final decisions lies an identical and single choice. The point is always to know whether one is making the choice of reason, which consists in making the reasonable decision of submitting the dividing line between the fair and the non-fair (or between the true and the non-true) to critical discussion or, on the contrary, if one is making the choice of unreasonableness, which consists in rejecting the reasonable perspective of a unanimous agreement, especially by refusing that any person should take part in the discussion. As the choice of the reasonable, the choice of reason is thus *ipso facto* the choice to acknowledge *alter* as *alter ego*.

Nonetheless, for Popper, it remains very clear that this choice is ultimately free. Moral choice is not the choice of coercion, and no argument, even the most convincing conceivable one, could lead someone who does not wish to argue to actually argue. It would thus seem that in the end, relativism and even the war of the gods (between those who make the choice of reason and those who refuse to do so) cannot be avoided. One way of reducing this new final decision would be to give it a final foundation in the reason. This is what Apel[8] set out to do.

Apel does not contemplates finding a deductive foundation (starting from something else, regarded as anterior) for the choice of reason. This would be leaving relativism in order to fall into dogmatism and anyway, such a foundation would imply admitting the principles which it seeks to found. He aims to find a 'transcendental' foundation, that is, such that the choice of reason may appear as an *a priori* imperative presupposition. His reasoning is, undoubtedly, very enticing, and may be summarised as follows: it is impossible to argue against the choice of reason, since this implies using reasons, and therefore making the choice of reason against which one aims at arguing. In other words, any challenge to the norms of reason leads to a 'performative self-contradiction' (Apel, 1975). The problem is that by saying that, one leaves the question which was asked unanswered: must I argue anything at all?[9] In brief, Apel does not answer to Beaumarchais (*The Marriage of Figaro*, Act I, Scene 1) or rather he still leaves Figaro speechless when facing Suzanne:

8 Karl-Otto Apel wrote many works on this issue, which have led him to break away (Apel, 1989) from Habermas following the objections addressed to him by the latter (Habermas, 1983).

9 Rather than: why should I argue? To those who put the question this way, Apel (1986) has every opportunity to reply that asking oneself 'why' is already to make the choice of reason. On the objections to the final foundation, Jean-Marc Ferry's work (1987) may be consulted.

> – *Suzanne (Figaro's fiancée):* And what are you measuring there, my dear?
> – *Figaro:* I'm just thinking about this fine bed which His Lordship is giving us. The question is: will it go here?
> – In this room?
> – This is the one he's letting us have.
> – Well *I* don't want it.
> – Why?
> – I just don't.
> – But why not?
> – I don't like it.
> – You might give a reason?
> – Suppose I don't want to?
> – Ay! Once they are sure of us…
> – Giving a reason for being right amounts to admitting I could be wrong. Are you my humble servitor or aren't you?

Argumentation cannot compel anyone to argue, and on this idea Nietzsche (1888, 'The Problem of Socrates', § 5) could easily fly to the rescue of Suzanne: 'Anything which needs first to have itself proved is of little value. Wherever it is still good manners to be authoritative, and people do not "justify" but command, the dialectician is a kind of buffoon: he is laughed at and not taken seriously. – Socrates was the buffoon who *got himself taken seriously*: what was actually going on here?' To those who purely and simply refuse to argue, what does Apel answer? Relatively to older texts, some of his recent reflections (Apel, 1986) seem to add more nuances:

> What we have shown is this: *those who argue with the required seriousness* and who sincerely seek the intersubjectively valid truth […] then necessarily decide too in favour of being moral. […] However, this does not prove that a man cannot decide against being moral and, consequently, also against being rational, in the sense of the will of truth. If this happened at the level of principles, this would amount to a self-destruction (which can be an extreme, hardly imaginable, pathological case).

In the end, we must stop at the viewpoint held by Popper, Kant, Rawls or Habermas (among others). To put it like Habermas: there is no final foundation for the discourse ethics. The choice of reason remains a free choice (which can be and is argued, but not compelled by argumentation itself), a choice of the will in favour of the reason, in a word, the choice to give the priority to the just and, as a result, it is 'the most fundamental decision in the ethical field' (Popper, 1945, II, p. 233). A consistent system of freedom cannot impose anything from the start, except being freely chosen. If an actor does not want to solve a conflict other than by force, if she wants to make the choice of egoism (being a free rider) or of altruism (by sacrificing herself in the name of an idea of the good, out of 'sanctity') rather than justice, in brief, if she rejects the reasonable, it is not the reasonable, precisely because it is the reasonable, which can impose itself as such.

### 2.4 *Convention and objectivity do not stand in opposition*

But it must be clear that outside unanimous agreement, this actor cannot pretend that her subjective reasons are, by miracle, objective too, that her choice is a moral choice. And as a matter of fact, with what arguments towards others could she do so, now that she has rejected the choice to argue or to justify herself publicly and reasonably? Consequently, lapsing again into relativism is avoided. We are not led to claim that all decisions are equal. One concession only: there exists a final decision which only has to do with the freedom of the subject. Denying it would be admitting a final heteronomy of the will and would open the floodgates for all determinisms. But only the choice of reason leads to moral choice. Only the reasonable is objective. Only unanimous agreement can serve as practical truth. The dividing line is very clear and entirely contradictory with relativism according to which, since the choice of reason is the product of a totally free final decision, almost anything can be called moral, or regarded as deriving from a good will. Acknowledging that the freedom of the subject is an intangible principle, were it only in order to be able to contemplate the perspective of unanimous agreement, is not at all recognising that from then on, any decision can claim to objectivity. It is even the exact opposite. An objective reason is a reason which can be accepted by everyone. As we know, it amounts to the same to say that it is – or at least may be – the basis of a unanimous agreement, or that it is reasonable. Someone who refuses the choice of reason rejects the reasonable. He can therefore not claim that he does so for reasonable motives. He will never convince those who, by making the choice of reason, demand that a reasoning be consistent. Here is again, formulated from a different angle, Apel's reasoning, but without drawing the same conclusion from it in terms of final foundation.

One must actually distinguish between two cases of refusal of agreement which do not amount to the same at all. The individual who turns down an agreement in the name of his right of veto does so in the context of the choice of reason. Whereas the person who rejects the choice of reason rejects the very principle of unanimous agreement. She denies that it is the fair way to settle the conflict opposing her to others. And if everyone did the same, there could be no agreement. It only turns out that, when everyone has given up on finding a reasonable solution, an open conflict unfolds and disagreements are solved through force. There is no unanimous agreement on the idea that everyone should renounce the choice of reason, if we accept that a conflict is at the very least a manifest disagreement, and that a disagreement is not an agreement. That in a given situation all the actors reject the choice of reason does not define in any way, except in the case of a sophism, a reasonable choice or an objectivity. This extreme but not impossible situation, as is a Hobbesian state of nature, does in no way mar the clarity and the neatness of the line separating the reasonable from the non-reasonable.

Admitting that the choice of reason is the consequence of a free final decision, it is clear that our claim is at one with some form of conventionalism. But this conventionalism has nothing to do with a relativism, a decisionism, or any nihilism. We are not brought back to the war of the gods. Acknowledging that the priority of justice is the outcome of a free will does not make it impossible to see in the unanimous agreement a stopping condition opening up a space of practical objectivity. Contrary to the relativist, for whom if everything is a convention, everything is equal, we are perfectly capable of distinguishing between objective motives and subjective ones, between the reasons of a fair spectator and those of a partial actor, between the categorical imperative and the hypothetical imperatives. In return, if the principle of a free will was not maintained, these distinctions would not be possible, or they would lose all their meaning. In the wake of Popper, for whom saying that laws are conventional does not amount to saying that they are all worth the same, we think that convention and objectivity are not opposed. But this demands two things: (i) abandoning a metaphysical conception of the truth; (ii) recognising that next to positive or theoretical objectivity, there is room for some practical objectivity and this is what is essential here.

## 3. Practical Objectivity

### 3.1 *Rejecting a metaphysical conception of the truth and not sticking to a positive objectivity*

The question of objectivity is all the more arduous as we must start by doing away with the metaphysical vision which is always more or less nagging minds. Objectivity does not reside in some in-itself. A thing is not good because it is in conformity with justice in itself. The good in itself, the just in itself, the true in itself, the thing in itself are unknowable. Whatever the way in which the problem is tackled, the thing in itself derives from an infinity which is fatally exterior to a finite subject which has no way of getting out of himself in order to get hold of this infinity. From the practical point of view, there results that it is within himself that a subject must find the reasons which lead him to want to live with others rather than in some exteriority or nature. The will to live together is an autonomous will, that is, one which is not determined by anything exterior (history, community, revelation of the in-itself, etc.). Determinism, no matter what its nature is, is denied. The Kantian critic of metaphysics opens the space of an autonomous subject or one freely submitting to the moral law, which means, as we know, that he or she assumes the reasons of a fair spectator because only these reasons, not being guided only by the good for oneself or for someone else, are capable of obtaining *everyone*'s assent. Objectivity thus has its foundation, as we have already pointed out, in intersubjectivity rather than in the relationship to some in-itself or in some exteriority which would determine the subjects or their relationships to be 'objective'. It is very clear that it is the unanimous agreement which serves as a matrix to objectivity, and especially that in this relationship between subjects everyone remains free to make their decisions. It is no less clear that consequently, it is not theoretical or positive objectivity which is being discussed here.

According to positivism, the conformity of an utterance with the fact that it describes or seeks to predict is, following the model of physics, the single criterion of truth (thanks to a rigorous observation or experimentation). There is no objectivity outside factual positivity and only the latter can be a source of truth.[10] In so far as this model has a pretension to be exported to moral and political sciences, one may speak of scientism. This is neither more nor less than thinking that only a discipline which can present positive models which are analogous to those of (mathematised) physics reaches objective or 'scientific' knowledge. If one confronts this way of considering objectivity with the Humian ban, one can see how devastating it may be to understand norms or values.

Prescriptive judgments can of course be the object of a positive science, since they are facts and like any other fact lend themselves to description or explanation. There may be some specific method difficulties when dealing with values, but they are not unsurpassable. Rules can be implemented, like the famous axiological neutrality of the analyst. However, on the ground of moral judgments, just as on any other ground, one cannot go beyond this factual aspect in order to found some objectivity. Again, we find Kelsen and the positivistic conviction which animates him. Hence the necessary degradation of this positivism into a relativism since, for the rest, everything is only subjective. We could go as far as to hold that a consistent positivism can only be relativistic. This is actually a source of difficulty for us, since we do not claim for a second to call into question positive objectivity. But the true difficulty does not reside in defining theoretical objectivity so much as in its pretension to be the one and only prevailing criterion of objectivity. On this aspect, we are at one with Sylvie Mesure and Alain Renaut (1996):

> For the war of the gods to seem inevitable, on the basis of the distortion which had appeared within reason, and which was expressed by the Humian ban, it was necessary in the first place to reduce any conceivable form of objectivity to the model of theoretical objectivity, that of the knowledge of natural phenomena ('facts'): because one had become convinced (according to the constitutive conviction of scientism) that some objectivity could be achieved only through this model […].

'Objective' morality is then that which is, which may be described, and since there is no ('scientific') passage from the descriptive to the prescriptive, any scientific discourse stops here. With such a description, the right is brought down to the fact, or what ought-to-be to what is. There is nothing

10 It must actually be noticed that facts being discussed can just as well be facts of fiction as facts of reality. The fact that Sherlock Holmes liked the violin is just as true as the fact that Louis XIV loved dancing; Edmond Dantès – future Count of Monte Cristo – was treated just as unfairly as Dreyfus.

outside positive right, and it is impossible to wonder whether a positive rule is objectively fair or not. This is indeed what liberalism, any liberalism, seeks to avoid at all costs, for in the end the fundamental principle of the subject's freedom is always denied, and this is why it maintains firmly the dualism of what ought-to-be and what is, even if this does not prevent it from seeking common regulating principles (in the reasonable).

Indeed, it should not be forgotten that there is not only one form of objectivity. Luckily, the alternative does not consist in choosing between the scientism of a reductive positivism and metaphysics. Without reverting to a metaphysical project, next to positive objectivity (of which we only challenge the reductive character, let us repeat it), there is room for some *practical objectivity* which, actually and as we shall see, occurs in two different ways. Scientific discourse thus does not stop where relativists would like it to stop. Good reasons, as objective reasons, are not only those which are voiced here or there in some argument or justification, but those conforming to this practical objectivity. And in order to back this point of view, it is not necessary to abrogate the Humian ban. One only has to disconnect it from positivism or dogmatism. It can then easily be seen that unanimous agreement as a stopping condition for the principle of sufficient reason is well and truly the ground where some objectivity is at work.

### 3.2 *Unanimous agreement as a stopping condition opens a space for objectivity*

Let us come back for a moment to the stopping condition issue and see what the relativist actually questions. It has been previously established that in order to judge on the theoretical or practical truth of an utterance, it was always necessary to distinguish at least three levels of speech. To confuse them is a sophism which leads inevitably to paradoxes such as Epimenides's. Level L1 is that of the utterance on which it is going to be necessary to pass a judgment (for instance: 'I am a Cretan'). Level L2 is that of the test (or the function) of truth (for instance, a lie detector). Level L3 is that of the stopping condition thanks to which the L2-level test is acknowledged as valid (this lie detector is a reliable device). The stopping condition is imperative by virtue of the principle of reason (or causality). Without this condition, we find ourselves inexorably confronted to an infinite regression. It can be located further than L3 in the chain of reasons. It can even be very far, since, following Leibniz, it is God as the Prime Mover which constitutes it. But it is at the minimum at level 3. In other words, it is admitted that the lie detector cannot be its own test of truth, just as it cannot be the Cretan who is speaking.

In one case, and only one, it is possible to postulate the absence of a stopping condition: the case when one accepts to remain *strictly* at level L1. Indeed, it is noticeable that, contrary to the utterance 'I am lying', the sentence 'I am telling the truth' contains no paradox.[11] Therefore, it cannot be logically refused, on the condition however that this universe of truth in itself remains confined to the domain which makes it possible: that of *utterances without evaluation.* If the sentence 'I am telling the truth' had to be evaluated, inevitably, a test and a stopping condition and thus, leaving level L1 would be required. This universe of utterances without evaluation is, however, extraordinarily poor. The true is possible there on the condition of never dissociating itself from the non-true! This universe, where the whole is everything, is certainly not the basis for an objective or scientific reflection, where evaluation is of course required. It is not such that it calls into question the imperative necessity of a stopping condition to establish a theoretical or practical truth. It seems to us that relativism does not challenge this point. Its challenge bears upon the consequences of the arbitrariness in a stopping condition which is set down conventionally by men. But this can be done in two ways.

First, the relativist may refuse any stopping condition at all. He then agrees with nihilism as radical scepticism: since any stopping condition is arbitrary, one must imperatively get by without it. However, such radicalism cannot even be uttered, since this very utterance implies admitting many stopping conditions. At the other extreme of the whole everything, which can only be true, since there is nothing outside everything, we are left with no reasons at all. Not a word, in the ordinary sense of the term, is possible. Maybe there is nothing left but a will to power? However, this is not the relativistic position discussed so far. 'Nothing is worthy' is not necessarily equivalent to 'anything goes'. According to the latter orientation, which is quicker to conceive that reason has become 'world', a stopping condition is needed and, moreover, it is indeed established by mankind. It does not result from some social determinism or other – which would of course represent another solution, but would take us out of the context of the

11 With the notations used above, it is written: $\forall p, p \in V \Leftrightarrow `p \in V' \in V$.

freedom of moral choice and therefore of the debate with relativism as to the consequences of such freedom. But, precisely, the relativist points out that such a stopping condition, as it results from a free and arbitrary choice, can only open up a space for subjectivity. The contrary position which we stand for consists in emphasising that it is arbitrary only from the viewpoint of a positive objectivity, and that it is not so at all from the viewpoint of some practical objectivity. Unanimous agreement as a stopping condition, though the latter is positively conventional, enables fully such practical objectivity to be effective. It is indeed because it forgets this that reductive positivism degenerates into relativism. A comparison between justice and language will be an opportunity to return to it with one last example.

### 3.3 *A theoretical and practical coherence*

There are many differences between language and justice, especially because in the case of the sign the link between the signifier and the signified is purely arbitrary, and does not have to fulfil transcendental conditions. But both are human conventions and in both cases a unanimous agreement on this convention is needed for it to perform its office: settling a conflict, making a communication possible. The words of language are like the supermarket cash desks of the previous example. At first sight, in order to refer to a table, any cluster of sounds is suited. However, communication only functions within a community if each of its members uses the same word to describe the same thing. Spaniards could say 'table', where French people could say 'mesa'. This is the gist of what the relativist tells us, and it is not much. He cannot see that in order to communicate with some French, one has to say 'table' or that, in order to communicate with Spaniards, 'mesa', and nothing else, must be used. Frederic may well tell Emmanuelle that, since every word is arbitrary, he can use 'table' or 'mesa' as he pleases, Emmanuelle will be right in objecting that as long as they have not agreed on the same convention, they will not understand each other. Subjectively, one may prefer, for aesthetic reasons, such or such cluster of sounds. But the demand for practical coherence leads to seek a unanimous agreement which, once reached, turns the chosen word into what must *objectively* be used for the communication initially targeted to be effective. In this respect, the same goes with justice. The norm which has been unanimously chosen becomes an objective norm.

Nevertheless, as we have said from the start, there is an important difference between language and justice. While any arbitrary cluster of phonemes may be a candidate to constitute a moneme, not any norm can be contemplated *a priori*. Whereas in the case of a language facts and right are as it were confused, in the case of justice, this is never true. To be valid, or legitimate or objective, a word does not need to be anything else than the universal convention adopted by a language. In order to be valid, a norm must moreover be universalisable *a priori*, and any gathering of words forming a (syntactically valid) rule submitted to the approval of a community does not meet this condition. This point has already been previously established, but it is worth recalling it in order to really make clear what separates Kantian conventionalism from relativism. One example, slightly more baroque than those proposed when we were illustrating the objectivity of the right of veto, will be enough. Let us suppose the rule: 'Considering that improving one's well-being is the supreme goal and that by appropriating the belongings of one's neighbour this end is reached, it is allowed, twice in one's lifetime, to kill one's neighbour and take all her belongings.' The rule seems impartial, an identical right is given to everyone, and a limit is even set in the hope of avoiding the state of war of all against all. And yet, applied on a broad scale, it will inevitably lead to the strongest taking hold of the belongings of the weakest, while decimating this population, who are obviously far less capable of defending themselves against the now-legitimate aggressions of their stronger neighbours. Under the guise of so-called impartiality, such a rule is nothing else than the 'law' of the strongest, and thereby simply contradicts the right of veto of the weakest. It can very well be *de facto* the object of a unanimous agreement; it could not be made universal *a priori*, since by denying the right of veto of some, it negates the very principle of unanimous agreement which, however, it claims to use in order to back its legitimacy. Even if it satisfies the criterion of a practical consistency, it does not satisfy that of a theoretical consistency, if what is meant by this is that it does not fulfil the conditions which make it a thinkable object *a priori*.

### 3.4 *Unanimous agreement as a practical truth by virtue of a double objectivity*

From the angle of the *discussion* of a norm, these two consistency criteria define reasons which the actors may use in order to seek a unanimous agreement, and from this practical angle, the nature of the mobilised objectivity appears more clearly. For the actors, a unanimous agreement defines a practical truth. Fair principles have the value of a practical truth or of correctness. Now, if of course a practical truth is not a theoretical truth, otherwise it would not be necessary to use two different phrases, it is also in both cases a truth. And, so that this same notion may be used in a non-exaggerated way, it must rest on some objective knowledge. This usually means two things: there must (i) be an agreement between the knowledge and its object, that is with its content or its matter and (ii) the form of knowledge should follow the logic (at least the principles of identity and non-contradiction) which defines the truth criteria for thinking in general and the understanding in particular which, otherwise, would fatally end up contradicting itself. It must be emphasised that the second condition is *sine qua non* but non-sufficient (Kant, 1787, I, II, introd., 3). We must therefore find out what are the adequation criteria which must be selected in the practical field.

The first criterion which springs to mind is, as we have seen, that of conformity to the fact. But, in the practical case, we have also seen that it is not possible to restrict ourselves to this empiricist or positivistic demand – unless we accept to bring what ought to be down to what is. Always in reference to the theoretical reason, a second path could be contemplated. Justice as a unanimous agreement has made it possible to exclude a whole series of situations from the field of this justice. Now, the reasons which have allowed such rejections are objective in so far as the maintenance of the principle of non-contradiction, and consequently of identity, has played a substantial part in this, in such a way as to avoid precisely any subjective reading which could turn against the very principle of agreement. Does this mean as a result that theoretical reason determines the agreements to which practical reason consents? According to us, this dogmatic interpretation of objectivity is not in the slightest more receivable than the positivistic conception. And, to understand this, we must ask ourselves what actors who verify or argue that this clause of objectivity is well respected actually do. In other words, in practical terms, how can we ensure that condition (ii) above is concretely respected?

It seems to us that for the actors this amounts to relying on their judgment in order to verify that there is indeed an agreement on what makes it possible to subsume the particular under the universal character of the rule. Here, this rule is a rule of the understanding, given *a priori* to reason. Judgment is therefore determinant; but obviously not in the sense that it determines action. It is not an analytical judgment, which would consist in inferring the fact of agreement from the formal logic presiding over this agreement. The logical form does not impose itself in this (deductive) way to practical agreements. It is out of the question to lapse into the dogmatism of a practical reason which would be absolutely deducted from theoretical reason. Judgment is determinant, in the sense that it 'decide[s] whether something is an object of pure practical reason or not' (Kant, 1788, I, II). It is always the will which is the determinant principle of action and 'the question is only whether we should *(dürfen)* will an action' (Kant, *ibid.*), that is, the *right*, relatively to *a priori* rules of the understanding, to want this very agreement, which is being discussed. From the point of view of an (only) empirical practical reason, we may want any rational agreement. But, from the point of view of pure practical reason, we demand it to be reasonable by not calling into question the very principle of agreement (equal liberty or everyone's right of veto, as preferred). This clause of theoretical consistency is necessary and not sufficient, but if it is observed, there is some objectivity, according to a first form, which may be called 'determinant' – on the condition that, as we have just emphasised, one endows the term with no deterministic or dogmatic bearing at all.

Endowing it with such bearing would be all the more detrimental since according to the second form of practical objectivity, it becomes all the clearer that it is impossible to grant it this meaning. The reason why not any intersubjectivity is at stake is also that questions raised in order to come to an agreement as to a fair norm are not ethereal questions where everyone can cling to their positions without seeking agreement, without it having some incidences for them and all the others. Norms are supposed to have a practical interest. The aim is to solve a conflict (or a problem) which everyone has to face, and this demands practical coherence. The convention which leads to the norm must be applied, and it must effectively have the power to solve the conflict other than by force. This demand for practical coherence refers to a *reflective* objectivity. As in the previous case, actors always call on their judgment in order to subsume the particular under the general, but this time the particular is given and the general (the universal of the rule) must be found. Judgment is therefore reflective. Here, the universal is not provided by the understanding, but this does not mean that this reflective judgment does not rest on some *a priori* principle. This principle (which is specific to it) consists, as we have seen, in satisfying some common aim. It is a principle of finality and from this viewpoint the reflective judgment is teleological (Kant, 1790). If this finality was only subjective, we would be dealing with an aesthetic judgment, but by expressing the common or the general will in the present case, this finality (as the *a priori* principle of a teleological reflective judgement) is objective.

Of course, one must not separate the two forms of practical objectivity – determinant and reflective objectivity. We did so here, but it goes without saying that one does not go without the other when considering the perspective of unanimous agreement.

We can then answer the question we were asking: to what extent is the knowledge of the moral law, in the form of justice as unanimous agreement, that of a practical truth? The moral value of a fair norm does not rest on its theoretical or positive objectivity. Such a norm is objective in practical terms only from a both determinant and reflective angle, as a result of which it satisfies the two conditions which were posed for one to speak of objective knowledge in general. Justice as a unanimous agreement is objective because it is adequate to its matter as a result of the demand for practical consistency which commands that a convention must reach the goal targeted by everyone (to overcome conflict and express the general will), and it respects the logical form of the understanding, by meeting a demand for theoretical consistency, because it must not be contrary to the transcendental conditions of unanimous agreement.

Therefore, the subjectivism of the relativist no longer has any firm holding to object from. The free choice of reason does not prevent in any way recognising these two forms of practical objectivity and setting down consequently rigorous procedures of validation. One would have to be very reductive, by wanting to bring everything exclusively down to positive objectivity, not to see this. Freedom is not the enemy of the reasonable. It is its condition. Only the choice of unreasonableness is the enemy of the reasonable. Holding that the free will of women and men is ultimately and fundamentally what characterises the choice between unreason and reason is not giving up on distinguishing objectively between the non-reasonable and the reasonable – quite the reverse. If agreeing in order to solve a conflict supposes everyone to want to give the priority to the right over the good, such a will would not be worth anything if it was not free. The reasonable would inevitably come to fade away into one form or another of heteronomy of the subject. In the end, and contrary to what the relativist thinks, it is not only possible but indispensable to keep the freedom of an actor and the objectivity of his reasonable choice together.

Of course, we still have to ask ourselves whether this freedom is not too formal to be also real. It is a problem which liberalism does not overlook and answers are plenty in contemporary works. It refers to the issue of knowing what must be compensated in terms of empirical inequalities when the latter are such that it is no longer possible to speak of freedom without using empty words (Dworkin, 1977). It is a thorny question, as we have seen when dealing with positive discrimination. It triggers formidable empirical dilemmas. Extremes – not compensating anything or compensating everything – are certainly unacceptable. For the rest, it falls upon the actors to find a reasonable balance. Nevertheless, one thing is certain. It is not by giving up the principles of justice as fairness that difficulties can be solved. Once more, it is actually the opposite. Giving up on freedom as a principle is giving up on freedom as a horizon, and consequently, putting oneself in the position of no longer being able to hear the reasons of a fair spectator. There is no denying that the irreducible conflict between simply partial actors which we are then facing is not the appropriate framework to devise solutions which are acceptable to all, especially when questions become as difficult as those which deal with real freedom. Maintaining, against relativism, that some objectivity is possible in the respect of the equal liberty of moral beings is on the contrary to maintain the perspective of a fair agreement. Without such a perspective, it is purely and simply real freedom which would become an empty word.

## 4. Two Consequences for a Sociological Analysis

### 4.1 *The empirical question of universality*

What has just been established as to the objectivity of reasonable choice settles the question of its universality. A rule which is unanimously agreed on, as long as it shows all the characteristics of practical objectivity, is justified from the standpoint of its universalisation. But a relativist can object that this universality remains in a way very 'theoretical'. And there is no doubt that, even if the rejection of subjectivism is admitted, justice as a unanimous agreement is far from being *empirically* observed at any time and place. In short, one could go as far as accepting the arguments touching on the objectivity of the reasonable, but it would be necessary to acknowledge that they do not – or very rarely – have practical consequences. Even if this objection (often of sociological origin) is only empirical, it is difficult to ignore it completely; all the more as what is required is to specify how a sociological analysis which admits the objectivity of the reasonable deals with its empirical universality.

Let us first note that in the wake of the categorical imperative, the reasons of a fair spectator do not constitute a mechanic which would determine any will in an absolute way. The interest for *ego* or *alter* may always prevail empirically over impartiality, and it is truly certain that we live neither in Kant's 'kingdom of ends', nor in Rawls's 'well-ordered society'. These concepts actually remind us that the two aspects of unanimous agreement must be distinguished: both reality and horizon. From the perspective of facts, while it is certain that justice is not universally applied, it is not non-existent either; and where it does not exist, it can still be an ideal. From the viewpoint of the right, the absence of any justice for a given community, at a certain point of its history, does not annihilate the principle of the right. And as a matter of fact, saying that there is no justice in such or such situation can only be done in relation to a definition of the just for which one admits that it could lead to an applicable norm in this situation. The impossibility of coming to an agreement on some definition of the right would then rather be at the core of the relativistic empirical objection, claiming that what is fair here can never be – except by accident – fair somewhere else. More precisely, the conception of justice which we have developed would be (possibly) valid for modern societies (aiming to be liberal and democratic), though still in an imperfect way, but, *by nature*, it would not be worth anything outside these societies. If we have to be more specific, however, we must distinguish between questions pertaining to the *foundations* of social ties and those pertaining to the *applications* of justice (Habermas, 1999). Procedural impartiality is relevant in both cases, but according to whether it is reserved for problems of application to specific conflicts, where only one comprehensive conception of the good prevails, or whether it serves (on its own) to found the norm of the right which makes it possible for several conceptions of the good to coexist, and is applied afterwards, we are confronted with two distinct societal configurations.

Under different names, their ideal types have been clearly identified by numerous sociologists. Each author does not insist exactly on the same traits, but there is still a broad consensus in opposing traditional societies to modern ones: mechanical solidarity *v.* organic solidarity according to Durkheim (1893), community *v.* society according to Tönnies (1887), traditional domination *v.* legal-rational domination according to Weber (1922), traditional community made of nested social circles *v.* modern communities where these circles intersect according to Simmel (1908), *homo hierarchicus v. homo æqualis* according to Louis Dumont (1977) – the list could be extended far beyond these. Some use a more ternary typology. For Weber, charismatic domination defines a third pole, but one which by definition cannot survive the disappearance of the leader's charisma. One must find a solution to the fading of this charisma and this can either lead back to tradition, or lead to legal rationalisation. Henri Mendras (1976) places between primary societies and industrial societies the intermediate type of peasant societies. Urban development already exists in them and, above all, the relationships of the various agrarian communities with an inclusive society are fundamental. For instance, these ties account for the fact that innovation is not impossible in this environment, even if these societies remain based on the respect of tradition. When it comes to describing a historical evolution in the best possible way, it is certainly better not too use an overly binary pattern.[12] It remains that the intermediary types are either temporary, or some sort of mixture between two poles which everything opposes. From the viewpoint of moral development and justice, if, in the wake of all these theories, one wishes to identify these two poles, it is necessary to distinguish between traditional societies, where only a comprehensive conception of the good prevails, and modern societies, where several conceptions cohabit for good.

In traditional societies, the same communitarian ethos and the same vision of the world are shared by all or almost all the actors, often in relation to prevailing religious beliefs. The same idea of the good lies at the *foundation* of social ties. It finds its legitimacy in an already-given custom, which says what the good life is. Actors only have to formulate their own moral judgments in specific cases. As for the rest, it is this unanimous conception

12 As for the psychology of morality, it invites us to distinguish several stages in moral development. And what prevails ontogenetically is certainly not devoid of phylogenetic relevance.

of the good which defines what is morally acceptable and serves to distinguish the various equivalence classes of rights and duties as well as their hierarchies. These hierarchies essentially rest on ascribed status (as opposed to achieved status): hierarchy of castes, lineages, sexes, ranks of birth, etc. These societies can be called 'holistic', in the sense that, in general, individuals usually come second to their status, but without it preventing either an individuation or an appearance of disagreements, arguments or conflicts. There are at least two reasons for this. First, the common vision of the world may have some dark places which are propitious to diverging interpretations and litigations. Moreover, supporting the same communitarian ethos is far from preventing the manifestation of all egoisms. For instance, when it comes to distributing the fruits of a reaping carried out by individuals of various statuses, it can be acknowledged as normal that those of the noble lineage receive more than those of the common one. But if a nobleman grants himself more than customs allow, the commoner may legitimately complain. Everyone knows this is unfair with respect to established rules. To settle the conflict with justice, a *third party*, unbiased, called the judge (individual or assembly), is used. And this is universal, in the sense that it would be recognised as unfair everywhere for the common individual not to be able to enforce his right in his society, either because nothing can be done against the force or the cunning of the other, or because nothing can be done against his wealth, which empowers him to bribe a corrupt judge, or because those who must judge are partial anyway, etc. Fairness, according to the prevailing perfection criterion, and procedural impartiality, which includes the judge's impartiality, are universally the attributes of what is called a just procedure to settle a conflict.

We have sufficiently proven that the perfection criterion under discussion is not neutral if one is dealing with objectivity. There remains that, even here, one must suppose a unanimous agreement on the impartiality of the procedure in order to speak of justice. It is true that the debate is already closed as to what to do in order to do the right thing. The good is decided on and even how to achieve it. But everyone must still grant that what has been decided was indeed respected in practice. Without this, without any objectivable connection between the principle that has been established and its application, everyone could virtuously exempt themselves from established rules. There would be no rules anymore. In other words, in this instance, the social contract is regarded as already signed, but this does not diminish in the slightest its value as a customary right recognised by all as an effective right. In this respect, let us add that the way in which these societies deal with change derives from this: the conception of the good, or customary right, is supposed to solve conflicts. Therefore, one only has to rely on an instance, a judge, who applies the right in the name of the good. But of course, in the face of novelty, in the face of the occurrence of an unheard-of conflict, one *must* pronounce on new bases. The most diverse solutions then exist. Most often, this is decided on according to the existing balance of powers, but it may happen that the latter is ritualised, or still that some neutral equity is sought (Popkin, 1979).

The situation changes radically when it is admitted that several diverging conceptions of the good can and must coexist pacifically within the same society. The pluralism of visions of the world and the disagreement on basic axiological criteria are still possible reasonably only if everyone agrees on the fundamental norms which make living together fair for everyone. Morality can no longer be an already-given reality. It must be built. Since norms are no longer meant to solve particular conflicts within the same axiological framework, impartiality, in so far as it is put at the basis, can no longer derive from a mere third party. For the norm to be founded, it must be so *by all the parties on an equal footing*, which does not make it impossible for one to wonder what, in order to solve a conflict, would be the position of a third party. The parties must convince one another reciprocally and reach a rule which is justified in the eyes of everyone through an equal consideration for the interest of each one. As Rawls (1980, p. 571) writes: 'The essential agreement in judgments of justice arises not from the recognition of a prior and independent moral order, but from everyone's affirmation of the same authoritative social perspective.' Hence equality, and since the point is to settle cross-cultural or interaxiological conflicts, it necessarily entails the universality and the abstraction of the procedure which can obviously not be deduced from a given perfection criterion borrowed as such from one or the other of the conflicting visions of the world. By thus serving to the foundation of the right, impartiality or procedural fairness[13] takes on a character which is at once universal, abstract and egalitarian. As a result, in modern societies, where the axiological consensus is not given in

13 Brian Barry (1995, p. 11) rightly distinguishes between this 'second-order impartiality' so as to found justice 'calls for principles and rules that are capable of forming the basis of free agreement among people seeking agreement on reasonable terms', and a 'first-order impartiality', that of a third party, which is simply incorporated in the precept of behaving 'without being motivated by private considerations'.

advance, justice is founded in everyone's eyes and in the same movement finds itself at the basis of life in common. It does not result from this that these societies no longer have to solve problems of application. These problems remain, and must still be solved impartially and fairly. But only these societies build with every freedom their norm of justice through some procedural impartiality, implying universality and equality, in order to place it at the foundation of social ties. It can be noticed that, when this is the case, 'natural right' – and thus universal right, which today is referred to by the phrase 'human rights' – is at the basis of a positive right.

All in all, when it comes to problems of application, the demand for an equitable and impartial procedure to settle a given conflict in a fair way is universal.[14] When this demand is not satisfied, only arbitrariness rules. On the contrary, what has just been said is enough to show that we do not think that all societies, communities, groups, or situations empirically meet the criteria of practical objectivity by giving the priority to the right over the good. But what allows one to draw a relativistic conclusion from this? Why, if the priority of justice is not universally widespread, should justice as an agreement lose some of its objectivity? As for us, we have emphasised the strong reasons which allow one to think the reverse; on the side of the detractors of this position, we cannot see any other justification than the norm of some reductive positivism. The priority of justice prevails in theory and in practice, and the fact it is not observed empirically everywhere only invalidates the correctness of this principle for those who bring what ought to be down to what is.

It is therefore not possible to claim that sociological analysis should be relativistic. The previous lines – even if we admit very willingly that they may be disputed – show that the objectivity of the reasonable, as the principle of a modelling, is far from being incompatible with a sociological approach. There actually results another consequence, which now hinges on the extent of what the sociologist can hold scientifically.

14 In social psychology, from several experiments, Tom R. Tyler *et al.* (1997, p. 250) conclude that the members of different ethnic or social groups agree that procedural justice is the key criterion for evaluating the fairness of dispute resolution conflicts. Their findings suggest that: 'A focus on the fairness of procedures is a phenomenon that exists in very different social and cultural groups.'

### 4.2 *An extension of the critic*

We have had the opportunity to underline the cost of putting the right and the good at the same level on several occasions. With relativism, which brings these two notions down to subjective values, there results a serious restriction of sociological analysis. If anything goes, the sociologist does not have any way at all of arguing for instance that a moral opinion advocating a negative discrimination rests on bad reasons. She may describe it, say that it comes from the youngest or the oldest, the executives or the workmen, etc., notice that it does not amount to the same as a morality which rejects such a discrimination, held up by other social categories, more or less numerous. She can show that each one is rational because it serves the economic interests of the groups or actors involved. She can also observe that it is the product of a rationality in value. But she cannot go beyond this. In the end, in a consistent relativistic perspective, a sociologist studying Europe in the 1930–40s would observe that a Nazi ethics is in conflict with a democratic ethics, but that, as a scientist, there is nothing else to add, since in the end, it is all the same. Admittedly, if there is indeed such a thing as a 'defeat of the mind',[15] this is the last straw. If the sociologist has no way of showing, not relatively to her own conception of the good which she is still free to voice as a citizen, but by only resorting to scientific reasoning itself, that some reasons holding certain moral opinions are not objective reasons, because they are not those of a fair spectator or do not pass the unanimous agreement test, or pass it by violating the transcendental conditions of this agreement – in other words, that these reasons may be rational in a narrow sense but are in no way *objectively* reasonable – then it is truly certain that her knowledge is not worth more than that of mere accountancy. Luckily, no one is doomed to such pessimism, nor to such a restriction of the scientific programme since, as we have just seen, it is rather the relativism which lies at its foundation which does not pass the test of close examination.

To sustain this position, it is not necessary to question the rule of axiological neutrality which imposes to the analyst not to pass any value judgment on the fact which she studies. It is of course not in the name of subjective values that reasons must be evaluated. It is only and precisely about doing what one does when one seeks to argue on some positive objectivity,

15 The phrase is borrowed from the title of an essay by Alain Finkelkraut (1987).

with the difference that as far as justice is concerned, it is practical objectivity which comes into play. Therefore the role of the analyst does not change. It always consists in describing and explaining scientifically the social phenomena which she observes. It leaves it to the politician or the citizen to intervene in the public debate, by using these explanations or not. The deontological bases of critical analysis, if we give this name to this programme, are thus not new, and as a result it is no longer necessary to dwell on them any longer. On the contrary, the research field is much broader than the one prevailing in standard analyses of social sciences, since by including the perspective of the reasonable, it can no longer restrict itself *a priori* to a phenomenology of justifications, to a mere acknowledgment of the fact of moral pluralism or to an analysis of a restricted rationality. These limitations are all the more damaging as, in order to overcome their narrowness, one only has to define properly correctness and objectivity for the practical reason, without giving up on anything as to the necessity of these criteria for a scientific analysis.

It should not be inferred from this that some euphoric optimism could come to replace relativistic scepticism. A liberal conception of justice as fairness or as unanimous agreement is not able to answer any question. In simple cases, such as that of negative discrimination, there is no doubt as to the answer, but in more complex cases, such as that of positive discrimination, one must recognise that beyond a few principles, which must be regarded as firm, there is matter for discussion. The alternative to relativism is in no way a triumphant science with an answer to everything, in everyone's place. Such a conception would be antiscientific, if one thinks that any knowledge (unless it is very basic) is incomplete, and would in any event be contradictory with the position we support, since this position is rooted in the principle of liberty whereby actors can argue in the context of a public discussion, leaving it to them to find the reasons and the coherent conventions which make it possible for them to live together when their arguments clash.

# Conclusion

A Kantian orientation in the analysis of social or economic facts is deeply rooted in freedom and reason in *all* its aspects. On the reverse, the competing theories have unceasingly tried to evacuate them in part or completely. But facts are stubborn and morality cannot bear the brunt of this process (Boudon, 2000). A theory of actions or opinions *must* account for them. But how, if men are deprived of their capacity to be autonomous and reasonable, if they are not responsible for the social order they make up?

For the competing theories, in the end, the recipe is always pretty much the same. Machines revealing or selecting morality are invented. Naturalism and theology are at one on this point. Sometimes these machines can be slightly shaky, but with the improvement of modelling techniques, they become increasingly sophisticated. We are told that morality is a product of natural selection,[1] or that it results from an optimisation of the good, or that it is inscribed in a totality or a history which overhangs everybody and is imposed on everyone. When there is a jam in the machine, when individuals do not behave or think in accordance with the theory, the holist starts speaking of false consciousness, irrationality or the unconscious, and the rational choice theorist includes arbitrarily some moral preferences in the utility functions to be maximised, just when it is these very preferences the model should account for.[2] In all cases, the social order which had to be explained is hidden or presupposed – when it is not simply spontaneous.[3]

1 Since this theory cannot by definition be verified, we have not dwelt on it in the preceding pages. An article by Michaël Ruse (1993), which Ferry and Vincent criticise (2000), provides a recent example of such Neo-Darwinism.

2 It only accounts for them if these preferences maximise the utility; now, since these preferences are moral or non-selfish, they are contrary to such a maximisation. A famous example is that of the voting paradox. In the absence of legal constraints, act-utilitarianism cannot explain why people vote (Boudon, 1997). As for rule-utilitarianism (Harsanyi, 1977), it predicts that participation rates can either be 0%, or 100%.

3 The latest development can be found in theories of self-organisation, chaos or bifurcations, on which Hayek already relied (1976). Put some men in a pot, bring to the boil, and you will see them behave like Bénard cells (a classic example of 'self-organisation' in physics). Let us forget about the energy spent, forget that social systems are not 'far from equilibrium' or highly instable in the sense of the dissipative structures theory, for-

The irony displayed by Kant (1788) towards the way Leibniz dealt with human freedom can easily be extended to the way in which all these theories deal with mankind and its freedom since, once more, in the end, it is only 'the freedom of a turnspit, which, when once it is wound up, accomplishes its motions of itself'.

There is no denying that building a morality-selecting machine can be tempting – just as it can be tempting to retort that although today we still do not know how to do so in a satisfactory way, one day, we will. Unfortunately, the limit is not to be found in the extraordinary difficulty of the problem to be solved, but rather in the project itself. All the current failures are not owed to the fact that the machine is not sophisticated enough. They come from what must necessarily be presupposed initially when one launches into such a programme, that is, that in one way or another, man is a nature. This is no doubt one of the most essential breaching points with the viewpoint we hold. For, according to this viewpoint, man is a reasonable being and consequently, he cannot be reduced to a nature: though he is affected by nature, this does not mean that he is absolutely determined by it. Any programme performing such a reduction is doomed to fail in the face of freedom.

However, if this is not a sufficient reason to lapse into scepticism, the procedure must be inverted. This is what we suggested from the very start of this work. Starting from freedom and reason without reducing it *a priori* and then rooting firmly any analysis in this starting point amounts to thinking that social sciences too may have their Copernican revolution. Of course, some analyses have already taken this direction, but they are almost non-existent in economics, and are only a small minority in sociology. Therefore, instead of starting by regarding, according to Durkheim's wish (1895), 'social facts as things', one must on the contrary avoid thinking that it is necessary to reify social ties to take up a scientific stance. Then one will find easily enough the long way which at the end of the 18th century led to conceiving fully the subject's autonomy (Schneewind, 1998).

In this context, justice is defined as a unanimous agreement to which the priority is given. We have accounted for this and of course we will not go back here to all the arguments we have put forward. However, it may be useful to emphasise the difference with an analysis which would aim at

---

get that an *epsilon* as small as one wishes is a notion which does not make any sense in a social or economic reality to provoke a 'butterfly effect' in it, etc.

formulating a theory of justice by listing up all its principles. We did not set ourselves this goal for essentially two reasons. First, even if one restricts oneself to modern societies, it is unlikely that all the positive principles leading to *one* theory of justice could be listed up (Boudon, 1995*b*). This is even truer if other forms of social and political organisation are considered. Moreover, this objective, assuming that it can be reached, does not necessarily have to be searched for. Unanimous agreement is enough.

Let us take the example of the three principles of justice enunciated by Rawls (1971). The first one is that of equal liberty for all. It is of course fundamental, but it is consubstantial with the idea of unanimous agreement. One simply cannot be conceived without the other. The second principle is that of a fair equality of opportunities. Here again, the reverse principle of an *a priori* limitation of what an individual may reasonably aspire to, before any confrontation with others' real talents and aspirations, would amount to calling into question her right of veto. The case of the third principle, called 'difference principle', which is expressed through the search for a maximal improvement of the plight of the least well off, is less simple. This is actually why it has found itself more widely debated than the previous ones. One of its consequences is that any increase of inequalities is not unfair. If the plight of the least well off improves as much as possible, there is nothing unfair *a priori* if the situation of those who are better off improves at the same time. The situation is unfair only if this improvement leads to a deterioration of that of the least well off. What is the answer from the viewpoint of unanimous agreement? For this latter proposition to be able to get everyone's assent, a study case must be ruled out. As we already remarked in chapter 2, altruism must be excluded; this is actually what Rawls does through construction. More precisely, it must be supposed that the least well off are not all altruists. With this reservation that at least one of the most deprived is not altruistic, then the proposition which consists in admitting the social injustice of the situation under discussion is the only one which is likely *a priori* to receive everyone's assent (without any abandonment of their right of veto). But the very fact of this argumentation is enough to show that one must, in a completely essential way, enquire about what the situation is in empirical terms.

Many other principles of justice can easily be inferred from unanimous agreement. Without trying to be exhaustive, we listed up some of them: no retroactive laws, no secret clauses, etc. They are no less important than the previous ones. Each is in its own way a negation of the very principle of unanimous agreement. Promulgating a retroactive law is just as much of a negation of the principle of unanimous agreement as a negation of equal liberty – a negation of justice therefore, if the latter is defined by this agreement. From this point of view, there is no hierarchy to be made. Unanimous agreement is enough, in the sense that, in the face of a principle about which one wonders whether it is or not *a priori* contradictory with justice, one only has to wonder whether it amounts to calling into question the right of veto of an individual.

Once this unanimity test has been passed, it must be acknowledged that questions are often too complex or too difficult to be settled on this mode. We have seen it by taking the example of positive discrimination and we are now going to return to it with another example. There results that a liberal theory of justice cannot be closed. This is actually why it must not set itself as a goal to list up all its principles. A liberal theory which would close itself in such a way would negate itself. It would do what it claims to avoid by anchoring itself firmly on the principle of freedom: start speaking in the place of the citizens. Taking to its term the Copernican revolution which we started from thus necessarily leads to an *open theory of justice*.

It is true that, as we have seen, this openness could put it at great risk. If the social order is indeed built up, it is only a human convention. And such conventionalism can easily degrade into relativism. Relativism is damaging in general, and would be especially so here, as it would stand in total contradiction with the essential characteristics of the proposed theory. But we have also seen that this danger could be avoided. It only threatens those who reduce objectivity to its mere positive form and do not see that in the practical domain there is also some room for a practical objectivity. The reasonable choice is an objective choice in this sense, and therefore there is nothing relative.

This openness, freed from the relativistic risk, can be better defined by observing that it makes it possible to highlight the link between the two parts of this book. In a certain way, this link can be made easily enough: the fair spectator is the schema of unanimous agreement. In other words, it is a method for evidencing the reasons of an actor who gives the priority to justice as a unanimous agreement. We have verified this by applying this method to the analysis of a statistical empirical poll and by observing that it made it possible to account for this data, when competing models failed or proved insufficient.

A more complete specification of this link raises difficult questions, however. It would be easy if there was a schema for freedom. But, precisely, there is none; this would be contradictory, with respect to the very principle of freedom. There results that the fair spectator as the schema of unanimous agreement is a formula which is not perfectly specified as long as one does not know to which link between morality and the law or politics it leads. All the problem of the autonomy of the law or of politics from morality is raised here. And, undeniably, solutions are far from being obvious. As a matter of fact, Kant and Fichte, who *did* agree on the essential in the mid-1790s, used to give opposite answers on this question. And even in the writings of the same author, such as Rawls, one finds an answer which clearly evolves between *A Theory of Justice* (1971) and *Political Liberalism* (1993).

As far as the autonomy of morality from politics is concerned, the question, in the end, is to know what gap there can be between the categorical imperative and the social contract. The former refers to the knowledge of the moral law; the latter, to the political construction of the law. It is true that some parallels should not be overlooked. In order to build a free society, everyone must be able to recognise for themselves the law and to understand its good reasons; conversely, no one knows the law unfailingly since it is impossible to anticipate absolutely the assent which others must necessarily give to make it possible to say that an agreement is fair. In both cases, it is always the public use of reason which is in the foreground, either in terms of principles, or effectively.

Nonetheless the gap is important as soon as one considers seriously that one may be the judge of the law and an active party. The categorical imperative only deals with the possibility of moral autonomy, while the social contract aims at political autonomy. The categorical imperative teaches me what I must do if I want to do the right thing, that is, if I want to show good will or act out of a moral duty. However, can one merely say that political autonomy is achieved from the very moment the legislator follows the categorical imperative? In total, what political value must be granted to the categorical imperative? In practice, the legislator is not the people, but a delegate, and the risk is obviously that this person speaks on behalf of the others. This is something to worry about since we are in the process of accepting a political limit to the use of reason. Freedom of thought is at risk of becoming purely formal since, beyond a certain limit, the freedom to influence the other through arguments is withdrawn: he speaks in our place.

That he should speak in our place and say the same thing is still fair enough, but if some reasons are deprived of a public debate, the problem becomes acute. If the legislator is not good-willed and grants himself the best part, he does not follow the categorical imperative and injustice is blatant. But, even if he is good-willed, he will only guess the fair agreement between people whom he understands. This would not be a difficulty if, in the end, the agreement only consisted in denying our differences. But of course, it cannot be reduced to this.[4] Using Rousseau's vocabulary, eventually, the question comes down to knowing how to shift from a set of particular wills to a general will.

The first way seems to get rid of all that differentiates us, and to reach through this abstraction device the idea of being free and reasonable. Each particular will meets the essence of this free and reasonable being; it then becomes identical with the others, and is nothing else than the general will. In this perspective, the categorical imperative does not fall back into solipsism, since it always presupposes a plurality of subjects; the form of the reasoning still demands it. This is the way followed by Kant and this is the reason why he supports the idea that the social contract is only a fourth formulation of the categorical imperative, reserved to the legislator. The range of the social contract, however, finds itself reduced. Those who orientate themselves thanks to this formulation of the categorical imperative simply verify that the contract is not logically vitiated by an implicit negation of the free and reasonable character of one of the subjects. As we have seen, this was hardly a mere trifle; but it is still fairly minor, since we are only describing all possible fair agreements. It is still necessary to choose among these agreements, and this choice is not indifferent. But there lacks a criterion here, and as a result it is hard to see, for now, what prevents a legislator, supposedly one of good will, to claim to be the only pure individual in the world and consequently declare that his particular will is tantamount to the general will.

Let us then consider the second way. According to Philonenko (1968), whom we are now following, Rousseau was far from holding the general will to be a mere procedure of abstraction. For him, it was rather a procedure to integrate differences. The general will conveys the idea of a collective, political autonomy, and the particular will is not annihilated, but *ex-*

4 For Philonenko (1968), it is on this matter that Fichte separates from Kant, and this led them to different judgments on the French Revolution.

*pressed* within the general will. This amounts to saying that, *a priori*, everything is made public and discussed. Benjamin Constant's (1806) critic on this matter, emphasising the border between private and public, is well-known. The idea which can be inferred from Rousseau's position rather seems to us to be that no one can draw some *a priori* border between the public and the private sphere, as if it was written somewhere that some particular wills should never be voiced, but annihilated. This would amount to reverting to the first way, where some reasons were robbed of a public debate, this time because of the fallibility of the good-willed legislator. In the end, the only points which are not debatable points, so to speak, derive from the logical structure of unanimous agreement (expounded in chapter 3). For the rest, differences in lifestyles and life plans, even those which are completely egotistic, are not negated in order to build the fair rules of life in common. They are acknowledged and subject to a reasonable discussion. It thus appears that the openness stipulated by a liberal theory of justice has a link with the criterion which was lacking at the outcome of the first way.

This can be argued by insisting on what brings closer the viewpoints of Rawls and Habermas. The reflective equilibrium of the former and the discourse ethics of the latter meet in Rousseau's conception of the general will. All three eventually make the public use of reason the pure procedure which defines justice. Consequently, the only confusion not to make is to regard Rawls's substantial proposals in his *Theory of Justice* as a re-definition of justice (cf. the remarks on Epimenides' paradox in chapter 3), whereas he expounds a procedure integrating contents which are reasonable (for him) in order to know the moral law. It is a debatable procedure, which does deserve to be debated – as proved by the last thirty years.

In this respect, the fair spectator theory is at the same level. It cannot be otherwise since knowledge is *for someone*, while the construction of a unanimous agreement demands *everyone*'s participation. In other words, unanimous agreement as a reason cannot, without a contradiction, escape unanimous agreement as an effective procedure. The one does not go without the other. The fair spectator as a position remains inscribed in the context of an ethics of discussion. It cannot overcome it. The openness advocated by a liberal theory is therefore not a sort of pragmatic demand, but an *a priori* necessity. In order to escape the difficulty which the first way can trigger, it is an intangible characteristic of the model.

This can be seen in a second way through the question of the autonomy of the law from morality. Once again, this is a complex question, but one can focus on the following debate. If the procedure which leads to a given law is correct, this law is necessarily fair. Contemplating that I may exempt myself from it is a self-contradiction. Therefore this would mean that there is no logical space for some autonomy of the right from morality. In other words, starting from a legitimate constitution, from legitimate elections, from legitimate legislators, it is hard to see how the laws adopted could not be legitimate themselves, and how it could be legitimate to exempt oneself from them. If the starting point is fair, the linking in conformity, then the arrival point is necessarily correct. But facts do not always go this way. And there is no doubt that laws which are voted legitimately can turn out to be unfair.

One brick in the edifice can help us overcome this dilemma. The subject, who is at stake in the system which leads to justice as unanimous agreement, is, as we have seen, a finite subject. Among other consequences this means, as Habermas (1999, chap. 6) reminds us, that in a discussion on the fairness of such or such rule, norm or law:

> Well-grounded moral norms can claim only validity *prima facie*. For *ex ante*, only the consequences and collateral effects of *typical* cases, which can be anticipated, are considered. Unanticipated constellations of conflict situations that occur subsequently give rise to a further need for interpretation that must be met from within the altered perspective of a discourse of *application*.

Let us add again here that, in these debates of application, secondary effects are not always predictable. In the public space of a reasonable discussion, there is clearly some room for some uncertainty, and it may well be that a law, or a norm, even if it is procedurally legitimate, turns out to be unfair. In this case, since contracts are never signed for an infinite duration, the essential is that everyone has retained their right of veto.

However, this does not solve the question, and it even bounces back, since in the facts, it is illusory to deny that a full exercise of this right can prove very difficult in order to lead to a change in a law (or a norm) which has become unfair. Therefore we can only acknowledge *a priori* everyone's right to civil disobedience. Since in some circumstances, this can become the only way of putting to practice one's right of veto, without this right, once more, it would be the right of veto which would be denied. Of course, the danger is that everyone may, according to their moods, invoke their right to civil disobedience in order to dodge the law.

But, between these two extremes which must certainly be rejected, the absence of any possible civil disobedience and the laxness of a disobedience which is allowed under any circumstance, there remains a margin which is far too important to claim that the question could be settled through this mere rejection. Of course two cases must be distinguished. In the case of a tyrannical society, the prevalence of individual rights is non-existent, human rights are infringed upon, and civil disobedience is obviously legitimate. It is in democratic societies, such as we know them today, that is to say, endowed with constitutions which on average are fair, without these societies themselves being perfectly fair, that the question is relevant. If the unjust character of a law is not a sufficient reason to disobey it, its legal validity is not a sufficient reason to conform to it. Like Rawls (1971, VI, § 57), we think that everything depends on the *degree* of injustice of the law. Now, if we accept this idea, it is truly certain that (Rawls, VI, § 55) 'we should not expect too much of a theory of civil disobedience'. We have the same situation here as in discussions on positive discrimination. In the end, it is not the theorists, but the citizens who must find the reasonable answers; hence, from a second viewpoint, the necessary openness of a liberal theory.

If, from a Copernican revolution which is taken to its end, there thus results a liberal and open theory of justice, we can now see in what way the fair spectator is the schema of unanimous agreement. For here, as Kant (1787, II, I, 2) remarks: 'It is absurd to expect to be enlightened by Reason, and at the same time to prescribe to it what side of the question it must adopt.' Such openness does not make it impossible to hold firmly the principle of unanimous agreement. The discussion of this principle is not at all on the same level as the controversies on the degrees of positive discrimination or civil disobedience which may be considered. In this discussion, the point is only to know whether one accepts or not the idea of justice as unanimous agreement. Its rejection, as we know, entails important consequences. Nothing prevents coercion and the law of the strongest from being the foundation of justice – so much so that we cannot even see any longer how such a word could keep on making any sense at all. If, on the contrary, one accepts justice as a unanimous agreement, then there is no other solution but to reject, as being objectively unfair, all the situations (slavery, negative discrimination, etc.) which violate its principle. Beyond, this principle still prevails, but the theorist withdraws, not through some sort of modesty or demission in the face of the complexity of practical questions, but because his theory indicates to him that such a withdrawal is imperative. It falls upon the citizen, upon any citizen, to determine how to implement the priority of justice as a unanimous agreement.

# Bibliography


Agresti A., 1984, *Analysis of ordinal categorical data*, New York, John Wiley & Sons.

Apel K.-O., 1975, The problem of philosophical fundamental grounding in light of a transcendental pragmatics of language, *Man and World*, 8(3), 239–275.

Apel K.-O., 1986, *Fondation de l'éthique de la communication [...]*, tr. fr. in 1998, *Discussion et responsabilité*, (tome II), Paris, Cerf, 85–133.

Apel K.-O., 1989, Normatively grounding 'Critical Theory' through recourse to the life-world? A transcendental-pragmatic attempt to think with Habermas against Habermas, in A. Honneth, T. McCarthy, C. Offe, A. Wellmer (eds), 1992, *Philosophical Interventions in the Unfinished Project of Enlightement*, Cambridge, Mass., MIT press, 125–170.

Arrow K., 1951, 2nd ed. 1963, *Social choice and individual values*, London, Yale UP.

Axelrod R., 1984, *The evolution of cooperation*, New York, Basic books.

Ballet J., 1998, Altruisme sacrificiel et altruisme rationnel, in F.-R. Mahieu, H. Rapoport (eds), *Altruisme, Analyses économiques*, Paris, Economica, 139–159.

Barry B., 1995, *Justice as impartiality*, Oxford, Clarendon Press.

Bentham J., 1789, 2nd ed. 1823, *An introduction to the principles of morals and legislation*, London, Athlone Press.

Bernheim B., Stark O., 1988, Altruism within the family reconsidered: Do nice guys finish last?, *American Economic Review*, 78, 1034–1045.

Berlin I., 1969, *Four essays on liberty*, London, New York, Oxford UP.

Berten A., Silveira P. da, Pourtois H. (eds), 1997, *Libéraux et communautariens*, Paris, PUF.

Boeri T., Börsch-Supan A., Tabellini G., 2001, Would you like to shrink the Welfare State? The opinions of European citizens, *Economic Policy*, 32, 7–50.

Boltanski L., Thévenot L., 1991, *De la justification, Les économies de la grandeur*, Paris, Gallimard.

Boudon R., 1995*a*, *Le juste et le vrai, Etudes sur l'objectivité des valeurs et de la connaissance*, Paris, Fayard.

Boudon R., 1995*b*, A propos des sentiments de justice: nouvelles remarques sur la théorie de Rawls, *L'Année Sociologique*, 45(2), 273–295.

Boudon R., 1997, Le 'paradoxe du vote' et la théorie de la rationalité, *Revue Française de Sociologie*, XXXVIII(2), 217–227.

Boudon R., 2000, Adam Smith: le 'spectateur impartial' et l'acteur partial, in *Etudes sur les sociologues classiques*, t. II, Paris, PUF, 21–62.

Boudon R., 2002, *Déclin de la morale? Déclin des valeurs?*, Paris, PUF.

Boudon R., 2003, *Raison, bonnes raisons*, Paris, PUF.

Bouretz P., 1998, Entre scepticisme et nihilisme: Max Weber et la guerre des dieux, in S. Mesure (ed.), *La rationalité des valeurs*, Paris, PUF, 59–80.

Broussolle D., 2001, Le recours à la rationalité maximisatrice peut-il dispenser l'économie de considérations morales?, *Economie appliquée*, 4, 125–156.

Cahuc P., Kempf H., 2000, L'altruisme est-il socialement efficace?, *Revue du MAUSS*, 15, 223–246.

Cibois Ph., 1993, Le PEM, Pourcentage de l'écart maximum: un indice de liaison entre modalités d'un tableau de contingence, *Bulletin de Méthodologie Sociologique*, 40, 43–63.

Cohen G. A., 1990, Marxism and contemporary political philosophy, *Canadian Journal of Philosophy*, suppl. vol. 16, 363–387.

Coleman J., 1990, *Foundations of social theory*, Cambridge, Mass., The Belknap Press.

Comte A., 1852, engl. tr. 1973, *The catechism of positive religion*, Clifton, N.J., A. M. Kelley.

Constant B., 1806, engl. tr. 2003, *Principles of politics applicable to all governments*, Indianapolis, Ind., Liberty Fund.

Dosi G., Marengo L., Bassanini A., Valente M., 1997, Les normes comme propriétés émergentes d'un apprentissage adaptatif, in B. Reynaud (ed.), *Les limites de la rationalité,* t. 2, *Les figures du collectif*, Paris, La Découverte, 45–64.

Dumont L., 1977, *Homo æqualis*, Paris, Gallimard.

Dupuy J.-P., 1992, 2nd ed. 1997, *Libéralisme et justice sociale: le sacrifice et l'envie*, Paris, Fondation Saint-Simon, Calmann-Lévy, 2nd ed. Hachette.

Durkheim E., 1893, engl. tr. 1984, *The division of labor in society*, New York, Free Press.

Durkheim E., 1895, engl. tr. 1982, *The rules of sociological method*, New York, Free Press.

Dworkin R., 1977, *Taking rights seriously*, London, Duckworth.

Elster J., 1989, *The cement of society, A study of social order*, Cambridge, Cambridge UP.

Ferry J.-M., 1987, *Habermas, L'éthique de la communication,* Paris, PUF.

Ferry L., Vincent J.-D., 2000, *Qu'est-ce que l'homme? Sur les fondamentaux de la biologie et de la philosophie*, Paris, Odile Jacob.

Ferry L., 1984, engl. tr. 1990, *Rights: the new quarrel between the Ancients and the Moderns*, Chicago, University of Chicago Press.

Feyerabend P., 1975, *Against method: outlines of an anarchistic theory of knowledge*, London, Atlantic Highlands, Humanities Press.

Fichte J. G., 1794, engl. tr. 1988, *The purpose of higher education: also known as the vocation of the scholar*, Mt. Savage, Md., Nightsun Books.

Fichte J. G., 1794–1795, engl. tr. 1988, Concerning the concept of the Wissenschaftslehre, in *Fichte: Early Philosophical Writings*, Ithaca, New York, Cornell UP, 94–135.

Fichte J. G., 1796–1797, engl. tr. 2000, *Foundations of natural right: according to the principles of the Wissenschaftlehre*, New York, Cambrigde UP.

Finkielkraut A., 1987, engl. tr. 1995, *The defeat of the mind*, New York, Columbia UP.

Forsé M., 1989, *L'ordre improbable, Entropie et processus sociaux*, Paris, PUF.

Forsé M., 1999, Libéralisme et interventionnisme, Analyse comparée des opinions sur le rôle économique de l'Etat et du gouvernement dans six pays, *Revue de l'OFCE*, 68, 219–240.

Forsé M., 2002, Les réseaux sociaux chez Simmel: les fondements d'un modèle individualiste et structural, in L. Deroche-Gurcel, P. Watier (eds), *La* Sociologie *de Georg Simmel (1908), Eléments actuels de modélisation sociale*, Paris, PUF, 63–109.

Frank R. H., Gilovich T., Regan D., 1993, Does studying economics inhibit cooperation? *Journal of Economic Perspectives*, 7(2), 159–171.

Friedman D., 1973, *The machinery of freedom, Guide to radical capitalism*, La Rochelle, NY, Arlington House.

Friedman M., 1987, Beyond caring: The de-moralization of gender, *Canadian Journal of Philosophy*, suppl. vol. 13, 87–110.

Gauthier D., 1986, *Morals by agreement*, Oxford, Oxford UP.

Gilligan C., 1982, *In a different voice: Psychological theory and women's development*, Cambridge, Mass., Harvard UP.

Grunberg G., Schweisguth E., 1990, Libéralisme culturel et libéralisme économique, in CEVIPOF, *L'électeur français en question*, Paris, Presses de la FNSP, 45–68.

Guerrien B., 1995, *La théorie des jeux*, Paris, Economica.

Haberman S. J., 1973, The analysis of residuals in cross-classification tables, *Biometrics*, 29, 205–20.

Habermas J., 1983, *Moral und Selbstbewusstsein*, fr. tr. 1986, *Morale et communication*, Paris, Cerf.

Habermas J., 1991, engl. tr. 1993, *Justification and application, Remarks on discourse ethics*, Cambridge, Polity Press.

Habermas J., 1995, Reconciliation through the public use of reason: remarks on John Rawls's political liberalism, *The Journal of Philosophy*, 92(3), 109–131.

Habermas J., 1999, engl. tr. 2003, *Truth and justification*, Cambridge, Polity Press.

Hare R., 1981, *Moral thinking*, Oxford, Clarendon Press.

Harrod R. F., 1936, Utilitarianism revisited, *Mind*, 45, 137–156.

Harsanyi J., 1977, Morality and the theory of rational behaviour, *Social Research*, 44(4), 623–656.

Hayek F., 1973, *Law, legislation and liberty*, Vol. 2, *The mirage of social justice*, London, Routledge & Kegan Paul.

Hayek F., 1988, *The fatal conceit, The errors of socialism*, London, Routledge.

Hirschman A. O., 1984, *L'économie comme science morale et politique*, Paris, Gallimard, Le Seuil, Hautes Etudes.

Hobbes Th., 1651, 1968, *Leviathan*, Baltimore, Penguin Books.

Homans G., 1974, rev. ed., *Social behaviour, Its elementary forms*, New York, Harcourt Brace Javanovich Inc.

Hume D., 1739 (Books I et II), 1740 (Book III), 1978, *A treatise of human nature*, New York, Oxford UP.

Hutcheson F., 1725, 1971, *An inquiry into the original of our ideas of beauty and virtue*, New York, Garland Pub.

Jacquemain M., 1995, Représentations de la justice sociale, *L'Année Sociologique*, 45(2), 401–432.

Kant E., 1785, engl. tr. 2002, *Groundwork for the metaphysics of morals*, New Haven, Yale UP.

Kant E., 1787, (1st ed. 1781), engl. tr. 2003, *Critique of pure reason*, Mineola, NY, Dover Publications.

Kant E., 1788, engl. tr. 2004, *Critique of practical reason*, Mineola, NY, Dover Publications.

Kant E., 1790, engl. tr. 2000, *Critique of the power of judgment*, New York, Cambridge UP.

Kant E., 1793, engl. tr. 1974, *On the old saw: that may be right in theory but it won't work in practice*, Philadelphia, University of Pennsylvania Press.

Kant E., 1797, engl. tr. 1999, *Metaphysical elements of justice, Part I of The metaphysics of morals*, Indianapolis, Hackett Pub. Co.

Kant E., 1798, engl. tr. 1978, *Anthropology from a pragmatic point of view*, Carbondale, Southern Illinois UP.

Kellerhals J., Coenen-Huther J., Modak M., 1988, *Les figures de l'équité, La construction des normes de justice dans les groupes*, Paris, PUF.

Kelsen H., 1979, engl. tr. 1991, *General theory of norms*, Oxford, Clarendon Press.

Kluegel J., Mason D., Wegener B. (eds), 1995, *Social justice and political change: public opinion in capitalist and post-communist states*, New York, Aldine de Gruyter.

Kohlberg L., 1981, *The philosophy of moral development*, San Francisco, Harper & Row.

Kymlicka W., 1990, *Contemporary political philosophy*, Oxford, Clarendon Press.

Kymlicka W., 1995, *Multicultural citizenship: a liberal theory of minority rights*, Oxford, Oxford UP.

Leibniz G. W., 1710, engl. tr. 1985, *Theodicy: essays on the goodness of God, the freedom of man, and the origin of evil*, La Salle, Ill., Open Court.

Lindbeck A., Snower D., 1988, *The insider – outsider theory of employment and unemployment*, Cambridge, MIT Press.

Locke J., 1690, 1979, *Treatise of civil government and A letter concerning toleration*, New York, Irvington.

MacCallum Jr. G. C., 1972, Negative and positive freedom, in P. Laslett, W. G. Runciman, Q. Skinner (eds), *Philosophy, politics and society*, series IV, Oxford, Blackwell, 174–193.

MacIntyre A., 1981, *After virtue, a study in moral theory*, Notre Dame, Ind., University of Notre Dame Press.

MacIntyre A., 1984, Is Patriotism a virtue?, reprinted in R. Beiner (ed.), 1995, *Theorizing Citizenship*, Albany, NY, State University of New York Press, 209–228.

Mandeville B., 1714, 1970, *The fable of the bees*, Harmondsworth, Penguin.

Marx K., 1859, engl. tr. 1971, *A contribution to the critique of political economy*, London, Lawrence and Wishart.

Marx K., 1875, 1972, *Critique of the Gotha programme*, Peking, Foreign Languages Press.

Maynard Smith J., 1982, *Evolution and the theory of games*, Cambridge, Cambridge UP.

Mendras H., 1976, *Sociétés paysannes*, Paris, Armand Colin.

Mesure S. (ed.), 1998, *La rationalité des valeurs*, Paris, PUF.

Mesure S., Renaut A., 1996, *La guerre des dieux, Essai sur la querelle des valeurs*, Paris, Grasset.

Mill J. S., 1859, 2004, *On liberty*, Lanham, Md., Rowman & Littlefield Publishers.

Miller D., 1999, *Principles of social justice*, Cambridge, Harvard UP.

Moessinger P., 1998, *Décisions et procédures de l'accord*, Paris, PUF.

Moore G. E., 1912, 2004, *Principia ethica*, Mineola, N.Y., Dover Publications.

Nagel Th., 1991, *Equality and partiality*, New York, Oxford UP.

Nietzsche F., 1888, engl. tr. 1998, *Twilight of the idols, or, How to philosophize with a hammer*, Oxford, Oxford UP.

Nozick R., 1974, *Anarchy, State and utopia*, Oxford, Basil Blackwell.

Olson M., 1965, *The logic of collective action*, Cambridge, Mass., Harvard UP.

Parodi M., 2004, *La modernité manquée du structuralisme*, Paris, PUF.

Peretti-Watel P., 2000, *Sociologie du risque*, Paris, Armand Colin.

Pharo P., 2001, *Les sens de la justice, Essai de sémantique sociologique*, Paris, PUF.

Philonenko A., 1966, *La liberté humaine dans la philosophie de Fichte*, Paris, Vrin.

Philonenko A., 1968, *Théorie et praxis dans la pensée morale et politique de Kant et Fichte en 1793*, Paris, Vrin.

Piaget J., 1932, engl. tr. 1948, *The moral judgement of the child*, Glencoe, Ill., Free Press.

Piaget J., 1973, *L'abstraction réfléchissante, Etudes d'épistémologie génétique*, vol. 34 et 35, Paris, PUF.

Popkin S., 1979, *The rational peasant, The political economy of rural society in Vietnam*, Berkeley, University of Californian Press.

Popper K., 1945, 1963, *The open society and its enemies*, vol. II, *The high tide of prophecy: Hegel, Marx and the aftermath*, Princeton, Princeton UP.

Rapoport A., Chammah A. M., 1965, *Prisoner's Dilemma*, Ann Arbor, MI, University of Michigan Press.

Rawls J., 1971, rev. ed. 1999, *A theory of justice*, Cambridge, Mass., Harvard UP.

Rawls J., 1980, Kantian constructivism in moral theory, *The Journal of Philosophy*, 77(9), 515–572.

Rawls J., 1993, *Political liberalism*, New York, Columbia UP.

Rawls J., 2000, *Lectures on the history of moral philosophy*, Cambridge, Mass., Harvard UP.

Renaut A., 1986, *Le système du droit, Philosophie et droit dans la pensée de Fichte*, Paris, PUF.

Renaut A., 1997, *Kant aujourd'hui*, Paris, Flammarion.

Renaut A., 1998, Libéralisme politique et polythéisme des valeurs, in S. Mesure (ed.), *La rationalité des valeurs*, Paris, PUF.

Roemer J., 1988, *Free to lose, An introduction to Marxist economic philosophy*, Cambridge, Mass., Harvard UP.

Rothbard M., 1973, *For a new liberty, The libertarian manifesto*, New York & London, Collier.

Rousseau J.-J., 1762, engl. tr. 2002, *The social contract; and, The first and second discourses*, New Haven, Yale UP.

Ruse M., 1993, Une défense de l'éthique évolutionniste, in J.-P. Changeux (ed.), *Les fondements naturels de l'éthique*, Paris, Odile Jacob, 35–64.

Sandel M., 1982, *Liberalism and the limits of justice*, New York, Cambridge UP.

Sandel M., 1988, The political theory of the procedural republic, *Revue de métaphysique et de morale*, 93(1), 57–68.

Scanlon Th., 1998, *What we owe to each other*, Cambridge, The Belknap Press of Harvard UP.

Schneewind J. B., 1998, *The invention of autonomy: a history of modern moral philosophy,* New York, Cambridge UP.

Sen A., 1977, Rational fools, A critique of the behavioral foundations of economic theory, *Philosophy and Public Affairs*, 6(4), 317–344.

Sen A., 1999, *L'économie est une science morale*, Paris, La Découverte.

Shaftesbury A. A. C., 1711, Inquiry concerning virtue or merit, in D. Walford (ed.), 1977, *Characteristics of men, manners, opinions, times*, Manchester, Manchester UP.

Shubik M., 1982, *Game theory in the social sciences: concepts and solutions*, Cambridge, Mass., MIT Press.

Sidgwick H., 1874, 1962, *The methods of ethics*, London, Macmillan.

Simmel G., 1908, *Soziologie*, fr. tr. 1999, *Sociologie, Essai sur les formes de la socialisation*, Paris, PUF.

Simmel G., 1917, *Grundfragen der Soziologie*, fr. tr. 1981, *Sociologie et épistémologie*, Paris, PUF.

Simon H., 1957, *Models of Man*, New York, John Wiley.

Slote M., 1985, *Common sense morality and consequentialism*, London, Routledge.

Slote M., 1989, *Beyond optimizing, A study of rational choice*, Cambridge, Mass., Harvard UP.

Smith A., 1759, 2002, *The theory of moral sentiments*, Cambridge, Cambridge UP.

Smith A., 1776, 2003, *The wealth of nations*, New York, Bantam Classic.

Spencer H., 1879, 1884, *The data of ethics*, New York, D. Appleton and company.

Swaan A. de, 1988, *In care of the state: health care, education, and welfare in Europe and the USA in the modern era*, New York, Oxford UP.

Taylor Ch., 1989, *Sources of the self*, Cambridge, Mass., Harvard UP.

Tönnies F., 1887, engl. tr. 1988, *Community and society*, New Brunswick, N.J., Transaction Books.

Tronto J., 1987, Beyond gender difference to a theory of care, *Signs*, 12(4), 644–663.

Tucker A. W., 1950, *A two-person dilemma*, Mimeographed paper, Stanford University.

Tyler T., Boeckmann R., Smith H., Huo Y., 1997, *Social justice in a diverse society*, Boulder, Westview Press.

Van Parijs Ph., 1991, *Qu'est-ce qu'une société juste? Introduction à la pratique de la philosophie politique*, Paris, Seuil.

Walzer M., 1983, *Spheres of justice, A defense of pluralism and equality*, New York, Basic Books.

Weber M., 1919, engl. tr. 1960 (3rd ed.), *Science as a vocation*, in H. H. Gerth, C. Wright Mills (eds), *From Max Weber: Essays in Sociology*, New York, Oxford UP, 129–156.

Weber M., 1922, engl. tr. 1978, *Economy and society, An outline of interpretive sociology*, Berkeley, University of California Press.

Wolfelsperger A., 2001, La modélisation économique de la rationalité axiologique. Des sentiments moraux aux mécanismes sociaux de la moralité, in R. Boudon, P. Demeulenaere, R. Viale (eds), *L'explication des normes sociales*, Paris, PUF, 63–91.

www.ingramcontent.com/pod-product-compliance
Ingram Content Group UK Ltd.
Pitfield, Milton Keynes, MK11 3LW, UK
UKHW021845100926
8556IPUK00019B/1051

9 783039 106585